The Summer of '63: Vicksburg and Tullahoma

Favorite Stories and Fresh Perspectives
from the Historians at Emerging Civil War

Edited by
Chris Mackowski & Dan Welch

The Emerging Civil War Series

offers compelling, easy-to-read overviews of some of the Civil War's most important battles and stories.

Recipient of the Army Historical Foundation's Lieutenant General Richard G. Trefry Award for contributions to the literature on the history of the U.S. Army

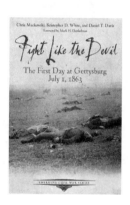

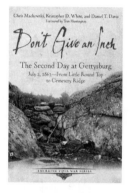

For a complete list of titles in the Emerging Civil War Series, visit www.emergingcivilwar.com.

The Summer of '63:
Vicksburg and Tullahoma

Favorite Stories and Fresh Perspectives
from the Historians at Emerging Civil War

Edited by
Chris Mackowski & Dan Welch

SB

Savas Beatie
California

First edition, first printing

ISBN-13 (hardcover): 978-1-61121-572-4
ISBN-13 (ebook): 978-1-95454-705-6

Library of Congress Cataloging-in-Publication Data

Names: Mackowski, Chris, editor. | Welch, Dan (Educator), editor.
Title: The summer of '63: Vicksburg and Tullahoma : favorite stories and fresh perspectives
    from the historians at Emerging Civil War / edited by Chris Mackowski, and Dan Welch.
Other titles: Favorite stories and fresh perspectives from the historians
    at Emerging Civil War | Emerging Civil War (Website)
Description: El Dorado Hills, CA : Savas Beatie LLC, [2021] | Series: Emerging Civil
    War anniversary series | Includes bibliographical references and index. | Summary: "The
    Summer of '63: Vicksburg and Tullahoma collects some of our historians' favorite
    stories, original research, and engaging voices from the historians at Emerging Civil War,
    anthologized from ECW's blog and podcast, and the annual Emerging Civil War Symposium
    at Stevenson Ridge. The volume also contains a few original pieces, plus maps and illustrations.
    When read with its companion volume, The Summer of '63: Gettysburg it contextualizes the
    events in Mississippi and middle Tennessee with the other great events of the Civil War's turning
    point summer"-- Provided by publisher.
Identifiers: LCCN 2021007557 | ISBN 9781611215724 (hardcover) | ISBN
    9781954547056 (ebook)
Subjects: LCSH: Vicksburg (Miss.)--History--Siege, 1863. | Mississippi--History--Civil War,
    1861-1865--Campaigns. | Tullahoma Campaign, 1863. | Tennessee--History--Civil War,
    1861-1865--Campaigns. | United States--History--Civil War, 1861-1865--Campaigns.
Classification: LCC E475.2 .S86 2021 | DDC 973.7/344--dc23
LC record available at https://lccn.loc.gov/2021007557

Savas Beatie
989 Governor Drive, Suite 102
El Dorado Hills, CA 95762
916-941-6896 / sales@savasbeatie.com / www.savasbeatie.com

All of our titles are available at special discount rates for bulk purchases in the United States. Contact us for information.

Proudly published, printed, and warehoused in the United States of America.

DAN:
To my great-great grandfather, Pvt. Uriah Roe,
100th Pennsylvania Volunteer Infantry. Thank you for your service.

CHRIS:
To Jenny Ann

We jointly dedicate this book to Sarah Keeney,
who has been indispensable in bringing
the Emerging Civil War Series to life,
in service to our readers and our writers.

Chris Heisey

Table of Contents

List of Maps
xii

Points of Interest
xiii

Editors' Note
xiv

Acknowledgments
xvi

Foreword
Matt Atkinson
xviii

Photographing Vicksburg
Chris Heisey
xxii

Assaulting the Bastion City
Kristopher D. White
1

Scenes from the Vicksburg Campaign
Chris Mackowski
7

"Praise the Lord and Admiral Porter":
Running the Vicksburg Batteries
Dwight S. Hughes
35

A Poet's Perspective: Melville on Running the Batteries at Vicksburg
Caroline Davis
42

The Soldier and the Sailor at Vicksburg: Grant and Porter
Dwight S. Hughes
48

Grierson's Raid
Angela M. Riotto
60

Sherman's "Demon Spirit"
Chris Mackowski
64

"Anxious to Make the Grand Trial": A Hoosier at Port Gibson
Daniel A. Masters
68

The Stakes of Vicksburg
Chris Kolakowski
72

"You Can Do a Great Deal in Eight Days":
Ulysses S. Grant's Forgotten Turning Point
Chris Mackowski
75

The Battle of Jackson—and Off to Moscow!
Chris Mackowski
83

"Our Army Was Thoroughly Beaten":
An English Rebel Remembers Champion Hill
Daniel A. Masters
95

Old Abe, the Eighth Wisconsin War Eagle: A Short Account of his Exploits in
War and Honorable—as Well as Useful—Career in Peace, with Emphasis
on the Vicksburg Campaign
Meg Groeling and Chris Mackowski
101

"The Forlorn Hope"
Andrew Miller
108

The Forlorn Hope at Vicksburg
Chris Mackowski
111

BookChat with Timothy B. Smith,
author of *The Union Assaults on Vicksburg*
Chris Mackowski and Timothy B. Smith
121

The Falling Out Between McClernand and Grant
Sean Michael Chick
127

Confederates Shoot a Maine Deserter at Vicksburg
Brian Swartz
133

Abraham: The Slave Who Was "Blowed to Freedom"
Meg Groeling
136

"To Rescue the Command":
Maj. Gen. John S. Bowen and the Surrender of Vicksburg
Kristen Trout
150

"Independence Forever!"
Chris Mackowski
154

The Civilian Experience at Vicksburg: In Their Own Words
Paige Gibbons Backus
162

A Sacred Service: Sister Ignatius Sumner and the Sisters of Mercy
during the Vicksburg Campaign 1862-63
Andrew Miller
168

In the Wake of Vicksburg,
U. S. Grant as Commander of the Army of the Potomac?
Chris Mackowski
172

A Question between Virginia and Mississippi
Chris Mackowski
177

From Civil War to World War:
The Missouri State Memorial at Vicksburg National Military Park
Kristen Trout
191

"All that I Have to Give You is from Memory":
William T. Rigby's Letter Writing Campaign
to Veterans of the Siege of Vicksburg
Andrew Miller
194

COVID and the USS *Cairo*: A Summer at Vicksburg
Caroline Davis
199

Gettysburg and Vicksburg as Turning Points of the Civil War
Matt Atkinson
203

Not Written in Letters of Blood: Tullahoma
Dave Powell
218

The 1863 Tullahoma Campaign
Chris Kolakowski
221

The Battle of Liberty Gap
William Lee White
242

"At Liberty Gap . . . Every Man is a Hero":
The Story of an Ohio Soldier
Jon-Erik Gilot
253

Tullahoma Campaign History
Written in a Confederate Cemetery
Brian Swartz
259

The Battle of Shelbyville:
The Saber Charge that Made the Union Cavalry
Sean Michael Chick
264

Battle at Bethpage Bridge
Dave Powell
268

"All In Our Favor": A Federal Officer
in the Midst of the Tullahoma Campaign
Daniel A. Masters
270

Forgotten? The Tullahoma Campaign
Chris Kolakowski and Chris Mackowski
274

Not Written in Letters of Blood, Redux
Dave Powell
286

Contributors
288

Postscript
292

Index
294

List of Maps

Essay Points of Interest (Edward Alexander)
xiii

Grant's Attempts at Vicksburg (Hal Jespersen)
xxx

Vicksburg Campaign (Edward Alexander)
8

Battle of Jackson (Edward Alexander)
88

Vicksburg Siege Lines (Edward Alexander)
109

Forlorn Hope (Edward Alexander)
113

Tullahoma Campaign (Edward Alexander)
233

Battle of Liberty Gap (Edward Alexander)
244

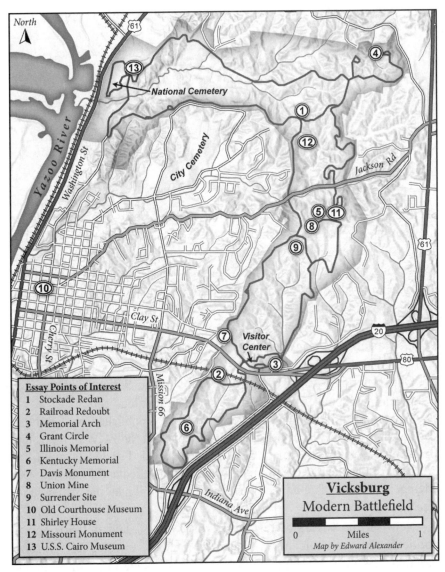

North

National Cemetery

City Cemetery

Jackson Rd

Visitor Center

Clay St

Essay Points of Interest
1 Stockade Redan
2 Railroad Redoubt
3 Memorial Arch
4 Grant Circle
5 Illinois Memorial
6 Kentucky Memorial
7 Davis Monument
8 Union Mine
9 Surrender Site
10 Old Courthouse Museum
11 Shirley House
12 Missouri Monument
13 U.S.S. Cairo Museum

Vicksburg
Modern Battlefield

0   Miles   1
Map by Edward Alexander

VICKSBURG: MODERN BATTLEFIELD—Particular points of interest discussed in some of the essays are marked on this map for easy reference. In addition, the National Park Service administers several additional sites non-contiguous with the main battlefield, such as Navy Circle and South Fort south of downtown along the Mississippi River, as well as a number of monuments along such places as Confederate Avenue. Following I-20 west across the river leads to Delta, Louisiana, the site of Grant's Canal; I-20 east leads to Jackson, Mississippi.

Editors' Note

Emerging Civil War serves as a public history-oriented platform for sharing original scholarship related to the American Civil War. The scholarship we present reflects the eclectic background, expertise, interests, and writing styles of our cadre of historians. We've shared that scholarship not only on the Emerging Civil War blog, but also in the pages of the Emerging Civil War Series published by Savas Beatie, in other general-audience and academic publications, at our annual Emerging Civil War Symposium at Stevenson Ridge, on our monthly podcasts, and even through social media.

Our Emerging Civil War 10th Anniversary Series captures and commemorates some of the highlights from our first ten years.

This compendium includes pieces originally published on our blog; podcast transcripts; and transcripts of talks given at the ECW Symposium. It also includes an assortment of original material. Previously published pieces have been updated and, in most cases, expanded and footnoted. Our attempt is to offer value-added rather than just reprint material available for free elsewhere.

Between the covers of this series, readers will find military, social, political, and economic history; memory studies; travelogues; personal narratives; essays; and photography. This broad range of scholarship and creative work is meant to provide readers with a diversity of perspectives. The combined collection of material is *not* intended to serve as a complete narrative of events or comprehensive overview. Rather, these are the stories and events our historians happened to be interested in writing about at any given time. In that way, the collection represents the sort of eclectic ongoing conversation you'll find on our blog.

As a collective, the individuals who comprise ECW are encouraged to share their own unique interests and approaches. The resulting work—and the respectful discussions that surround it—forward ECW's overall effort to promote a general awareness of the Civil War as America's defining event.

Another of ECW's organizational priorities is our ongoing work to identify and spotlight the next generation of "emerging" Civil War historians and the fresh ideas they bring to the historical conversation. (Some of us were "emerging" when ECW started up ten years ago and have perhaps since "emerged," but the quest to spotlight new voices continues!)

Most importantly, it is the common thread of public history and the ideals of interpretation that so strongly tie our seemingly disparate bodies of work together. America's defining event should not be consigned to forgotten footnotes and dusty shelves. As public historians, we understand the resonance and importance history's lessons can have in our modern world and in our daily lives, so we always seek to connect people with those great stories and invaluable lessons. Emerging Civil War remains committed to making our history something available for all of us—writers, readers, historians, hobbyists, men, women, young, old, and people of all races and ethnicities—and by doing so, making it something we can engage, question, challenge, and enjoy.

Please join us online at www.emergingcivilwar.com.

Acknowledgments

First and foremost, thanks to our colleagues at Emerging Civil War, past and present. ECW has always been and remains a team effort. We've worked with some wonderful historians, writers, and "emerging voices" over the past decade, and we're proud to show off some of that work here.

Thanks, too, to Theodore Savas and his team at Savas Beatie, with a special thanks to our editorial liaison, Sarah Keeney. Together, ECW and Savas Beatie have produced some great work, and we're thankful to Ted for agreeing to help us celebrate ECW's tenth anniversary by allowing us to produce more great work. We thank everyone at Savas Beatie for all they do to support the efforts of Emerging Civil War.

Thanks to cartographers Edward Alexander and Hal Jespersen for their great maps, which continue to be a distinctive feature of ECW books.

Thanks to Chris Heisey for always being willing to contribute *one more* photograph as the design of our anniversart books continuted to evolve.

Thanks to John Foskett and Patrick McCormick, who both reviewed the text and made valuable suggestions and observations. Thanks also to Denise Hardy for her transcriptions.

At ECW, thanks to Sarah Kay Bierle, ECW's managing editor, whose work made it a lot easier for us to collect the material we've assembled in this volume. Our official un-official archivist, Jon-Erik Gilot, has helped us make it easier to access our past work. Christopher Kolakowski, as our chief historian, provides overall quality control for our work.

Finally, we'd like to thank Terry Winschel, retired chief historian at Vicksburg National Military Park, and Jim Woodrick, licensed battlefield guide at Vicksburg NMP and retired Mississippi state archivist, for their thorough readings and thoughtful feedback on this volume. Their eyes were invaluable.

*   *   *

Chris:

When we began assembling material for this volume and its companion volume about Gettysburg, I was surprised to discover I had written a lot more about Vicksburg in the past ten years than Gettysburg. I grew up near Gettysburg, I've been there far more times, and I've written books about the battle—but I've somehow blogged more about Vicksburg, a place I've been fortunate to visit only twice.

I want to thank the American Battlefield Trust and, specifically, Senior Education Manager Kris White for sparking my interest in the Vicksburg Campaign.

Thanks to Timothy B. Smith, a historian I deeply admire, for encouraging me along in my studies. Thanks, too, to historians Matt Atkinson, Parker Hills, Andrew Miller, Dave Powell, Angela Riotta, Jim Woodrick, and the legendary Terry Winschel for sharing their time and expertise at various times. (I'm not sure Gen. Hills would even remember me, but my two days in the field with him and Kris were unforgettable to me!). I also thank Charles Grear and Steven Woodworth for their excellent essay collections on Vicksburg, published by Southern Illinois University Press..

Finally, as always, my thanks to my family, especially my kids, Stephanie, Thomas, and Sophie Marie (my first grandchild!); Jackson; and Maxwell James. Most of all, thanks to my wife and partner, Jenny Ann, to whom I dedicate this volume.

*   *   *

Dan:

My continued appreciation to Chris Mackowski and Ted Savas for providing me with an opportunity to learn the role of an editor for this series. Their continued support during this volume afforded me more growth in this role. Thank you both.

As an Eastern Theater guy, it was an incredible learning experience working with all of the contributors in this volume. It has been a true delight to learn from colleagues and peers in the field of this critical 1863 campaign.

Finally, I would like to thank my family. These types of projects do not come to fruition without many hours at the keyboard and in front of a screen. Often that means missing family gatherings or activities to meet the next hurdle, the next deadline. Their understanding, patience, and support of this endeavor made all those late nights and long weekends easier. I could not have completed this volume without them.

Foreword

by Matt Atkinson

The landscape blossomed with every hue of green imaginable, and a soft scent of honeysuckle and pine mingled with the mockingbird's shrill chirp wafting through the air—it was the spring of '63. Those blossoms portended the humidity, though, which, coupled with the increasing daily heat, foretold of summer on the way. The change in weather also brought increased pressure from Washington: Advance!

Seeking to further entice, the War Department sent an offer to all field commanders: a major general's commission in the Regular Army for the first victory.

In the bayous and floodlands of Louisiana, the Union army toiled away fruitlessly trying to bypass Vicksburg. It had been a hard winter and many brave and patriotic boys lay buried in the only dry place available—the river levees—dead from disease and sickness, a glorious sacrifice for the nation. But the irony of any story always comes last: the only place to bury their poor souls was also the only place available for the remaining souls to keep living. Dry land was in scant supply.

Leading this army was 41-year-old Hiram Ulysses Grant, otherwise known as Ulysses. His friends called him Sam, and his character was stone cold stolid. With a cigar in his mouth, he led the opening of the Tennessee heartland. While initially on a roll, he had his hat handed to him in the first round of Shiloh. When told he'd had "the devil's own day," he responded, "yes, but [we will] lick 'em tomorrow." He proceeded to accomplish just that.

Indeed, Capt. Sam Grant had known the devil's own day. In 1854, while stationed away from his wife and kids, Grant heard the cry of "that lonesome whippoorwill." He battled the bottle but lost. It cost him his commission and sent him drifting with his family from job to job for the next six years. The Civil War's onset brought a need for professionally trained military officers, and Grant needed work. With the backing of a local politician and a little luck, Grant got one of the four stars Illinois gave out in 1861. He parlayed his chance with successive victory after victory—until Shiloh. Lincoln stood with the man from Galena, though, remarking, "I can't spare this man. He fights."

And here he was now, in the spring of 1863, nine years after leaving the army, standing in the Louisiana mud, commanding the largest amphibious invasion in American history up to that time against the Confederacy's toughest target.

Try as he might, Grant had already failed multiple times to capture Vicksburg. The Union army's fruitless efforts only served to give more unique names to the lexicon of the Civil War: Chickasaw Bayou, Holly Springs, Duckport, Yazoo Pass, Lake Providence, and Grant's Canal. Even the patient Lincoln grew concerned. As cigar smoke ringed his head, Grant knew this was his last chance.

Meanwhile, in the rocky hills of Tennessee, the Army of the Cumberland stood poised at Murfreesboro to strike. Their commander, William Starke Rosecrans, however, was in no hurry to pull the trigger. The 43-year-old Union general came from the Buckeye State, just as Grant had. Both were West Point graduates, possessed of high intellect, self-confidence, and fearlessness. Although teammates, in 1863, they were also rivals.

Journalist Henry Villard recalled Rosecrans's "narrow, long face with kindly blue eyes, strong nose and mouth, and scanty full grayish beard. His general expression was very genial." Indeed, many of his soldiers loved "Ol' Rosy," the general who worked indefatigably for their welfare. On the battlefield, none were braver than him. And no man clung to the tenets of Roman Catholicism more than this praying general. "He carries a cross attached to his watch seal," wrote James Garfield, his chief of staff, "and as he drew his watch out of [the] side [of his] pants pocket his rosary, a dirty-looking string of friar's beads came out with it. Before retiring he took out his rosary and knelt for five or ten minutes before his bed."

Rosecrans entered the war under the tutelage of George McClellan and quickly rose to command of Union forces in West Virginia. He bested none other than Robert E. Lee at Cheat Mountain, solidifying Union control of the area. With victory came promotion and a Western command under John Pope (who himself had a future date with Lee). At the battle of Iuka, Rosecrans teamed with Grant in an unsuccessful pincer movement against "Pap" Price. Two weeks later, Rosecrans's forces administered a sound defeat at Corinth to the "Gallant" Earl Van Dorn. A lackluster pursuit of the defeated Confederates and Rosecrans's penchant for going off "half-cocked" led to a rift with Grant that never healed. In the end, perhaps the irascible "Ol' Rosy" clashed too much with the taciturn Sam. Not because of these differences but, instead, because of their similarities, Lincoln still put his faith in these two commanders.

Were the stakes ever higher for the nation?

In the following pages are the stories of heroes and villains, cowards and stalwarts, slaves and freedmen, and people who simply wanted to survive. The historians at *Emerging Civil War* make the story come alive. On a moonless night, watch as the acrid smoke from heavy cannons floats across the Mississippi while Union gunboats race past Confederate batteries. On May 3, stand with Grant as another momentous decision lies before him. Listen to the sound of hoofbeats as Grierson's Raiders ride hell-bent for leather toward Baton Rouge. After a pouring rain, watch while the United States flag is raised over Mississippi's capital. A few days later, feel the tension as Union soldiers charge in a forlorn hope against the Stockade Redan. Take a ride with Abraham on his way to freedom. Empathize with Grant as he battles not only the Rebels in his front but enemies in his rear. Look on curiously as Grant's old friend rides out to see him about a surrender. Then travel to Tennessee where infighting among Confederate generals rivals the bickering among the generals of the Vicksburg's army, and where a bold Union offensive movement pays off almost bloodlessly. Finally, in the aftermath, just like the burgeoning springtime, see the seeds planted by the old veterans for a new park, a place to be remembered.

Welcome to the stories of the Vicksburg and Tullahoma campaigns.

Chris Heisey

Photographing Vicksburg

by Chris Heisey

Vicksburg National Military Park, in western Mississippi, is exactly 1,000 miles from my home in Pennsylvania, and I have had the good fortune to visit the town perched atop the steep bluffs overlooking the mighty Mississippi River four times. Each time I've visited has been a rich experience as a photographer and Civil War enthusiast.

Vicksburg's battlefield landscape is adorned with beautiful statuary that not only celebrates the heroic Confederate defense, but also the Union's persistence at forcing the surrender of some 30,000 nearly starved southerners. And Vicksburg's surrounding landscape features dramatic rivulets and sand hill formations that make capturing the moonlike battlescapes a delight for any discerning photographer interested in taking evocative images.

My first visit occurred in the midst of a July heatwave in the 1990s that saw the temperature soar to 107 degrees with a heat index of 121. The foam padding on my camera tripod melted to the metal, and the experience brought home to me the oppressive weather that climatic campaigning in the Deep South must have been like for both sides in May through July 1863.

On another summer visit, I was pumping gas at a humble gas station in town when an old 1950s totally rusted Chevy pickup truck pulled up behind me at the only pump the station had. When an African-American man far older than the truck climbed out, he saw my Pennsylvania license plate and asked me if I would pump gas for him as his hands were too arthritic to squeeze the nozzle. "Put in 35 cents," he said with a smile that disclosed his toothless mouth as he handed me seven nickels with his swollen, deformed fingers. "That will get me home."

That transaction remains the best Civil War-related $20 I have ever spent.

Page vi: The Mississippi African American Memorial *Chris Heisey*
Page xxi: A dismounted cavalryman from the Wisconsin Memorial *Chris Heisey*
Page xxiii: Detail from the Mississippi Monument *Chris Heisey*
Pages xxiv-xxv: The Federal position at Raymond is marked by a line of 22 cannon *Chris Heisey*
Pages xxvi-xxvii: The Illinois Memorial *Chris Heisey*
Pages xxviii-xxix: The Ulysses S. Grant equestrian statue *Chris Heisey*
Pages 216-217: Stones River at McFadden's Ford *Chris Heisey*

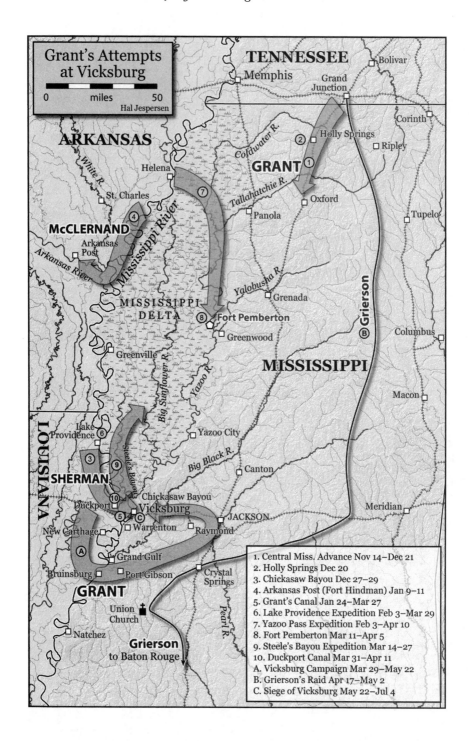

Grant's Attempts at Vicksburg

0   miles   50

Hal Jespersen

TENNESSEE

Bolivar

Memphis   Grand Junction

Corinth

ARKANSAS

Holly Springs

②

Ripley

GRANT ①

Helena

Tallahatchie R.

Oxford

St. Charles

Panola

Tupelo

⑦

McCLERNAND

④

Arkansas Post

Mississippi River

Yalobusha R.

Grenada

Grierson

MISSISSIPPI DELTA

⑧ Fort Pemberton

Columbus

Greenwood

Ⓑ

Greenville

MISSISSIPPI

Macon

Lake Providence ⑥

Yazoo City

LOUISIANA

③   ⑨

Big Black R.

Canton

SHERMAN

⑩   Chickasaw Bayou

Duckport   Vicksburg

Meridian

⑤ Ⓒ

Warrenton   JACKSON

New Carthage   Raymond

Ⓐ   Grand Gulf

Bruinsburg   Port Gibson   Crystal Springs

GRANT

Union Church

Natchez

Grierson
to Baton Rouge

1. Central Miss. Advance Nov 14–Dec 21
2. Holly Springs Dec 20
3. Chickasaw Bayou Dec 27–29
4. Arkansas Post (Fort Hindman) Jan 9–11
5. Grant's Canal Jan 24–Mar 27
6. Lake Providence Expedition Feb 3–Mar 29
7. Yazoo Pass Expedition Feb 3–Apr 10
8. Fort Pemberton Mar 11–Apr 5
9. Steele's Bayou Expedition Mar 14–27
10. Duckport Canal Mar 31–Apr 11
A. Vicksburg Campaign Mar 29–May 22
B. Grierson's Raid Apr 17–May 2
C. Siege of Vicksburg May 22–Jul 4

Assaulting the Bastion City

by Kristopher D. White

*This article first appeared in the winter 2020 issue of
the American Battlefield Trust's magazine,* Hallowed Ground.
It has been adapted from Battle Maps of the Civil War: The Western
Theater *(2020) by Kris White and with maps by Steven Stanley.*

Obtaining full control of the Mississippi River was an early and vital war aim for the Federals because the waterway served as a highway to move men and materials from places as far as way as Pittsburgh to New Orleans and the Gulf of Mexico. By early 1863, only three Confederate strong points stood between the Federals and dominance of the mighty river: Vicksburg and Grand Gulf, Mississippi, and Port Hudson, Louisiana.

The first, Vicksburg, was the "Gibraltar of the Confederacy." Situated atop dominating bluffs overlooking a sweeping bend of the river, Vicksburg was a tough nut to crack. Time and again, Maj. Gen. Ulysses S. Grant had tried and failed to approach the bastion city. A late 1862 advance south from Tennessee ended with Confederates severing Grant's supply lines. Major General William T. Sherman attempted to storm the city but came

OPPOSITE: GRANT'S ATTEMPTS AT VICKSBURG—Beginning in the fall of 1862, Grant made a number of attempts on Vicksburg, foiled time and again by the swampy terrain of the Mississippi Delta and the temperamental waters of the Mississippi River itself. When his attempts to approach Vicksburg from the north and circumvent it to the west failed, he finally crossed the river to the south and marched overland. When he could not conquer the city by battle, he subdued it by siege.

up short at Chickasaw Bayou. Canals were dug and abandoned. Levees were blown up to create floodplains, only to carry the boats too high in the water, literally among the branches of the trees. Nothing seemed to work.

In late April 1863, however, Grant finally struck gold. Utilizing some diversions, he marched his army down the western side of the river while Rear Adm. David Dixon Porter ran his flotilla of gunboats and transports past the Confederate guns of Vicksburg. The two forces reunited some 30 miles south of the city, and on April 29–30, Porter's sailors transported Grant's army across the river to Bruinsburg, Mississippi, unopposed.

Now on the Vicksburg side of the river, Grant's men marched toward their first objective, Port Gibson, situated roughly 10 miles to the east, which commanded the local road network. Fighting for control of the strategic crossroads was fierce and included rare nighttime combat. On the afternoon of May 1, Federals repulsed a desperate Confederate counterattack, leaving the Southerners to retreat and evacuate the remaining garrison at Grand Gulf the next day. The battle of Port Gibson was a resounding Union victory that secured Grant's beachhead east of the Mississippi River and cleared the way to the Southern Railroad supplying Vicksburg.

From there, rather than move directly on Vicksburg, Grant and his Army of the Tennessee drove along a northeastern axis of advance. Grant's ultimate goal was to isolate Confederate Lt. Gen. John C. Pemberton and Vicksburg from the rest of the Confederacy. Grant also aimed to disrupt the railroads and communications lines in and out of the city. The destruction of the Southern Railroad of Mississippi in the central part of the state was a vital objective.

Grant's army advanced over a broad front in hot, dusty conditions, with water scarce. On May 12, Grant directed his three corps to various crossings of Fourteen Mile Creek to secure a source of water for his men and animals. This would also move his army into position for the planned lunge against the railroad.

Meanwhile, Confederate Brig. Gen. John Gregg had been dispatched to Raymond, Mississippi, with 3,000 men and orders to strike the Federals in the flank or rear as they advanced. Faulty intelligence led him to believe that he would only face a small contingent of Union troops, but he was actually confronted by a powerful 10,000-man corps. Although outnumbered, Gregg ordered an attack, with units splashing *en echelon* across the creek to slam into the Federals. The blue line began to waver and break in places, but was rallied by the presence of division commander Maj. Gen. John A. Logan.

Union resistance stiffened, and once reinforcements arrived in the early afternoon a counterattack compelled Gregg to abandon the field and retreat toward Jackson. With a victory in hand, Grant divided his columns. One continued north toward the Southern Railroad; the other pressed east toward Jackson. The maneuvers resulted in a pincer movement that closed in on the state capital from the northwest and southwest, squeezing out Confederate defenders. The city fell on May 14.

The Raymond battlefield has been an incredible preservation success story, just as Champion Hill has been. Unfortunately, essentially all of the battlefield at Jackson has been lost. *Chris Mackowski*

Grant left one corps in the city to destroy anything of military value while he sent the second back out into the field to rejoin his third corps, guarding the army's left flank against a possible move by Pemberton, who had sallied forth from his Vicksburg defenses.

As the first streaks of dawn appeared in the eastern sky on May 16, 1863, a train heading east on the Southern Railroad near Clinton, Mississippi, found the tracks ahead destroyed. The brakeman and the baggage-master were escorted by Union soldiers into the presence of Maj. Gen. Ulysses S. Grant. When questioned, they informed him that the Confederate army defending Vicksburg, which they estimated numbered 25,000 men with 10 batteries, had advanced as far as Edwards Station and was preparing to attack Grant's army. This was not a bad estimate of the Confederate forces, which consisted of 23,000 men and 15 batteries. Grant ordered his troops, 32,000 in all, to march on Edwards along three parallel roads.

Although the opening shots of the battle of Champion Hill were fired along the lower road around 7:00 a.m., it was not until 9:45 a.m. that the

Union vanguard turned a bend in the upper road and reached the country home of Sid and Matilda Champion. A half-mile southwest of the house was the bald crest of Champion Hill, which dominated a strategic crossroads that

CHAMPION HOUSE SITE

In 1855, the land now known as Champion Hill was given to Sid and Matilda Champion as a wedding present from her father, Eli Montgomery. They erected a two-story white-frame house along the Jackson Road that overlooked the railroad. In 1862, Sid joined the 28th Mississippi Cavalry, leaving Matilda in charge of the plantation. On May 16, 1865, as the Battle of Champion Hill erupted, Grant claimed the Champion House as headquarters while Matilda took the children down to the cellar where they remained until the firing ceased. The house was used as a Union hospital then burned after the fall of Vicksburg. In 1865, Sid and Matilda returned and built a modest house down by the railroad, on a site known as Midway Station.

The home of Sid and Matilda Champion sat near the modern location of the Champion Hill Missionary Baptist Church. *Chris Mackowski*

would be vital to the final assault on Vicksburg.

Grant arrived on the field shortly after 10:00 a.m. and ordered his powerful battle line to advance. With a mighty cheer, the Federals slammed into the Confederates at the base of the hill, and a wild hand-to-hand brawl ensued.

Union soldiers swept over the crest of Champion Hill and drove hard toward the crossroads only 600 yards farther south. Despite a murderous fire of musketry and artillery, the Federals seized the crossroads and stood on the verge of victory.

But Confederate Gen. John Pemberton ordered a desperate counterattack that struck the Union position before they consolidated their hold on the crossroads. The gray wave surged over the crest of Champion Hill and pushed the Federals back to the Champion House. Their success, however, was short-lived, as two more Union divisions charged the hill. Threatened in flank and rear, the Southerners were compelled to fall back. When the Federals again seized the crossroads, Pemberton ordered his army off of the field and back toward the defenses of Vicksburg. Union victory at Champion Hill—and the next day at the Big Black River Bridge—forced the Confederates into a doomed position inside the fortifications of Vicksburg.

On the evening of May 17, Pemberton's beleaguered army poured into the defensive lines around the Confederate Gibraltar. Looking for a

Somber mustaches were about the only thing Ulysses S. Grant and John C. Pemberton had in common. The most notable difference: the Vicksburg Campaign saw Grant rise to the occasion even as Pemberton was overwhelmed by it. *LOC/LOC*

quick victory and not wanting to give Pemberton time to settle in, Grant ordered an immediate assault. Of his three corps, only Maj. Gen. William T. Sherman's XV Corps, northeast of the city, was in position to attack on May 19. Sherman's assault focused on the Stockade Redan, named for a log stockade wall across the Graveyard Road connecting two gun positions. Here, Mississippi troops reinforced by Col. Francis Cockrell's Missouri Brigade manned the rifle pits, with the 27th Louisiana Infantry manning a lunnette just to the west of the redan.

Sherman's men moved forward down the road at 2:00 p.m. and were immediately slowed by the ravines and obstructions in front of the redan. Bloody combat ensued outside the Confederate works. The 13th United States Infantry, once commanded by Sherman, planted its colors on the redan but could advance no farther. Capt. Edward C. Washington, the grandnephew of George Washington, commanding the 1st Battalion, 13th U.S., was mortally wounded in the attack. After fierce fighting, Sherman's men pulled back.

Undaunted by his failure, Grant made a more thorough reconnaissance of the defenses prior to ordering another assault. Early on the morning of May 22, Union artillery opened fire, and for four hours bombarded the city's defenses. At 10:00 a.m., the guns fell silent, and Union infantry advanced on a three-mile front. Sherman attacked again down the Graveyard Road, Maj. Gen. James B. McPherson's corps moved against the center along the Jackson Road and Maj. Gen. John B. McClernand's corps attacked toward the south at the 2nd Texas Lunette and the Railroad Redoubt, where the Southern Railroad crossed the Confederate lines. Fronted by a ditch 10 feet deep and walls 20 feet high, the redoubt offered enfilading fire for rifles and artillery. After bloody hand-to-hand fighting, Federals breached the Railroad Redoubt, capturing a handful of prisoners. The victory, however, was the only Confederate position broken that day, and even that was for only a brief time.

Grant's unsuccessful attacks gave him no choice but to invest Vicksburg in a siege. Pemberton's defenders suffered from shortened rations, exposure to the elements and constant bombardment from Grant's army and Porter's navy gunboats. Reduced in number by sickness and casualties, the garrison of Vicksburg was spread dangerously thin. Civilians were particularly hard hit. Many were forced to live underground in crudely dug caves due to the heavy shelling.

By early June, Grant had established his own line of circumvallation surrounding the city. At thirteen points along his line, Grant ordered tunnels dug under the Confederate positions where explosives could be placed to destroy the Rebel works. At the end of the month, the first mine was ready to be blown. Union miners tunneled 40 feet under a redan near the James Shirley House, packed the tunnel with 2,200 pounds of black powder, and on June 25 detonated it with a huge explosion. After more than 20 hours of hand-to-hand fighting in the 12-foot-deep crater left by the blast, the Union regiments were unable to advance out of it and withdrew back to their lines. The siege continued.

By July, the situation was dire for the Confederates. Grant and Pemberton met between the lines on July 3. Grant insisted on an unconditional surrender, but Pemberton refused. Rebuffed, Grant later that night offered to parole the Confederate defenders. At 10:00 a.m. the next day, Independence Day, some 29,000 Confederates marched out of their lines, stacked their rifles and furled their flags. The 47-day siege of Vicksburg was over.

With the loss of Pemberton's army and a Union victory at Port Hudson five days later, the Union controlled the entire Mississippi River, and the Confederacy was split in half.

Scenes from the Vicksburg Campaign

by Chris Mackowski

To commemorate the 155th anniversary of the Vicksburg Campaign in 2018, the American Battlefield Trust conducted a series of Facebook LIVE programs from Mississippi. ECW co-founder Kris White, in charge of the trip as the Trust's Senior Education Manager, invited me to come along as co-host. The Trust's Social Media Manager, Connor Townsend, came along as well, as our technical director and cameraperson.

We landed in Jackson, Mississippi, the state capital, on May 15, 2018, to kick off our tour. Although it meant presenting the campaign a little out of order, we wanted to take advantage of being in the city to recap the May 14, 1863, battle there, so Jackson became our first program of the trip. Most notably, I ended up with Johnny and June Carter Cash's song "Jackson" stuck in my head for days. (If you don't know the song, beware: It's a heck of an earworm![1]*)*

Unfortunately, because we had so much to cram into our two-and-a-half days, I didn't have the time to write a travelogue as we went along, but I did post dozens of photos on the blog so I could share with ECW readers some of the amazing things I was seeing and experiencing. That series, "Scenes from Vicksburg," which ran May 16-19, 2018, serves as the basis for the travelogue that follows. I've also incorporated work from posts I wrote during a week-long road trip with historian Dan Davis in May 2015.

---

1 Take a listen: https://youtu.be/AAca-M-9xpY

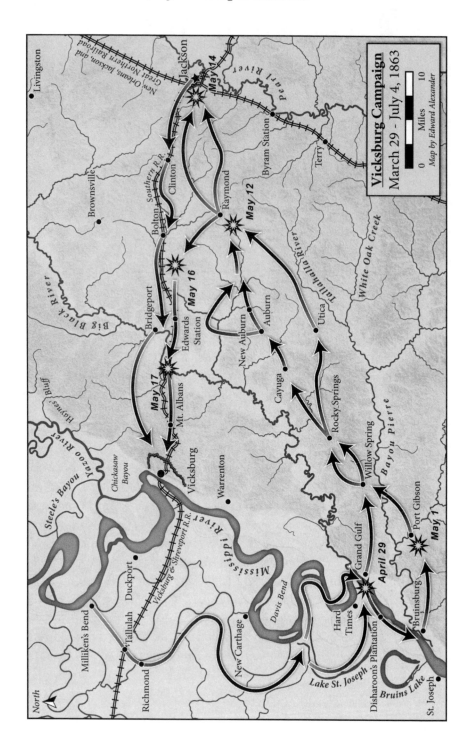

The landing area today is a wide flood plain, but in 1863, the riverbank ran right along the edge of the light brown grass in the foreground. *Chris Mackowski*

In the interest of narrative flow, I've reordered the segments a bit compared to the order in which they first appeared on the blog.

*   *   *

Bruinsburg

The flood plain along the east bank of the Mississippi looks like a bed ready for military inspection, flat and smooth. Brigadier General (Ret.) Parker Hills, formerly of the Mississippi National Guard and now proprietor of Battle Focus Tours, looks across the panoramic flatness and chooses a

OPPOSITE: VICKSBURG CAMPAIGN—Unable to clear a way across the river at Grand Gulf on April 29, Grant instead moved his army to the east bank of the Mississippi at Bruinsburg beginning on April 30. Moving inland, he fought battles at Port Gibson, Raymond, Jackson, Champion Hill, and the Big Black River before closing on Vicksburg from the east. Two failed attempts to take the city on April 19 and 22 led to a siege that lasted until July 4, 1863.

spot near an old road trace that comes up from the riverbank. "This is the road Grant's men used," he tells us.

We're in Bruinsburg, where Ulysses S. Grant landed his army on April 30-May 1, 1863, to kick off his overland campaign to take Vicksburg. "It was 'Grant's D-Day,'" Kris White says, "but with no Germans waiting for him." The World War II analogy is not far off. When David Dixon Porter's navy ferried Grant's army to the east bank, it would be the largest amphibious landing in U.S. history until American forces landed on the beaches of North Africa in 1942.

Major General John McClernand's 20,000-man XIII Corps crossed first, followed by Maj. Gen. James McPherson's 17,000-man XVII Corps. Major General William T. Sherman's 20,000-man XV Corps, for the time being, remained on the west bank to guard the Federal supply depot at Milliken's Bend and distract Confederate commander Lt. Gen. John Pemberton in Vicksburg.

Parker has brought us, with permission, onto private property so we could get to the actual debarkation site itself. We had descended a breakneck dirt road—the

This road trace is the path Grant's men took from their disembarkation point along the river onto the eastern shore of the Mississippi. *Chris Mackowski*

historic Bruinsburg Road, now a farmer's driveway—and driven along a wide plain of dust-dry mud and brown wind-swept grass where, on the far side, a team of tractors has begun turning over the field for the season's planting. Along the tree line, lush and green, empty deer stands look with hollow eyes out over the fields.

High water at the time of Grant's arrival forced his men to move along

High water necessitated that Grant's men march along a dike to get away from the riverbank. Here, as the dike runs through the forest, note how the ground slopes away on either side of the green strip right down the middle of the image (that's the dike). The river would have been to the left of the camera. *Chris Mackowski*

a dike elevated above the mire. Eventually, they reached the road that took them up the same breakneck way we descended.

Parker sets up an easel with a laminated map of the war's Western Theatre on it. He has two dry-erase markers taped together, Union blue on one end and Confederate red on the other. He marks the maps with colorful precision, showing how Federals used the rivers to facilitate the inexorable advance of their armies overland from Kentucky and Illinois into the Confederacy's interior.

That march took Grant from Ft. Donelson down the Tennessee River to Shiloh and, from there, down to the Mississippi rail junction of Corinth. From there, Vicksburg became the next key, but its capture eluded him. He tried six times, unsuccessfully, to find a way in or around the Hill City. The seventh time, which we're about to trace, would be the charm.

Port Gibson

From the bottomlands, we retrace our way up the historic Bruinsburg Road to the paved route that will take us to Port Gibson. A witness tree stands at the intersection.

As we continue on, the road twists and turns as valleys and chasms yawn open out of nowhere. I recall Grant's description of the terrain:

A witness tree stands at the intersection where the historic Bruinsburg Road meets the modern road that runs back into Port Gibson. *Chris Mackowski*

> The country in this part of Mississippi stands on edge, as it were, the roads running along the ridges except when they occasionally pass from one ridge to another. Where there are no clearings the sides of the hills are covered with a very heavy growth of timber and with undergrowth, and the ravines are filled with vines and canebrakes, almost impenetrable.[2]

"The country," he told Halleck in a May 3 letter written after his victory at Port Gibson, "is the most broken and difficult to operate in I ever saw."[3]

Federals pushed about ten miles inland to secure the network of roads that ran into Port Gibson. Controlling them would give Grant greater options

---

2   Ulysses S. Grant, "The Personal Memoirs of Ulysses S. Grant," *Grant: Memoirs and Selected Letters*, Mary Drake McFeely and William S. McFeely, editors (New York: Library of America, 1990), 321.

3   Grant to Halleck, 3 May 1863, O.R. XXIV, Pt. 1, 34.

At Windsor Ruins, a state historic site, twenty-three columns remain standing, each 45 feet tall. Wrought iron balcony fencing still connects columns along the former front of the building, and each column is topped by additional ornamental ironwork. *Chris Mackowski*

for his approach to Vicksburg, particularly since they would ease navigation through Bayou Pierre to the north. As McClernand advanced his XIII Corps, his skirmishers ran into Confederate skirmishers posted along the road about 4.2 miles outside town. It was just after midnight. Fighting escalated, but by 3:00 a.m. petered out for a few hours.

The next morning, McClernand went in with everything, including reinforcements from McPherson's XVII Corps coming up behind him. Confederates had reinforcements of their own arrive, but they could not hold back the Federal onslaught as McClernand leaned into the fight. By late afternoon, Confederates withdrew, and Grant held not only the field, but the roads, the momentum, and a number of options.

"The road to Vicksburg is open," Grant crowed to Sherman. "All we want now are men, ammunition, and hard bread."[4] That served as Sherman's

4   Grant to Sherman, 3 May 1863, O.R. XXIV, Pt. 3, 269.

cue to come join the rest of the army. He did, securing a supply route for Grant's army as he did so.

On our way into town, we stop at Windsor Ruins, the skeletal remains of an opulent plantation house accidentally destroyed by fire after the war. Built in 1861 in the Greek revival style, it burned in 1890 when a guest, after lighting a cigarette, threw his match into a kitchen wastepaper basket. Unfounded rumor circulated years later that Sherman and his men burned the house a la his 1864 March to the Sea.

Grand Gulf

Grant's victory at Port Gibson uncovered the Confederate bastion along the Mississippi River at Grand Gulf, forcing its evacuation. Grant rode into the village and down to the river on the evening of May 3, where he met up with naval officers tied up along the riverbank in the U.S.S. *Louisville.*

Days earlier, on April 29, Porter had tried to reduce the two Confederate forts at Grand Gulf so Grant could cross his army there. Forts Wade and Cobun took a beating but held; Porter's fleet took a beating, too, and after five hours Porter called off the assault. Unable to dislodge the Confederates, Grant chose Bruinsburg as his alternative crossing point.

The failure of the Navy to capture Grand Gulf must have been a relief to Sherman. In a letter that day to his wife, he offered a pessimistic prediction. "[W]hen they take Grand Gulf they have the elephant by the tail . . ." he wrote. "[M]y own opinion is that this whole plan of attack on Vicksburg will fail, must fail."[5]

Grant, in contrast, felt optimistic about the town's capture. "This army is in the finest health and spirits," he wrote to Halleck. "Since leaving Milliken's Bend they have marched as much by night as by day, through mud and rain, without tents or much other baggage, and on irregular rations, without a complaint, and with less straggling than I have ever before witnessed."[6]

---

5   Sherman to wife, 29 April 1863, *Sherman's Civil War: Selected Correspondence of William T. Sherman, 1860-1865*, Brooks D. Simpson and Jean V. Berlin, eds. (Chapel Hill: University of North Carolina Press, 1999), 465.

6   Grant (in Grand Gulf!) to Halleck, 3 May 1863, O.R. XXIV, Pt. 1, 33.

You know you live right along the banks of the Mississippi River when. . . . *Chris Mackowski*

When we arrive at Grand Gulf, we first stop in at the Grand Gulf Military Park visitor center, which has a cool little museum filled with an eclectic collection that stretches well beyond the Civil War (I particularly like the mastodon bone). Outside, a collection of historic buildings creates an ersatz village: a blacksmith shop; the original town jail; a water wheel; and the original Grand Gulf cemetery. There's a 1768 log cabin called the "dog trot" house, so named for the open breezeway that connected the two halves of the home, and the 1868 Sacred Heart Roman Catholic Church (now non-denominational), formerly of Rodney, Mississippi, one of the last examples of "carpenter gothic church architecture" in the state—meaning the exterior bears a striking resemblance to an ornate old-fashioned gingerbread house. There's also an antique fire engine, a Civil War ambulance, and a restored 1861 Parrot gun.[7] The ruins of Fort Wade squat along a hillside.

7   https://www.grandgulfpark.ms.gov/tour.

High water has brought the Mississippi up enough that it reaches the historic riverbank, so we stand at the water's edge just as it would have been in April 1863. Federal gunboats were able to steam up to almost point-blank range to blast at Fort Wade, which in turn blasted back. Fort Cobun, a mile upstream, took and delivered similar punishment.

Next to us, a mobile home on metal stilts towers over us like a Martian tripod from an H.G. Wells novel. Elsewhere in the park, we've been told, roads and parking lots are under water. It all reminds us that the "Father of Waters" is ready to do battle of his own at any time.

Raymond

From Grand Gulf, we follow the route of Grant's supply train from the Mississippi up toward the modern Raymond battlefield. One of the myths of the campaign is that Grant lived off the land, a la Sherman's later March to the Sea, but in fact Frank Blair's division of Sherman's corps ensured Grant had a well-protected supply line. Round road signs that say "Grant's March 1863" point the way, similar to the Civil War Trails signs I'm familiar with back east.

Parker admits he is especially proud of the route, which he helped research and map out. It takes us through Mississippi backcountry, although the terrain seems a little less hostile than it did on the other side of Port Gibson. "Sherman, McPherson, and all of us worked and marched and moved, sleeping on the ground, our army in the lightest marching order," Grant once said of his time on the road.[8]

The well-marked route of Grant's march winds through some beautiful back-country. *Chris Mackowski*

I call to mind a comment from a friend—a native Mississippian who once worked at Vicksburg before moving to a park in the east—when I asked him for travel advice on following Grant's route. "You're heading into banjo country," he laughed.

---

8   John Russell Young, *Around the World with General Grant* (Abridged Edition), Michael Fellman, ed. (Johns Hopkins University Press, 2002), 621.

The Confederate artillery position has a reconstructed Whitworth cannon and two Napoleons. Whitworths were breech-loading pieces, so Parker opened up the breech to offer us a look inside. Its hexagonal rifling allowed for greater accuracy over its longer range. This piece was loaded with "birdshot"–filled with birds' nests! *Chris Mackowski*

We finally arrive in Raymond and the splendid little battlefield outside of town. A great volunteer organization, The Friends of Raymond Battlefield, maintains the site. Together with the American Battlefield Trust, the Friends have helped preserve more than one hundred acres of this battlefield, which was once destined to become a strip mall. Parker is a former president of the Friends, and there is again pride in his voice as he shows off the row of 22 cannons that mark the Federal position.

We set up a Facebook LIVE shot near the guns, with a panorama of thigh-high corn behind us. Parker again wields his double-ended dry-erase markers with military precision and quick attacks. When he shifts away from the easel to show off the guns, Connor smoothly keeps up with him.

Raymond started as a Confederate success when Texans and Tennesseans under Brig. Gen. John Gregg surprised lead elements of McPherson's XVII Corps, but McPherson shifted the odds by exerting his overall numerical edge—including the 7-to1 artillery advantage represented by the impressive line of artillery.

Confederates had a cool artillery feature of their own, though: a breech-loading British Whitworth cannon. Its hexagonal barrel, which could fire a shell six miles, far-outdistanced anything the Federals had. Because of their fitted shape, the shells made a terrifying shriek as they traveled. Parker takes us to the Confederate artillery position to show us Raymond's Whitworth. With the magic powers and know-how that come from his former position as the Friends' president, he even opens the breech of the piece to give us a peek inside.

In all ways, the preservation and interpretation successes at Raymond make the site a centerpiece for visiting Grant's overland campaign through Mississippi. *Chris Mackowski*

The two shiny Napoleons that sit nearby sulk like ugly stepsisters as we ooh and ahh over the Whitworth.

We break for lunch in Raymond, where a giant water tower stands in the center of town looking even more like a menacing Martian war machine than the stilted house did at Grand Gulf. Beneath it, an artillery piece and a high-polish black monument show off the town's Civil War cred. The monument, commemorating 150th anniversary of "The Campaign for Vicksburg," also offers a map and guide to the campaign trail.

Jackson

I've been to Battlefield Park in Jackson, Mississippi, once before, but people warned me against it. My ECW colleague Dan Davis, who went with me that initial time, looked up the address and said, "Uh-oh. Two people

A pair of Spanish-American War-era artillery pieces at Battlefield Park represent the Confederate position. Confederates had four guns here during the (short) battle. The sign mis-identifies the works as Confederate built, but they were constructed by Federals durng the July siege. *Chris Mackowski*

were killed there last January, and a body was found there on May 11."[9] Even today, online reviews say "Stay away. High crime area" and "a cute, tidy park in a bad area of Jackson, MS. It's not worth the possible danger to visit here. Highly advise against visiting. Bad enough to drive by."[10]

By the sounds of it, the battle of Jackson is still ongoing on some level. That seems to be happening on more than one level, though. "Battlefield Park fights for its reputation," one newspaper headline declares.[11]

When we arrive at Battlefield Park, the day could not be more pleasant, and the park looks almost idyllic. We get there midafternoon and find easy parking in a lot off tree-lined West Porter Street. There's some litter scattered against the curb, including an empty beer bottle and a used condom, but otherwise the park looks clean and inviting. I see tennis courts, and somewhere I can hear the thonk-thonk-thonk of a dribbling basketball. Plenty of shade trees—the kind that might cast sinister shadows at night—keep the sun off us.

9 L. Nave, "Battlefield Park Fights For Its Reputation," *Jackson Free Press*, 28 January 2015. https://www.jacksonfreepress.com/news/2015/jan/28/battlefield-park-fights-its-reputation/ (accessed 30 December 2020).

10 https://www.tripadvisor.com/Attraction_Review-g43833-d13440165-Reviews-Battlefield_Park-Jackson_Mississippi.html#REVIEWS

11 Nave.

At 54 acres, Battlefield Park is the largest park in the city, although its main purpose is recreational, for not historical.[12] It supposedly preserves a small area where Confederate artillery fired on Federals from William T. Sherman's advancing XV Corps during the battle of Jackson on May 14, 1863, although, in fact, the shin-high line of earthwork are actually the remains of Brig. Gen. Alvin Hovey's XIII Corps division, built during the siege of Jackson in July. The two artillery pieces—really, the two incomplete skeletons of artillery pieces—that sit in the park to (incorrectly) mark the Confederate position are Spanish-American War-era guns. A nearby sign offers context:

> This park and the surrounding area was involved in the Civil War action which occurred in Jackson on May 14, 1863, and July 9-17, 1863. The earthworks here constitute the most tangible remains of the extensive fortifications which were erected around the city. The property was acquired by the city of Jackson in 1927.

"It was all created out of thin air by the UDC, as best as I can figure, when the park was established in 1927," Jackson-based historian Jim Woodrick later tells me. "So, other than identifying the trenches as Confederate, and pointing the guns in the wrong direction, and the guns being from the wrong war—the kind ladies got everything right!"[13]

Because my oldest son is named Jackson, and because I'm a Stonewall Jackson fanboy, I volunteered before our trip to become our crew's "instant expert" on the battle of Jackson.[14] So when it's time to roll camera, Kris plays host and I play historian, and in the middle of our talk, Kris starts chuckling. Usually he's the one rolling off the micro-tactics, so watching us switch roles amuses him.

"It's like cramming for a test," I tell him afterwards. "I'll forget all this tomorrow!" I've amassed a huge stack of notes for this, though. "I'll have to write something up so I can put 'em to use," I say.[15]

---

12 https://westjxn.com/2016/06/21/city-of-jackson-completes-walking-trail-in-battlefield-park/. It's not, however, the oldest park, as mentioned on the website. That honor belongs to Smith Park in downtown Jackson.

13 James Woodrick to Chris Mackowski, email, 23 May 2021.

14 The city, by the way, was named for Andrew Jackson, not Stonewall.

15 See "The Battle of Jackson—and Off to Moscow!" in this very book!

Historians Tim Smith, Kris White, and Parker Hills, and the Trust's social media guru, Connor Townsend. *Chris Mackowski*

Champion Hill

We cap off our first day on the campaign trail with a visit to Champion Hill on the 155th anniversary of the battle. As a historian, it's always a special treat for me to walk a battlefield on the anniversary of the battle. And to make it even better, we're joined by the guy who wrote the book on the battle, Tim Smith. Professionally, he goes by his full name, Timothy B. Smith, so as not to confuse people with Gettysburg historian Tim Smith. Kris refers to them "Tim Smith of the East" and "Tim Smith of the West."

I'm in full "Civil War Nerd" mode to be out on the field, on the anniversary, with some of the world's greatest experts on the battle.

We start at the Crossroads where state historical markers and a couple monuments tell not only the story of the battle but also the story of the site's preservation. (Since our visit, the Trust has installed a monument on the site to Ed Bearss, former Chief Historian of the National Park Service and former historian at Vicksburg, who had a special place in his heart for Champion Hill.)

The Crossroads is only a "T" now; it had once been a "four-corners," but one of the roads has devolved into an overgrown trace. Dan Davis and I once found the other end of that road trace behind the Champion Hill Missionary

Baptist Church. "Oh, you couldn't pay me enough to go walking down through those woods, all the rattlesnakes down there," said Ray, a carpenter who greeted us warmly when we pulled into the church's lot. His words all came out as a single syllable in a smooth Mississippi accent.

Champion Hill is the largest battle of the Vicksburg campaign. Confederate Lt. Gen. John C. Pemberton, under confusing orders from his superior, Gen. Joseph E. Johnston, left the safety of Vicksburg to link up with Johnston

Someone decked out the Crossroads for the 155th anniversary of the battle. *Chris Mackowski*

in Jackson only to find himself blundering in-to a battle with Grant instead. Outnumbered 22,000 to 32,000, Confederates found themselves knocked back on their heels, although a powerful counterattack by Brig. Gen. John Bowen, who'd tried to mount the stiff defense at Port Gibson on May 3, nearly cracked the Federal army. I'm coming to appreciate Bowen as a "go-to guy" in this campaign and wondering how he might've done with more to work with.

Because of connectivity issues, we shoot our Facebook segments in two parts, one at the Crossroads and one walking up to the very top of the hill. We walk and talk as what appears to be an old logging road winds upward. At the tip-top, there's a sitting area with a bench, which surprises me for some reason, and a historic marker that tells the story of the "hill of death." Much of the top of the hill was stripped away, though, by a gravel-mining operation early in the 20th century. "There are parts of Champion Hill scattered all across the county now," Parker Hills suggested. Trees obscure the view, but what feels like a wilderness stretches out around me for miles and miles.

The plaque on the historical marker at Champion Hill had been stolen once upon a time, but apparently, the thief, feeling guilty, sent the plaque back from Florida. *Chris Mackowski*

Vicksburg

My first (and only other) trip to Vicksburg happened in May 2015. My friend and ECW colleague Dan Davis and I had decided to road-trip through the Western Theater for a week. My daughter, Stephanie, recently graduated from college and a big Civil War buff herself, asked to join us.[16] We drove to Kennesaw Mountain and Atlanta, then down to Andersonville and turned west, hitting Montgomery and Selma, Meridian and Jackson. We hit up Raymond, Champion Hill, and even the Big Black River.

We rolled into Vicksburg just after lunch. By then, the heat index had soared into the low 200s. Celsius. The thermometer actually said something like 89, but it was hard to read with all the sweat stinging my eyes. The humidity was high enough to choke a cat—or a Yankee. I might have lived in Virginia, but my body had acclimated to Northern climes for 45 years, so my physiology didn't care about the address on my driver's license. That Mississippi afternoon redefined "brutal" for me.

I kept myself hydrated, but that only barely kept me going. A sandwich now and then didn't help much, either. There's something about the heat that always saps me. "This isn't like Virginia heat," said Dan, who was feeling it, too. "I'm used to that heat back home. This is something different entirely."

---

16   http://emergingcivilwar.com/tag/civil-war-trip-2015/. Dan now works as education manager at the American Battlefield Trust.

The Memorial Arch near the entrance to the park's loop road has its origins in a 1917 veterans' reunion. It was dedicated in 1920, originally placed on Clay Street; deemed a traffic hazard, it was related to the loop road in 1967. *Chris Mackowski*

By late May 1863, the Federal army had settled into siege lines around Vicksburg. Heat, dirt, flies, and humidity—ugh. But at least they had food and water. The Confederates trapped in the city had ever-decreasing supplies. Pemberton cut rations in half, then cut them in half again. Dogs and cats began to disappear. Then horses. Starvation was their slow, inexorable companion.

That had to be bad enough, but to suffer like that in the sweltering heat must have been misery of a kind I hadn't been able to really appreciate until this visit.

Grant had 50,000 Federals ringing the city, with 31,000 Confederates bottled up inside. On May 19 and again on May 22, Grant assaulted the Southern works but was repulsed both times; that's when he settled on a siege.

After a stop at the Visitor Center to get oriented, we passed beneath the park's memorial arch and followed the Tour Road as it snaked along the Federal and then the Confederate lines, first in a northern, and then in a smaller, southern loop—sixteen miles of road in all. Thirteen hundred monuments, tablets, and markers dotted the landscape, putting the battlefield in the same league as Gettysburg or Chickamauga as far as monumentation.

Unlike those two battlefields, though, where there's tremendous variety and character to the monuments, the monuments from each state are more standardized at Vicksburg. Indiana's look like thick, low rectangles with inscriptions on their tabletop surfaces. Ohio's look like small, partially unrolled scrolls. Iowa's look like miniature Greek temples.

One really surprising thing I liked: a tremendous number of regimental colonels have monuments dedicated to them, ornamented with bas-relief portraits. Similarly, most general officers have larger-than-life busts on pedestals along the Tour Road. A few have statues. A few governors even have statues.

Grant dominates the landscape. He sits astride his horse, Kangaroo, looking out across the battlescape. Two carved granite benches flank him, inviting visitors to sit a spell, but Grant's pose does not suggest that he wants to chat.

Ulysses S. Grant was widely recognized as one of the best horsemen in the army—so good he could make his horses stand as still as statues. *Chris Mackowski*

There's no path up to the benches, either, further discouraging visitation. The day's raw, open sun and suffocating humidity discourage us, too.

The only other Union officer who has an equestrian statue is Grant's perpetual pain in the ass, John McClernand, who sits near the Iowa monument—which also includes a magnificent equestrian statue—on the southern end of the line. Leave it to McClernand to try to outshine his commander, even here, even now. Grant gave McClernand the boot after the corps commander issued an order to his men patting them—and himself—on the back for action on May 22 while badmouthing the other corps.

Sherman is nowhere to be found. Neither is McPherson. McPherson gets forgotten so often that I wasn't surprised, but Sherman's absence struck me as an act of postwar passive-aggressiveness. He doesn't get a lot of love in the South, even now.

The thing that impressed me most is the battlefield's landscape. The terrain rolls and splashes like the massive waves of an angry ocean. The earthworks are well preserved, but the really stunning thing is that the land between the lines still bears the scars of bombardment. Time and time again, we pulled over, got out, and couldn't believe the view.

If there's a temple anywhere on any battlefield, it's the Illinois Memorial near the Shirley House. It's a highly symbolic structure: the 47 steps to get inside, for instance, represent the number of days of the siege. McClernand and Logan—whose division attacked along the nearby avenue, and who has a statue not far from here—both had Illinois connections, too, as did Lincoln and Grant, of course. The state also had more men participate in the siege than any other state.

The most peculiar monument I saw anywhere

A gold eagle atop the domed roof of the Illinois monument is often mistaken for "Old Abe," the mascot of the 8th Wisconsin—wrong state. *Chris Mackowski*

on the field was the plaza-like Kentucky Memorial. Installed in October 2001, it sits between the lines on the south end of the field where Kentuckians of both sides squared off against each other. The memorial features Lincoln and Davis—both Kentucky born—standing on the state seal. The inscription "United we stand. Divided we fall." wraps around them. Other text points out Kentucky's contributions to both sides during the war, including both presidents. Lincoln and Davis have freakish proportions, though, and look especially awkward and un-lifelike. I like the monument's concept, with a huge emphasis on commonalities and reconciliation, but overall it's a little surreal, to be honest,

The sculptor of the Kentucky monument originally wanted Lincoln and Davis shaking hands to replicate the figures in the state seal who are shaking hands, but the two men never actually met, so a handshake, no matter how much artistic license one might excuse, would have been too historically inaccurate. *Chris Mackowski*

Nearby, among a row of six Bluegrass generals, is a bust of John Breckinridge, depicted with postwar muttonchops so outrageous that they looked like an act of spite. I took a photo for my wife, a collateral descendent.

We ran into Jeff Davis elsewhere on the field where he was carrying a semi-furled Confederate flag over his left shoulder. He looked positively invigorated by Mississippi's heat and humidity. Davis, as a former resident of the Magnolia state, gets a lot of love in Mississippi. The Old Courthouse Museum downtown, which we also visited on the trip, has an entire room devoted to him.

There was actually much to see outside of the park. The national

For the record, John Breckinridge didn't sport this style of facial hair until after the war, although now he has it forever. (And you thought Ambrose Burnside had crazy facial hair. . . .) *Chris Mackowski*

military park used to encompass the entire siege line, but in the 1960s the Park Service turned over the lower third of its property to the city in exchange for some road closures elsewhere in the park. There are still monuments aplenty along what is now South Confederate Avenue but stopping to admire them as we did on the Tour Road was a lot more dangerous. My Virginia license

The best way for a president to show he loves his country is for him to hug the flag—just as Jefferson Davis does on the Vicksburg battlefield. *Chris Mackowski*

plates probably didn't engender any sympathy as a fellow Southerner; the glares I got pegged me as just some out-of-town rubbernecker.

We finally made it to the river's edge undented, where a stocky artillery piece dominated the heights. This was the Louisiana Circle, a position so formidable Federals never assaulted it. I could see Louisiana on the far side of the river and wondered how these soldiers felt to be so close to home yet so far away.

A little farther to the south were two other detached units of the park: South Fort and Navy Circle.

We grabbed some dinner and, somewhere between the breadsticks and the mushroom pizza, we realized we weren't going to make our late-day drive to Tupelo. The heat had sapped us. Vicksburg wore us down to the point that we couldn't leave.

Which turned out to be just fine. We ended up breaking out a few cigars and sat atop the defenses at Navy Circle and watched the sun set over the Mississippi. The Father of Waters flowed unvexed to the sea, and we were happy to spend some time watching him. He brought a breeze with him. We all felt better.

The siege of Vicksburg ended just fine.

Grant's Canal

When Kris and Connor and I arrive in Vicksburg on our 155th expedition, our first stop is actually on the far side of the Mississippi, a small park unit on DeSoto Point in what is, today, Delta, Louisiana. As hilly as the Vicksburg side of the river is, the Louisiana side is low and flat—river flood plain, for sure, at least once upon a time.

Just off the interstate exit sits a local convenience store filled with snacks, drinks, tobacco, beer, wine, and hard liquor. A trailer selling frozen daiquiris sits at the other end of the parking lot. Welcome to Louisiana.

We turn in the other direction, though, and cross some railroad tracks. Old Highway 80 parallels them for a while, but before we get into the little village of Delta itself we turn again and pass under I-20. Grant's Canal—a tiny unit of Vicksburg National Military park—sits nearby.

Originally built to be sixty feet wide by six feet deep, the remains of Grant's Canal look like little more than a 100-yard-long grassy driveway to nowhere. Most of the canal has been "obliterated through agricultural operations,"

Little remains of the canal, although it's distinct enough to see well in person. The far end, shown here, still collects water. *Chris Mackowski*

according to the Park Service, and what remains has largely been filled in by erosion.[17] Trees line the banks, and on the east side a sidewalk runs the length, dotted by wayside signs and aluminum War Department tablets. Water fills the far end, and I can easily imagine a couple alligators in there, invisible, watching me.

I am fascinated! Just the idea of the canal intrigues me. After Grant's repulse at Chickasaw Bayou December 26-29, 1862, he turned to the canal as a possible avenue for bypassing Vicksburg altogether.

17 https://www.nps.gov/vick/learn/historyculture/grants-canal.htm

The idea wasn't his, though. In the summer of 1862, 3,000 men under Brig. Gen. Thomas Williams dug the first attempt at a canal through here. Toiling in the Mississippi summer and malarial swamp, his men began to succumb to exhaustion, heatstroke, and disease. Williams tried to compensate by impressing "Between 1,100 and 1,200 blacks, gathered from neighboring plantations by armed parties," but by July 24, work stopped. "The labor of making this cut is far greater than estimated by anybody," Williams reported.[18]

Grant picked up the task in January. "The canal don't amount to much," groused Sherman, still grumpy after his repulse at Chickasaw.[19] At one point, the canal flooded and workers had to scramble to re-do much of

The 9th Connecticut monument honors one of the regiments that helped build the initial canal in the summer of 1862. A close-up of the monument shows men suffering from disease and heatstroke while working. *Chris Mackowski*

their work. Finally, in March, as Grant developed other plans for cracking Vicksburg, he abandoned the canal altogether, proving Sherman right in the end. The canal didn't amount to much.

A bronze marker atop a squat stone pillar tells the story of Grant's Canal; the marker, erected by the village of Delta, dates to 1936[20]. There's also a tablet commemorating the work of Black troops during the siege and at the battle of Milliken's Bend on June 7, 1863. Most impressive, because of its size, polished black surface, and laser etching, is the Connecticut State

18   Ibid.

19   Ibid.

20   https://www.hmdb.org/m.asp?m=84469

Memorial, erected in 2008. The memorial recognizes the work of the 9th Connecticut, part of Williams' summer excavation force. Of the 845 men in the regiment, 153 died during the four-week canal project. Etchings on the monument reproduce portraits of members of the regiment; others depict the sufferings of the men.[21]

Kris, Connor, and I try to do a live shot from canalside, but we have poor connectivity. We end up doing the shot in three segments, wrapping up the last one in short order before a disconnection wraps it up for us involuntarily. Besides, I'm sure there's an alligator waiting for me to turn my back long enough that it can pounce.

Vicksburg National Military Park

For our first shoot of the day in Vicksburg National Military Park, Kris kicks things off in front of an artillery display near the visitor center, and fire ants swarm up his leg. He doesn't notice them at first, but they get thick fast. As he talks to the camera, he tries subtly shaking his leg the way a cow might try to twitch away an errant fly. He quickly realizes what's going on—this is no fly—so he pitches the program over to Parker and smoothly slides out of the frame. Off-camera, there's much swatting and beating and aerosol clouds of bug spray.

We hit several key locations during the day, accompanied by Parker and Tim, as well as the

14-year-old drummer boy Orion Howe earned the Medal of Honor for actions in front of the Stockade Redan, relaying information to Sherman. *Chris Mackowski*

21 https://www.nps.gov/vick/learn/historyculture/connecticut-state-memorial.htm

The *Cairo* spent 102 years underwater before being recovered in the 1960s. The hole created by the explosion, below the ship's waterline, is still visible today. Amazingly, no one was killed in the explosion even though two gun crews were working in close proximity. *Chris Mackowski*

park's chief of interpretation, Scott Babinowich. These places are iconic: The Shirley House, the Illinois Monument, the 3rd Louisiana Redan. We walk in the footsteps of the "Forlorn Hope" assaulting Stockade Redan. We watch a special black powder rifle-firing demonstration put on exclusively for us. We see Federal efforts to build a mine and blow open part of the Confederate line.

The whole battlefield is an extravagant sculpture park, amazing to behold.

USS *Cairo*

At the northern tip of the park, we visit the USS *Cairo*. The *Cairo* was a city-class brown water ironclad protected by tons of armor plating on its sides. The bow of the ship even had extra protection called "railroad armor" because it was literally made of railroad rails; the full ship couldn't get the extra armor because it would've made it too heavy.

Not that all that iron ended up doing the *Cairo* any good in the end. The ironclad has the distinction of being the first ship ever sunk by an electronic mine—or, as NPS historian Ray Hamel describes it, what today we'd really describe as an IED. Ray gives us a great tour and then, as a special bonus, lets us check out the museum's collection of ordnance recovered from the *Cairo*.

Now-retired park historian Terry Winschel lets Kris White pick his brain about the siege of Vicksburg. *Chris Mackowski*

Vicksburg National Cemetery

We wrap up our Facebook LIVE broadcasts with a segment from Vicksburg National Cemetery. Seventeen thousand men are buried here; 14,000 are unidentified.[22]

As a special treat, the park's former chief historian, Terry Winschel, joins us to conclude the siege and discuss the aftermath of the battle. Terry is a legendary figure and a Southern gentleman (even though originally from Pittsburgh), so it's a real treat for me to meet him. We all stroll through the cemetery, and Terry shares story after story, sparked by different headstones we pass—and we're not even broadcasting yet. It's tragedy told compellingly and compassionately.

A giant Indian mound—which is just a landscaped hill, not an actual Indian mound (like the ones at Shiloh, for instance)—a stands on

22 https://www.nps.gov/vick/learn/historyculture/tour-stop-8-national-cemetery.htm

The Indian mound near the back corner of Vicksburg National Cemetery isn't actually an Indian mound. It was once just a hill but was reshaped as part of the same landscaping that created the cemetery's terraces. *LOC*

the back side of the cemetery. A brick staircase gives us access to the top where a gazebo—a "rest pavilion," as described by the park—provides a contemplative space.[23] The drop from the top of the mound, at least a couple stories, is precipitous, and I keep worrying I'll fall to my doom if I get within ten feet of the edge. On camera, I try to keep up my energy, but one eye is always watching for that edge. This final perch, though, from the top of the Indian mound, offers a stunning view of the national cemetery—and a poignant reminder of the cost of war.

---

23   https://www.nps.gov/articles/rehabilitation-of-the-indian-mound-steps-in-vicksburg-national-cemetery.htm

"Praise the Lord
and Admiral Porter":
Running the Vicksburg Batteries

by Dwight S. Hughes

*Originally published as a blog post on Emerging Civil War
on November 4, 2020*

"We still live," wrote Lt. Elias Smith of the USS *Lafayette*. "The whole gunboat fleet passed the Vicksburg batteries on Thursday night [April 16, 1863], without receiving material damage. All praise to the Lord and Admiral Porter." As far as he knew, no Union lives had been lost; about a dozen were wounded, two seriously, out of some two thousand men.

The U. S. Navy now had six river ironclads, one wooden gunboat, and two troop transports in Rebel territory below the city. "How we escaped the firing ordeal as well as we did, is a mystery to us all. We were under fire for over an hour: and such fire! Earthquakes, thunder and volcanoes, hailstones and coals of fire; New York conflagrations and Fourth of July pyrotechnics—they were nothing to it."[1]

Smith's observations were recorded in letters to friends and then published in the *New York Times*. The ironclad ram *Lafayette*—converted from a 280-

---

1 H. Walke, *Naval Scenes and Reminiscences of the Civil War in the United States, on the Southern and Western Waters During the Years 1861, 1862 and 1863 with the History of that Period* (New York: F. R. Reed & Company, 1877), 353-359. All subsequent Smith quotes from this source.

foot sidewheel steamer—was a mainstay of Rear Admiral David D. Porter's Mississippi River Squadron supporting Maj. Gen. Ulysses S. Grant in his campaign to take the Gibraltar of the West with the Army of the Tennessee.

The admiral and the general made a powerful team, melding maritime mobility and firepower with hard fighting on land. It had been a long slog, however. In late December 1862, Grant sent Maj. Gen. William T. Sherman downriver with a major amphibious force, landing at Chickasaw Bayou northeast of Vicksburg only to be repulsed with heavy casualties.

Porter's attempt to send gunboats up the Yazoo River and outflank the Confederate army facing Grant also failed, losing the ironclad USS *Cairo* to a Rebel torpedo—the first ship to be sunk by an electronic explosive device detonated remotely by hand.

During the winter and spring of 1862/63, Grant and Porter conducted a series of intense operations to outflank the city from north and east by digging canals, blowing up levees, flooding the Mississippi Delta, and pushing ironclads, gunboats, and troop transports through tiny, choked, and sluggish channels and swamps. All fruitless.

Grant's final option was to march the army through the swamps down the west side of the Mississippi, crossing the river south of and getting behind Vicksburg. Admiral Porter would have to sneak his gunboats and fragile transports downriver past powerful and plentiful enemy batteries on the bluffs with enough vessels surviving to suppress opposition and get the army safely across the Big Muddy.

Porter assumed this was a one-way, one-time run; it would be suicidal to creep back up against strong current. If the Navy failed, the Army of the Tennessee could be trapped on the wrong side.

It had been unthinkable in previous centuries for delicate wood and canvas men-of-war—dependent on fickle wind and armed with smaller weapons—to take on shore emplacements. Steam, iron, and increasingly powerful naval artillery had evened the odds between ship and shore. Ironclads were still vulnerable, however, especially to plunging shot; transports had no protection.

The Union navy first successfully ran Rebel batteries at Island Number 10 upriver just the previous year, but only with two ironclads (and no transports) against less formidable batteries on low sandbanks.

At about 9:30 p.m. on a clear, moonless night, *Lafayette* slipped her

The naval ram *Lafayette* didn't look pretty, but she got the job done. Note the iron casing around the ship's sidewheel paddles. *Naval History and Heritage Command*

moorings. The wooden gunboat USS *General Price* and a heavily-laden coal barge were lashed alongside to starboard where *Lafayette*'s armored casemate would at least partially shield them. Just ahead of *Lafayette* was the big ironclad USS *Benton*, lead ship in the column with Admiral Porter aboard; the rest of the squadron followed.

In the swirling river, the cumbersome *Benton* "persistently refused to point her head down stream," continued Lieutenant Smith. "It was an hour later before the fleet were under way in her wake." Admiral Porter recalled: "We started down the Mississippi as quietly as possible, drifting with the current. Dogs and crowing hens were left behind." Engines were silent. Chains, cotton bales, hay bales, and logs piled along the decks provided additional protection.

A grand ball was to be held in the city that night; the admiral hoped "sounds of revelry" would mask their approach. "As I looked back at the long line I could compare them only to so many phantom vessels. Not a light was to be seen nor a sound heard throughout the fleet."

Benton's low, dark shadow crept around the point below the heights looming up 280 feet. "We will, no doubt, slip by unnoticed," the admiral remarked to the boat's captain, "the rebels seem to keep a very poor watch."[2] *Lafayette* followed, her men standing silently to their weapons. Portside guns—9" and 11" Dahlgren smoothbores and a 100-pounder rifle—were

---

2 David Dixon Porter, *Incidents and Anecdotes of the Civil War* (New York: D. Appleton and Company, 1885), 175-177. All subsequent Porter quotes from this source.

ready, some at decreased elevation against lower Rebel emplacements and others elevated to strike middle and upper tiers.

"The whole heavens were suddenly illuminated," wrote Smith. "The lurid flames, as they shot up from the opposite shore, almost to mid heavens, converted the star-lit night into the brightness of noonday." On the west bank, a railroad station, outbuildings, and prepositioned barrels of tar burst into flames, backlighting the fleet.

"We had not surprised them in the least," noted Porter. "The upper fort opened its heavy guns upon the Benton, the shot rattling against her sides like hail. . . ." But the blistering deluge made little impression on four inches of iron plating over forty inches of oak. "There being no longer any concealment possible, we stood to our guns and returned the enemy's fire."

"Every fort and hill-top vomited forth shot and shell, many of the latter bursting in the air and doing no damage, but adding to the grandeur of the scene. As fast as our vessels came within range of the forts they opened their broadsides, and soon put a stop to any revelry that might be going on in Vicksburg."

"At 11.20, the first shots greeted us from the batteries," continued Smith. "The 'Lafayette' seemed to attract particular attention." Tall chimneys and wheelhouse with a steamer alongside made her a good mark, "two birds with one stone." "Standing there amidst that silent group of rough but earnest men, periling their lives for their country, I thought of the kindness of our 'dear Southern Brethren,' as shot after shot swept over us with the scream of tigers eager for prey. . . ."

"Five hundred, perhaps a thousand, guns were discharged, *but not more than one in ten struck, or did any damage to the fleet.* They mostly went over. . . . In such a case, it was hard to 'turn the other cheek;' in fact, it was more satisfactory to give than to receive."

The Union column hugged the east bank to get under the line of fire, so close they could hear Rebel gunners shouting orders while shells zinged overhead.

Through open gun ports, Lieutenant Smith had a good view down enemy barrels, "which now flashed like a thunder-storm along the river as far as the eye could see; but the incessant splatter of rifle balls, the spray from falling shot, the thunder of steel-pointed projectiles upon our sides, did not incline one to take a very *protracted view* of the scenery."

Lafayette's gunners got off a few discharges of grape, shrapnel, and

Admiral Porter's Fleet Running Rebel Batteries at Vicksburg, April 16th, 1863. Currier & Ives Lithograph, New York, 1863. *Naval History & Heritage Command*

percussion shell "in the very teeth of the Confederate batteries. . . . At each round the rebel artillery-men gave a shout, which seemed surprisingly near." The ironclad wafted by not one hundred yards from Vicksburg wharves.

Lafayette became almost unmanageable, swinging in river eddies until she was "*looking the batteries in the face*." Roiling gun smoke and the glare of burning buildings blinded the pilot. Bursting shells singed his hair but left him unhurt.

"The enemy, supposing we were disabled, set up a fiendish yell of triumph. We soon, however, backed round, and once more presented our broadside to them, and slowly drifted past, as if in contempt of their impotent efforts." Shells sank the coal barge, "thus relieving us of one great obstacle to our movements."

Wrought iron and steel-pointed missiles, 18-24 inches long, 6 to 8 inches in diameter, and about 100 pounds "were thrown by some of the heaviest rifle guns known to modern warfare," continued Smith. "Nine shots struck the ship, and several of them penetrated the casemates, making large holes and scattering their fragments, and that of the wood-work. . . ."

Lafayette's armor was 2.5" of plate and 2" of India rubber (which proved useless) over 3" of oak plank, but the armor thinned to 1" plate and 1" rubber aft where most shots came through.

One round smashed through the pilothouse just missing the pilot. A 100-pounder skimmed over the boiler, obliterated a wood partition, and showered wood chips over *Lafayette*'s captain. Another passed through the paddlewheel housing, clipped the crank arm, and buried itself two feet into solid shaft supporting timber.

Smith's stateroom was wrecked. He found his mattress sacking turned to pulp amongst two bushels of corn shucks—finely ground—along with piles of pine chips, the ruin of a straw hat, blankets and clothing, "all covered with the debris of the room, which had been most elegantly ventilated." And yet not one of the two hundred crewmen received a scratch.

On *Benton*, a gunner had his leg taken off; another crewman was wounded by a rifle ball through a gun port. Back down the line, the transport *Henry Clay* was hit hard, recorded Admiral Porter, but "the courageous pilot . . . stood at his post and, with his vessel all ablaze, attempted to run past the fleet." Men jumped into the water while the vessel floated until she burned up. The pilot was rescued.

Blazing cotton bales blanketed the river, "looking like a thousand lamps." The superstructure of the *Forest Queen* was nearly cut in two, but she made it through in repairable condition. The other transport, *Silver Wave*, suffered minor damage.

"The enemy's artillery fire was not much to boast of," concluded the admiral, "considering that they had over a hundred guns firing at us as we drifted down stream in such close order that it would seem to have been impossible to miss us."

"The sight was a grand one, and I stood on deck admiring it, while the captain fought his vessel and the pilot steered her through fire and smoke as coolly as if he was performing an everyday duty. The Vicksburgers must have been disappointed when they saw us get by their batteries with so little damage."

"We suffered most from the musketry fire. The soldiers lined the levee and fired into our port-holes,—wounding our men, for we were not more than twenty yards from the shore. Once only the fleet got into a little disorder, owing to the thick smoke which hung over the river, but the commanding officers, adhering to their orders 'to drift only,' got safely out of the difficulty."

On the night of April 22, six more transports loaded with supplies made the run with little damage. Then, under cover of naval artillery, General Grant ferried his army across the river, and surrounded and laid siege to Vicksburg, which surrendered on July 4, 1863.

It was one of the most brilliant campaigns of the war, at least as important as the simultaneous victory at Gettysburg. Admiral Porter and the Mississippi River Squadron transported the army, dominated the river, blockaded the city from the west, and provided continuous heavy shore bombardment.

A Poet's Perspective: Melville on Running the Batteries at Vicksburg

by Caroline Davis

Originally published as a blog post at Emerging Civil War on April 16, 2021

It was the spring of 1863, and Union Gen. Ulysses S. Grant was concocting a plan to seize the city of Vicksburg, Mississippi. As President Abraham Lincoln had made clear, Vicksburg was key to achieving victory over the Confederates and ending the war.

With help from Admiral David Dixon Porter, Grant launched a plan that in modern terms could be described as a "Hail Mary" in the fourth quarter with one final chance to score. The plan required Porter and his fleet to navigate a miles-long stretch of the Mississippi controlled by the Confederates. Porter made his pass on April 16, 1863.

The scene as described by poet Herman Melville:

> A moonless night--a friendly one;
> A haze dimmed the shadowy shore
> As the first lampless boat slid silent on;
> Hist! and we spake no more;
> We but pointed, and stilly, to what we saw.

Running the batteries at Vicksburg: A Confederate perspective. *LOC*

We felt the dew, and seemed to feel
The secret like a burden laid.
The first boat melts; and a second keel
Is blent with the foliaged shade--
Their midnight rounds have the rebel officers made?

Unspied as yet. A third--a fourth--
Gun-boat and transport in Indian file
Upon the war-path, smooth from the North;
But the watch may they hope to beguile?
The manned river-batteries stretch for mile on mile.[1]

Porter's primary objective was to ferry supplies to Federal troops stationed at New Carthage, Louisiana, and then to bring those troops to the east bank of the Mississippi. To accomplish this, Porter's boats would have to sneak past the Confederate river batteries at Vicksburg. Failure would mean the destruction of Porter's squadron, his career, and possibly his life.

---

1 All selections from Melville's poem come from Herman Melville, *Battle Pieces: The Civil War poems of Herman Melville* (Edison, NJ: Castle Books, 2000), 75-78.

Porter steamed downriver with seven ironclad gunboats and three transports, ordering his men to extinguish all lights and cover all ports until the vessels were close enough to open fire on the enemy. "Before starting, the hour of departure will be given, and every vessel will have her fires well ignited, so that they will show as little smoke as possible," said Porter.[2]

The plan seemed to be working until Porter's fleet rounded De Soto Point—when all of a sudden the enemy troops began lighting fires to illuminate the passing boats.

Melville wrote of this terrifying moment in his poem:

Herman Melville made his literary reputation writing about nautical themes, so it's little wonder he found Porter's adventures so fascinating. *LOC*

A flame leaps out; they are seen;
Another and another gun roars;
We tell the course of the boats through the screen
By each further fort that pours,
And we guess how they jump from their beds on those shrouded shores.

Converging fires. We speak, though low:
"That blastful furnace can they thread"
"Why, Shadrach, Meshach, and Abed-nego
Came out all right, we read;
The Lord, be sure, he helps his people, Ned."

How we strain our gaze. On bluffs they shun
A golden growing flame appears--
Confirms to a silvery steadfast one:

2   C.B. Boynton, *The History of the Navy During the Rebellion,* Vol. 2 (Cambridge, MA: D. Appleton & Company, 1886), 386.

"The town is afire!" crows Hugh: "three cheers"
Lot stops his mouth: "Nay, lad, better three tears."

A purposed light; it shows our fleet;
Yet a little late in its searching ray,
So far and strong, that in phantom cheat
Lank on the deck our shadows lay;
The shining flag-ship stings their guns to furious play.

Porter's fleet became more vulnerable with each torch that appeared on the bluffs, and it didn't take long for the Confederates to open fire. Porter's vessels took shelter against the riverbank, but every single boat was struck at least once. It is estimated that the Confederates fired more than 500 rounds into the fleet. Here's the action as described by Melville:

How dread to mark her near the glare
And glade of death the beacon throws
Athwart the racing waters there;
One by one each plainer grows,
Then speeds a blazoned target to our gladdened foes.

The impartial cresset lights as well
The fixed forts to the boats that run;
And, plunged from the ports, their answers swell
Back to each fortress dun:
Ponderous words speaks every monster gun.

Fearless they flash through gates of flame,
The salamanders hard to hit,
Though vivid shows each bulky frame;
And never the batteries intermit,
Nor the boats huge guns; they fire and flit.

Anon a lull. The beacon dies:
"Are they out of that strait accurst"
But other flames now dawning rise,

Not mellowly brilliant like the first,
But rolled in smoke, whose whitish volumes burst

Though bruised and battered, most of Porter's flotilla made it successfully through the gauntlet. One transport wasn't so lucky, having caught fire when a shell struck a bale of hay.

A baleful brand, a hurrying torch
Whereby anew the boats are seen—
A burning transport all alurch!
Breathless we gaze; yet still we glean
Glimpses of beauty as we eager lean.

The effulgence takes an amber glow
Which bathes the hill-side villas far;
Affrighted ladies mark the show
Painting the pale magnolia--
The fair, false, Circe light of cruel War.

The barge drifts doomed, a plague-struck one.
Shoreward in yawls the sailors fly.
But the gauntlet now is nearly run,
The spleenful forts by fits reply,
And the burning boat dies down in morning's sky.

All out of range. Adieu, Messieurs!
Jeers, as it speeds, our parting gun.
So burst we through their barriers
And menaces every one:
So Porter proves himself a brave man's son.

Porter's flight down the Mississippi took less than three hours but had a permanent impact on the Union's position. And, despite the heavy shelling, not a single life was lost. All sailors aboard the destroyed transport ship were relocated to nearby vessels. Thanks to Porter's bravery, General Grant was now in a position to launch a ground assault against the fortifications at

Vicksburg. The first objective was to move his men across the Mississippi, an effort that would lead to more fighting.

It began in Grand Gulf, Mississippi. On April 29, seven Union ironclads opened fire on Fort Wade and Fort Cobun, using their massive guns to blow holes in the riverside defenses. The guns of Fort Wade were silenced before 10:00 a.m. Fort Cobun remained defiant, though, and targeted the USS *Benton*— Porter's flagship in

Grand Gulf Military Park, opened in 1962, is dedicated to preserving the memory of both the town and the 1863 battle that occurred there. *Kris White*

the run at Vicksburg—and successfully handicapped the vessel by destroying its wheel. Porter himself was struck in the head by a shell fragment, causing an injury that forced him to start using his sword as a cane.

All told, Union forces suffered a total of 75 casualties (18 dead, 57 wounded) while Confederate forces suffered 22 casualties (3 dead, 19 wounded). The USS *Benton* and the USS *Tuscumbia* suffered significant damage but were able to remain with the fleet.[3]

At this point Porter and Grant abandoned their plans to make an amphibious landing at Grand Gulf. Instead, they launched a second attack on Fort Cobun to distract the Confederates while the transport vessels continued south toward Disharoon Plantation and made a successful landing at Bruinsburg, Mississippi.

The final campaign to take Vicksburg had begun.

3 See OR of the Union and Confederate Navies, Vol. 24 at 610-11, 613.

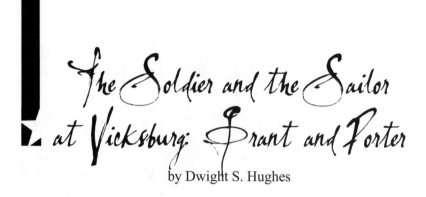

The Soldier and the Sailor at Vicksburg: Grant and Porter

by Dwight S. Hughes

On a late September day in 1862, Acting Rear Admiral David Dixon Porter was ushered into the presidential office. He had just been promoted over several ranks and several more senior contemporaries to command the Mississippi River Squadron. "I promised you," said Abraham Lincoln, "that you should see Vicksburg fall, and now you shall do it." The president inquired how the task should be accomplished. His plans were simple, replied Porter: "A large naval force, a strong body of troops, and patience, were the only means. . . ." Not long ago, continued the admiral, Vicksburg easily could have been taken, "but it is now a second Gibraltar, and the navy alone could do nothing. . . ."

"Well," said the President, "whom do you think is the general for such an occasion?" "General Grant, sir. Vicksburg is within his department; but I presume he will send Sherman there, who is equal to any occasion." Lincoln countered with another candidate: Maj. Gen. John A. McClernand, "an old and intimate friend of mine," the man who "saved the battle of Shiloh" and who was "a natural born general." McClernand, a prominent Illinois Democrat, had appealed personally to the president for an independent command with orders to campaign against the Confederate bastion.

"Why, Mr. President," Porter answered, "the general impression is that Grant won the battle of Shiloh; as he commanded the army, he would seem entitled to the credit. . . . With all due deference to you, I don't believe in natural-born generals except where they have had proper military training, and it seems to me the siege of Vicksburg is too important a matter to trust to anybody except a scientific military man; besides, if you take troops from Grant and Sherman to give them to McClernand, you will weaken the army." [1]

This exchange is recorded in Porter's *Incidents and Anecdotes of the Civil War* (1885) in which the admiral was wonderfully descriptive and often funny. He also was relentlessly self-promoting and occasionally creative or misremembering.

The reconstructed narrative does, however, introduce us to an underappreciated partnership— an army-navy partnership—that played a monumental role in a critical campaign: Maj. Gen. Ulysses S. Grant commanding the Army of the Tennessee and Admiral David D. Porter commanding the U. S. Navy Mississippi River Squadron while Maj. Gen. William T. Sherman contributed.

Sailors tell tall tales, as Adm. David D. Porter's memoirs often demonstrate. They're still well worth a read. *LOC*

Given the unprecedented nature of riverine warfare, success of this collaboration would hinge on the personalities and wills of these commanders and their subordinates down to individual units and vessels. Americans had no experience before 1862 with extensive operations on inland waterways requiring specialized classes of war vessels commanded and manned by naval personnel cooperating with land forces. The U. S. Navy began the war with no shallow-water warships, no tactics, no command structure, no

---

1   David Dixon Porter, *Incidents and Anecdotes of the Civil War* (New York: D. Appleton and Company, 1885), 137-138.

infrastructure. Below the commander in chief, there was no joint army-navy commander, no joint staff, and no protocols or mechanisms for directing joint operations.

Most officers considered their professions as disparate preserves of land and sea bounded by the hightide mark. Neither service was versed in the relatively new—less than a half-century old—business of steam rivermen and rivercraft now swarming heartland waters. Traditionally, officers of one service could issue no orders to an officer of the other service, respective rank notwithstanding. Military cultures with distinct organizations, technologies, and skills were required to cooperate within a common strategic framework. When respective service leaders failed to plan and execute together effectively, tactical missteps and lost strategic opportunities followed. Efficient partnerships produced hard won victories, but it was a learning process.

"I assumed command of the Mississippi Squadron at Cairo, Illinois, in October, 1862," Porter continued. "There were the sturdy ironclads that had fought their way-from Fort Henry to Donaldson, to Island No. 10, and White River, and destroyed the enemy's navy at Memphis. All had done good service under their gallant commanders, [Flag Officer Andrew H.] Foote and [Flag Officer Charles H.] Davis.

"The [ironclads] *Benton, Carondelet, Cairo, Baron de Kalb, Mound City*, and *Cincinnati. . .* became famous in the annals of the navy," recalled Porter. "Besides these were the [timberclads] *Tyler, Conestoga*, and *Lexington. . . .* The rest of the vessels under my command were not very formidable, consisting of some side-wheel river steamboats and three or four 'tin-clads,' and this was the force with which the navy was expected to batter down Vicksburg."[2]

General Grant and Flag Officer[3] Foote had teamed up for the capture of Forts Henry and Donelson in February 1862, but Foote was wounded

---

2 Ibid., 140.

3   The rank of "flag officer" was established in 1857 designating a senior officer commanding a group of war vessels—a squadron—and authorized to fly a distinctive banner on this "flagship." Until then, the senior U. S. Navy rank had been captain, equivalent to army colonel. The navy had no general officer equivalents because it had never deployed squadrons of more than a few ships, commanded by the senior captain present. With the massive expansion of the navy, admiral ranks would be established later in 1862, equivalent to army generals. David G. Farragut was the first admiral; David D. Porter was the second.

and reassigned. Coordinating with the army, navy gunboats now under Flag Officer Davis methodically cleared the Mississippi down to Vicksburg. But Navy Secretary Gideon Welles thought Davis was "not an energetic, driving, fighting officer, such as is wanted for rough work on the Mississippi; is kind and affable, but has not the vim, dash, recklessness perhaps is the better word—of Porter."[4]

Porter's appointment was an experiment, Welles confided to his diary, "and the results not entirely certain." Many senior officers would be dissatisfied, but juniors might be stimulated. "The river naval service is unique. Foote performed wonders and dissipated many prejudices. The army has fallen in love with the gunboats and wants them in every creek. Porter is wanting in some of the best qualities of Foote, but excels him perhaps in others. The service requires great energy, great activity, abundant resources. Porter is full of each, but is reckless, improvident, often too presuming and assuming."[5]

Welles's diary contradicts Porter's recollection of the discussions surrounding his promotion. According to the suspicious secretary, the admiral (who had never met Grant) expressed satisfaction at Lincoln's appointment of McClernand to command an independent army against Vicksburg and would readily cooperate with him. "[Porter] dreads and protests against association with any West Point general; says they are too self-sufficient, pedantic, and unpractical." This was partly, thought Welles, because the navy officer "feared he should be compelled to play a subordinate part with [a West Pointer], while with a civilian general he would have superiority." The admiral was "given to cliquism."[6]

From Cairo, Porter advised Grant by messenger that he had taken command of the naval forces and that he "should be happy to co-operate with him in any enterprise he might think proper to undertake." On November 20, the admiral was enjoying a supper party aboard the army quartermaster's steamboat when a short, travel-worn person in civilian dress was ushered in and introduced as General Grant. Though evidently tired and hungry, the

4 *Diary of Gideon Welles, Secretary of the Navy under Lincoln and Johnson*, 3 vols. (Boston; New York: Houghton Mifflin Company, 1911), vol. 1, 157-158.

5 Ibid., 167.

6 Ibid., 167, 220.

general commenced business at once, as again recalled by Porter.

"When can you move with your gun-boats, and what force have you?" "I can move to-morrow with all the old gun-boats and five or six other vessels. . . ." "Well, then," said Grant, "I will leave you now and write at once to Sherman to have thirty thousand infantry and artillery embarked in transports ready to start for Vicksburg the moment you get to Memphis. I will return to Holly Springs to-night, and will start with a large force for Grenada as soon as I can get off."

"I thought this plan an admirable one," noted Porter. "This was the preliminary step to the capture of Vicksburg."

"Grant and myself never indulged in long talks together," continued the admiral. "It was only necessary for him to tell me what he desired, and I carried out his wishes to the best of my ability. . . . Grant, in his plain, dusty coat, was, in my eyes, a greater general than the man who rides around, all feathers and fuss. Here in twenty minutes Grant unfolded his plan of campaign, involving the transportation of over one hundred thousand men, and, with a good supper staring him in the face, proposed to ride back again over a road he had just traveled without tasting a mouthful, his cigar serving, doubtless, for food and drink."[7]

Porter was conflating events. Grant initially planned a multi-pronged land advance on Vicksburg from the north and asked Porter how he might cooperate. But a few weeks later, the general decided to send Sherman by water to the mouth of the Yazoo River a few miles upstream from Vicksburg, his thinking undoubtedly influenced by the admiral.

Porter's concerns about obnoxious West Pointers were erased by this unassuming officer who fully involved a sailor in planning, and readily accepted advice from him. The general appeared eager to incorporate naval assets as integral combat and logistical arms. Neither of them had heard from McClernand, who remained in Springfield recruiting troops and enjoying his honeymoon. Grant wanted to move before the pesky political general showed up, and Porter wanted action.

A Porter biographer put it this way: "The growth of mutual respect between Porter and Grant began at their first meeting." Both exhibited

---

7 Porter, *Incidents and Anecdotes*, 140-142.

directness of character and expression with nothing artificial in thought, speech, or manners. They confronted problems head on and felt contempt for sham or pretense. Each understood his profession and grasped complex situations in minute detail.[8]

But socially the admiral and general were opposites. Grant was reserved, serious, and often grave; Porter was expansive, and, although stern in matters of discipline and war, had a natural buoyancy of temper and a quick, often satirical wit. "Between them, however, no personal intimacy existed, and as time passed they simply functioned as two colleagues with common objectives."[9]

The soldier was the son of an Ohio tanner who dispatched the youngster to West Point to make a man of him. Grant was compelled to resign his commission to avoid court martial for drunkenness and was a general failure at civilian life. The sailor hailed from a distinguished navy family, including his father, Commodore David Porter, hero of 1812. The young Porter went to sea in 1814 at age 10, sailed the world, and chafed under a glacial promotion system. He served for years at the U. S. Coast Survey, mapping harbors and strategic coastal positions and developing a practiced eye for terrain that now would serve him well.

A historian of the Vicksburg campaign noted that Grant and Porter "were a formidable combination, hyperaggressive and strategically astute." One was "a ground commander with an inborn understanding of topography" and the other "a river warrior masterful at using enemy waters to his advantage." More accurately, the ocean sailor was rapidly becoming a masterful river warrior. Despite the common element of water, rivers and oceans are decidedly different operating environments calling forth distinct skills and maritime adaptations.[10]

Porter recollected a November 1861 meeting with the president and navy secretary in which he suggested a plan to seize New Orleans from the sea. Lincoln liked the idea and concluded: "while we are about it, we

---

8 Chester G. Hearn, *Admiral David Dixon Porter* (Annapolis: Naval Institute Press, 1996), 155.

9 Ibid.

10 Donald L. Miller, *Vicksburg: Grant's Campaign That Broke the Confederacy* (New York: Simon & Schuster, 2019), XVI.

can push on to Vicksburg and open the river all the way along." Porter's ersatz foster brother, Flag Officer David G. Farragut, would command the expedition while then-Commander Porter would lead the mortar-boat squadron. In April 1862, Farragut blasted his big warships past the forts and secured the city. Having achieved that objective, the orders required him to "push a strong force up the river to take all their defenses in the rear."[11]

Farragut fought his deep-water squadron on up to Vicksburg but, assessing the fortress as unassailable without the army, returned to New Orleans. Navy Assistant Secretary Gustavus Fox wrote to Farragut of the president's distress: "This retreat may be a fatal step as regards our western movements. . . ." Secretary Welles instructed the flag officer: The president "requires you to use your utmost exertions . . .to open the river Mississippi and effect a junction with . . . the Western Flotilla."[12]

Farragut struggled back upriver where Porter joined him with the mortar boats and Flag Officer Davis came down from his recent victory at Memphis with the river squadron. Through June and July, this massive U.S. Navy armada—including Porter's mortars—relentlessly bombarded Rebel fortifications taking return fire without results. Farragut pleaded to theater commander Maj. Gen. Henry W. Halleck for assistance: "Can you aid me in this matter to carry out the peremptory order of the President?" He awaited the general's reply "with great anxiety." Halleck's response: "The scattered and weakened condition of my forces renders it impossible for me" to cooperate at Vicksburg.[13]

After the battle of Shiloh in April and the capture of Corinth in May, Grant and Sherman wanted to go to Vicksburg, but Halleck sidelined Grant and sent Sherman elsewhere. Falling water levels, disease, and low coal supplies compelled Farragut to withdraw his ocean vessels downriver. "It was a fatal mistake," recalled Sherman, "that halted General Halleck at

---

11   Porter, *Incidents and Anecdotes*, 69; United States War Department, *The War of the Rebellion: A Compilation of the Official Records of the Union and Confederate Navies in the war of the Rebellions*, 29 vols. (Washington D.C.: Government Printing Office, 1894-1922), Series I, volume 18, p. 7 (hereafter cited as *O.R.N.*, I, 18, 7).

12   *O.R.N.*, I, 18, 499, 502.

13   *O.R.N.*, I, 18, 590, 593.

Corinth, and led him to disperse and scatter the best materials for a fighting army that, up to that date, had been assembled in the West."[14]

Secretary Welles groused to his diary in January 1863: "Had the army seconded Farragut and the Navy months ago, Vicksburg would have been in our possession. Halleck was good for nothing then, nor is he now."[15] Thus, to the consternation of President Lincoln, was strategic opportunity lost and Porter's distrust of the army reinforced—until he met Grant.

Porter led his squadron down the Mississippi and found General Sherman embarking his troops on a long line of river steamers. "We departed from Memphis as arranged, and reached the Yazoo in good time." What followed was the disastrous battle of Chickasaw Bayou, December 26–29, 1862, in which Sherman's four divisions suffered a bloody repulse against formidable defenses in rain-soaked swamps. But as the first major amphibious landing, the operation was wholly successful.[16]

Overseeing 7 gunboats and 59 transports, Porter delivered Sherman's 32,000 men to the riverbanks, covered their landing, cleared torpedoes from the river (losing the ironclad USS *Cairo* in the process), suppressed enemy batteries and troop concentrations, and neatly extracted Union forces when the odds turned. A powerful team effectively melded maritime mobility and firepower with hard fighting on land. Sherman and Porter became life-long friends.

General McClernand materialized in early January 1863 at the mouth of the Yazoo and, being senior, co-opted Sherman's troops into his army. Sherman suggested that Porter transport the army forty miles up the Arkansas River and clear out the Rebel Fort Hindman at Arkansas Post. McClernand agreed without notifying Grant. Recalled Porter: "I attacked [the fort] with three ironclads and several smaller vessels and in three hours disabled all the guns. General Sherman surrounded the place with his troops, and, after heavy losses, it surrendered." McClernand intended to capture Vicksburg on his own, but Grant assumed overall command and relegated him to corps

---

14 William T. Sherman, *Memoirs of Gen. William T. Sherman — Volume 1* (Kindle Edition) 179.

15 Welles Diary, vol. 1, 218.

16 Porter, *Incidents and Anecdotes*, 143.

command. After attacking Vicksburg, Grant finally was able to fire the overly ambitious general with Porter's and Sherman's enthusiastic backing.[17]

During that flooded and disease-ridden winter of '62–'63, wrote Porter, General Grant "saw from the first that there was no use in sitting down before Vicksburg and simply looking at it." The general and the admiral conducted a series of intense operations to outflank the city from north and east by digging canals, blowing up levees, flooding the Mississippi Delta, and pushing ironclads, gunboats, and troop transports through sluggish swamps, timeless forests of gigantic trees, and tiny, choked channels. In all of which, "I have to say that we failed most egregiously."[18]

The Yazoo Pass expedition involved 2 ironclads, 4 light-armed "tinclads," and about 4,000 troops in 13 transports. Slowed by natural obstacles, the operation was halted in narrow byways and turned back by rapidly constructed Rebel gun emplacements. Porter complained about disunity of command after the army commander, Brig. Gen. Leonard F. Ross, refused to attack at the request of the navy officer in charge, Lt. Cmdr. Watson Smith. "There was a kind of 'stand-off' between the army and the navy" and "no disposition to act in concert."

The admiral, who was not known for unquestioning deference to authority, drew on his relationship with Grant: "Though he had no control over me whatever, and I was never tied down by any orders from the Navy Department, but left to my own discretion, I always deferred to his wishes in all matters, and went so far as to give orders to those under my command that they should obey the orders of Generals Grant and Sherman the same as if they came from myself. Hence we always acted with the most perfect accord. In this case the officer commanding the troops should have been subject to the orders of the naval officer."[19]

The next attempt to cross Steele's Bayou was, wrote Porter, "one of the most remarkable military and naval expeditions that ever set out in any country. . . ." The admiral took personal command to push five ironclads and four mortar rafts towed by tugs through dense and deeply inundated forest

17   Ibid., 148.

18   Ibid., 155-156.

19   Ibid., 162.

and along narrow, twisting channels flanked by high banks. They rammed over ancient trees and knocked bridges into kindling.

"Sometimes, when we would strike against one of these trees, a multitude of vermin would be shaken out on the deck—among them rats, mice, cockroaches, snakes, and lizards, which would be swept overboard by the sailors standing ready with their brooms. Once an old coon landed on deck, with the life half knocked out of him, but he came to in a short time and fought his way on shore." On another occasion, slaves stared from the bank in amazement at the doings of "Mas' Linkum's gun-boats." "What dey gwine ter do nex'?" said an old patriarch (according to Porter).[20]

Confederates began chopping down huge trees in front and behind while deploying sharpshooters and field pieces. Porter was trapped and prepared to destroy his boats, but Sherman rushed to the rescue, clearing the Rebels for the Navy to back out. "Old Tecumseh" came riding up, recalled the admiral: "Halloo, Porter. What did you get into such an ugly scrape for? So much for you navy fellows getting out of your element; better send for the soldiers always. My boys will put you through. . . . Your gun-boats are enough to scare the crows; they look as if you had got a terrible hammering."[21]

The troops joined in the fun: "Halloo, Jack," one fellow sang out, "how do you like playing mud-turtle? Better stick to the briny." "Don't go bushwhacking again, Jack," said another, "unless you have Sherman's boys close aboard of you; you look as if your mothers didn't know you were out." "Dry up," called a sailor, "we wasn't half as much used up as you was at Chickasaw Bayou!" for which the old tar got three cheers.[22]

"It was with the greatest delight that we got out of that ditch and into the open woods again, with plenty of 'sea room' and no lee shores. We took our time, went squirrel-hunting in the few boats we had left, and got a fine mess of turkey-buzzards out of the old oaks which surrounded us."[23]

20   Ibid., 170, 179. The dialect—which may be offensive to modern ears—is that used by Porter.

21   Ibid., 191-192.

22   Ibid., 193.

23   Ibid., 196.

Although these expeditions are mostly forgotten, that they were attempted at all attests to the grit and determination of all concerned. With a few altered circumstances and a little "luck," they might have been among the most renowned episodes in United States Navy history.

"I had had in contemplation the whole winter the movement by land to a point below Vicksburg," Grant recalled, subject only to "the possible but not expected success" of the previous expeditions. "My recollection is that Admiral Porter was the first one to whom I mentioned it. The co-operation of the navy was absolutely essential to the success (even to the contemplation) of such an enterprise. I had no more authority to command Porter than he had to command me. . . . Porter fell into the plan at once, and suggested that he had better superintend the preparation . . . as sailors would probably understand the work better than soldiers." Grant was, as usual, ready to trust and to delegate.[24]

On April 16, 1863, a clear night with no moon, seven gunboats and three transports got underway with Porter in the lead boat. "Every fort and hill-top vomited forth shot and shell, many of the latter bursting in the air and doing no damage, but adding to the grandeur of the scene." On April 22, six more boats loaded with supplies made the run. Only two transports were lost total, thirteen men wounded, and none killed.[25]

Of many effusive congratulations Porter said he received, one came from a beaming German-American brigadier general named Peter Osterhaus: "Now, dose dampt fellers, dey'll catch it; give dem gun-boat soup!" Sherman remarked (referring to the Steele's Bayou expedition): "You are more at home here than you were in the ditches grounding on willow-trees. Stick to this, old fellow; it suits Jack better." Porter: "[General Grant] had marched some thirty-two thousand men to the point opposite Grand Gulf, and gun-boats and transports were all assembled there, waiting to go whithersoever they were wanted."[26] One obstacle remained.

"The battle of Grand Gulf was fought April 29, 1863, and won by the navy, and it was as hard a fight as any that occurred during the war,"

---

24   John F. Marszalek, ed., *The Personal Memoirs of Ulysses S. Grant* (Cambridge: Harvard University Press, Kindle Edition, 2017), 319.

25   Porter, *Incidents and Anecdotes*, 200.

26   Ibid., 202, 207. The dialect is that used by Porter.

wrote Porter. "For more than five hours the gun-boats engaged the enemy's batteries at close quarters, the latter having thirteen heavy guns placed on commanding heights from eighty to one hundred and twenty feet above the river. We lost seventy-five men in killed and wounded, and silenced all the enemy's guns. We passed all the transports by the batteries without damage, and General Grant was at liberty to cross the Mississippi and commence operations on the Vicksburg side as soon as he thought proper." The admiral is exaggerating the results if not the intensity of the fight. Not all Rebel batteries were silenced; Grant was compelled to cross farther south at Bruinsburg after which Confederates abandoned Grand Gulf. [27]

In his memoirs, Ulysses S. Grant concluded: "The navy under Porter was all it could be, during the entire campaign. Without its assistance the campaign could not have been successfully made with twice the number of men engaged. It could not have been made at all, in the way it was, with any number of men without such assistance. The most perfect harmony reigned between the two arms of the service." These two superb commanders (three, counting Sherman) set the tone and the example in a conflict that suffered numerous disastrous leadership clashes.[28]

In Admiral Porter's opinion, the Vicksburg campaign was, "The most remarkable and most successful military operation of the civil war, and was the crowning move toward placing the Father of Waters once more under the absolute control of its legitimate rulers. . . . I realized my proudest hopes . . . and lived to see all my predictions fulfilled. I was one of the first who urged that all the power of the Government should be exerted to get possession of this stronghold, and I gave my whole attention during the siege to bring about this most desirable event."

"Old Tecumseh and myself hold on," Porter continued, "two tough old knots, with a good deal of the steel in us yet, and quite enough vitality to lay out any number of those who pride themselves upon what they can do. We can sit down and write out our reminiscences for the benefit of the young men who are coming along, and perhaps they may learn something from our experience."[29]

---

27   Ibid., 207.

28   Marszalek, ed., *Memoirs of Ulysses S. Grant*, 396.

29   Porter, *Incidents and Anecdotes*, 198, 210, 219.

Grierson's Raid

by Angela M. Riotto

If Vicksburg was the key to Union victory in the Western Theater, Jackson was the key to Vicksburg. By spring 1863, Maj. Gen. Ulysses S. Grant had made four failed attempts to seize Vicksburg by conventional means. Pressured by President Abraham Lincoln and Maj. Gen. Henry Halleck to capture the city, Grant opted for a new type of warfare: hard war.[1] The Army of the Tennessee's activities on the march to and from Jackson and Sherman's demolition of that city combined with Col. Benjamin Grierson's cavalry raid through the state initiated this strategy during the Vicksburg campaign.[2]

Geographically, politically, and economically, Jackson is the heart of Mississippi; and in 1863 it was the lifeline to Vicksburg. As the state's major industrial city and capital, Jackson boasted the intersection of Mississippi's two railroads, numerous rail yards and equipment shops, the state arsenal, mills, foundries, and food depots. Confederate war materials, packaged food items, cotton, and troops streamed from this epicenter to Mississippi's four corners. Confederate units waiting for resupply and reinforcement in Vicksburg relied on these items to come through Jackson. Realizing that he

---

[1] Mark Grimsley, *The Hard Hand of War: Union Military Policy Toward Southern Civilians 1861-1865* (Cambridge: Cambridge University Press, 1995); Buckley T. Foster, *Sherman's Mississippi Campaign* (Tuscaloosa: The University of Alabama, 2006); Michael Ballard, *Vicksburg: The Campaign that Opened the Mississippi* (Chapel Hill: University of North Carolina Press, 2004); Michael Ballard, *The Civil War in Mississippi: Major Campaigns and Battles* (Jackson: University Press of Mississippi, 2011); Timothy B. Smith, *Mississippi and the Civil War: The Home Front* (Jackson: University Press of Mississippi, 2010).

[2] Angela M. Riotto, "Furnish the Balance: The 1863 Roots of Hard War Strategy," M.A. Thesis (University of Southern Mississippi, 2012), 35.

required multiple plans to take Vicksburg, General Grant coordinated with Maj. Gen. Stephen A. Hurlbut, commander of the XVI Corps, to plan a diversion.[3] Hurlbut applauded the idea and expressed a desire to coordinate his movements with Grant's, declaring "this cavalry dash I desire to time so as to co-operate with what I suppose to be your plan, to land below Vicksburg, on south side of Black River. . . ."[4]

To lead the operation, Hurlbut selected 37-year-old Col. Benjamin H. Grierson of the 6th Illinois Cavalry Regiment. Grant expected Grierson to "strike out by way of Pontotoc, breaking right and left, cutting both [rail] roads, destroying the wires, burning provisions, and doing all the mischief they can, while one regiment ranges straight down to Selma or Meridian, breaking the east and west [rail] road thoroughly, and swinging back through Alabama."[5] In short, Grierson and his cavalrymen were to destroy supplies, raise the alarm throughout the state, and deceive the Confederates as to Grant's next move.

Col. Benjamin Grierson led a band of cavalry that historian Timothy B. Smith has called "the real horse soldiers." *LOC*

In a preview of the Union's nascent hard war strategy, Grierson's 1,700 cavalrymen abandoned their supply lines as they maneuvered throughout Mississippi. When planning the raid, Hurlbut encouraged Grierson to move quickly and live off the land. This served two main purposes. First, like Grant's justification to "make the country furnish the balance" during his own advance, foraging enabled units to move quickly in enemy territory

---

3   United States War Department, *The War of the Rebellion: A Compilation of the Official Records of the Union and Confederate Armies,* 70 vols. in 128 parts (Washington D.C.: Government Printing Office, 1880-1901), Series I, volume 24, part 3, p. 49-50 (hereafter cited as *O.R.,* I, 24, pt. 3, 49-50).

4   *O.R.,* I, 23, pt. 2, 214.

5   *O.R.,* I, 24, pt. 3, 185.

without pausing for resupply.[6] This allowed Grierson to maintain his high operational tempo, destroy Confederate infrastructure, and seize objectives before the enemy could effectively respond.[7] Second, mass foraging demoralized the civilian population in the area. Lasting for seventeen days and spanning 600 miles from Tennessee, through Mississippi, and ending in Louisiana, Grierson's raid discouraged Southern civilians loyal to the Confederacy and helped to decimate the state's military economy. *(See the map on page xxx to follow Grierson's route.)*

By April 29, Union commanders in the Western Theater considered Grierson's raid a success.[8] The former music teacher confounded Confederate Lieut. Gen. John C. Pemberton and preoccupied Rebel troops required to block Grant's advance south of Vicksburg. The Confederate redeployment of troops in an attempt to stop Grierson's destructive raid weakened Pemberton's force at Vicksburg, and also removed the possibility of a fierce defense of Grant's advance from Bruinsburg to Jackson and then to Vicksburg.[9]

The psychological effect of the Union raid upon the general population as well as the military leaders also cannot be underestimated. One Mississippi newspaper disparaged Pemberton's negligent failure to respond to and impede Grierson's raid. The author complained, "We have information that the enemy entered Brookhaven yesterday evening, burnt the railroad depot, cut the wires, and after doing what other damage they pleased, leisurely retired (a portion of them at least) in an easterly direction."[10] Grierson's raid demonstrated the United States Army's alarming ability to bring the war— hard war—and its effects home to Mississippians.

Grierson's raid as part of Grant's 1863 Vicksburg campaign was a fundamental step in the Union's development of hard war strategy as well as toward Vicksburg's eventual surrender. Afterward, Grant proudly reported "On April 17, this expedition started, and arrived at Baton Rouge on May 2,

---

6 Ulysses S. Grant, *Memoirs of U.S. Grant* (New York: Charles L. Webster and Co., 1885), 262.

7 Riotto, "Furnish the Balance," 30.

8 *O.R.*, I, 23, pt. 2, 291.

9 Grant, *Memoirs*, 261-262; Riotto, "Furnish the Balance," 29.

10 *Daily Mississippian*, 30 April 1863.

Grierson and his men made the front cover of *Harper's Weekly*
on June 6, 1863—a dash of good news during a spell when the
North needed some good news. *LOC*

having successfully traversed the whole State of Mississippi. This expedition
was skillfully conducted, and reflects great credit on Colonel Grierson and
all of his command. The notice given this raid by the Southern press confirms
our estimate of its importance. It has been one of the most brilliant cavalry
exploits of the war, and will be handed down in history as an example to be
imitated."[11] As planned, it demoralized the enemy, frightened the citizenry,
and created chaos along the way. Grierson himself recalled, "no one can
pass through that country without knowing that the Confederacy is broken
up. It is a mere shell with nothing in it."[12]

11 *O.R.*, I, 24, pt. 3, 58.

12 "The Romance of War," *New York Times*, 18 May 1863.

1. Sherman's "Demon Spirit"

by Chris Mackowski

Originally published as a blog post on Emerging Civil War on January 27, 2021

In a letter written on April 29, 1863, to his wife Ellen, William T. Sherman privately expressed his misgivings about the Vicksburg campaign Ulysses S. Grant was just then launching. "My own opinion is that this whole plan of attack on Vicksburg will fail must fail, and the fault will be on us all of course," he wrote.[1]

The entire letter is quite extraordinary, but what really jumps out at me is the venom Sherman holds for fellow corps commander John McClernand. McClernand, a highly influential political general commanding the XIII Corps, was the most senior of Grant's subordinates. Sherman despised McClernand, who outranked him and thus superseded him in command following Sherman's defeat at Chickasaw Bayou in late December 1862. That replacement, Sherman later admitted, was "the severest test of my patriotism."

"The Noises & clamor have produced their fruits. Even Grant is cowed & afraid of the newspapers," Sherman wrote, suspecting machinations behind the outcry.

---

1 William T. Sherman to Ellen, 29 April 1863, *Sherman's Civil War: Selected Correspondence of William T. Sherman, 1860-1865*, Brooks D. Simpson & Jean V. Berlin, eds. (Chapel Hill, NC: University of North Carolina Press, 1999), 464-6.

Should as the papers now intimate Grant be relieved & McClernand left in command, you may expect to hear of me at St. Louis, for I will not serve under McClernand. He is the impersonation of my Demon Spirit, not a shade of respect for truth, when falsehood is easier manufactured & fitted to his purpose: an overtowering ambition and utter ignorance of the first principles of war. I have in my possession his orders to do "certain things" which he would be ashamed of now. He knows I saw him cow at Shiloh. He knows he blundered in ignorance at the Post & came to me beseechingly, "Sherman what shall we do now?" And yet no sooner is the tempest past, and the pen in hand, his star is to be brightened and none so used to abuse, none so patient under it as Sherman. And therefore Glory at Sherman's expense.

"Demon Spirit"! Can you believe that? He calls out McClernand as a liar and a coward, too, with "overtowering ambition." Harsh words.

The reference to "the Post" was Arkansas Post, a Confederate garrison 45 miles upstream from the mouth of the Arkansas River. Federal forces captured it on January 11, 1863, as part of their operations against Vicksburg. McClernand wrote a self-adulatory report of the battle, ignoring Sherman's key role, further insulting the bruised feelings of the resentful Sherman.

Even after Grant arrived from Memphis in early February to take personal command of operations in the field, tensions between Sherman and McClernand continued to simmer, and Sherman became convinced it was only a matter of time before McClernand slipped him a Brutus-like dagger. "I avoid McClernand, because I know he is envious & jealous of everybody who stands in his way," Sherman told Ellen earlier in April. "He knows I appreciate him truly and therefore he would ruin me if he could."[2]

"Appreciate" here serves as a euphemism for "see through him clear as day and recognize him as the smarmy political snake he is." While that's my translation, not Sherman's exact words, he does express a similar sentiment in a February 6 letter to Ellen. "[H]e is a most deceitful man, taking all possible advantage and having no standard of

---

2   William T. Sherman to Ellen, 23 April 1863, *Sherman's Civil War*, 456.

truth & honor but the public clamor," he wrote.[3]

The context of the April 29 letter, though, stands out because it seems to be written while Sherman was sunk in one of the dark moods he was sometimes prone to. He did not have confidence in Grant's overall plan for crossing the Mississippi and making an overland attempt on Vicksburg from the rear. Sherman's own part of that plan entailed making an up-river demonstration against Confederate forces on the Yazoo River to keep their attention fixed there while Grant moved downriver and crossed. "I think Grant will make a safe lodgment at Grand Gulf," Sherman confided to Ellen, "but the real trouble is and will be the maintenance of

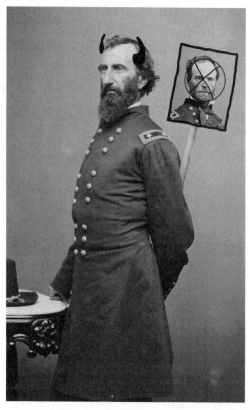

John "Demon Spirit" McClernand had no more love lost for Sherman than Sherman had for him. *LOC/Chris Mackowski*

the army there. If the capture of Holly Springs [on December 20, 1862] made him leave the Tallahatchie, how much more precarious is his position now below Vicksburg with every pound of provision, forage and ammunition to float past the seven miles of batteries at Vicksburg or be hauled thirty-seven miles along a narrow boggy road?"

Sherman himself would eventually supply the answer to this very question. Grant would assign the division of Maj. Gen. Francis Preston Blair, Jr., of Sherman's XV Corps to oversee the movement of supplies from

---

3   William T. Sherman to Ellen, 6 February 1863, *Sherman's Civil War*, 393.

Grand Gulf up to the rest of the army as it moved through the Mississippi interior. Sherman characterized Blair in the same category of political general as McClernand, "mere politicians who come to fight not for the real glory & success of the nation, but for their own individual aggrandizement."[4] Yet Blair would rise to the challenge and keep Grant's army supplied as it moved, even as the army's successes made a believer of the dutiful-but-pessimistic Sherman along the way.

Those successes, though, did nothing to soften Sherman's attitudes toward McClernand, who performed solidly during the overland campaign and at least as well as the other corps commanders in the assaults against Vicksburg itself. Sherman condemned him, by his own actions, as a man "full of vain-glory and hypocrisy" and enamored by a "process of self-flattery," and there was no changing his mind.[5] The venom Sherman expressed toward his "Demon Spirit" in his letter to Ellen only deepened over time, as McClernand would come to regret.

* * *

You can read the full text of Sherman's April 29, 1863, letter to Ellen at General Sherman's Blog, *created by a "JJ Brownyneal" during the Civil War Sesquicentennial to offer a day-by-day account of Sherman in the war. Other correspondence is also reprinted there, although the blog's first-person "voice of Sherman" is a fictional construct. Visit https://sherman150. wordpress.com.*

---

4 William T. Sherman to Ellen, 26 February 1863, *Sherman's Civil War*, 411.

5 United States War Department, *The War of the Rebellion: A Compilation of the Official Records of the Union and Confederate Armies*, 70 vols. in 128 parts (Washington D.C.: Government Printing Office, 1880-1901), Series I, volume 24, part 3, p. 162-3.

"Anxious to Make the Grand Trial": A Hoosier at Port Gibson

by Daniel A. Masters

Originally published as a blog post on Emerging Civil War on May 1, 2021

The 8th Indiana Infantry was among the first troops from the Hoosier State to enlist in the Civil War, but it wasn't until the battle of Port Gibson in May 1863 that the regiment came under serious fire. As related by Capt. Samuel H. Dunbar of Co. B, the regiment was among Grant's vanguard in the thrust across the Mississippi River that marked the opening land operation of the Vicksburg campaign. The regiment was part of Gen. William P. Benton's First Brigade of Gen. Eugene Carr's Fourteenth Division of John McClernand's XIII Corps. It was in the midst of a night march aiming to take the riverside batteries at Grand Gulf when four Confederate cannons lit the night. "This was the first positive salute of the kind that Co. B had ever received," Dunbar wrote. "Notwithstanding the obstruction, the column moved steadily on. The 1st Indiana Battery took position and opened upon the enemy to aid us in making the advance. After we got in range, the shot and shell came thick and fast booming and bursting on both sides of us and above our heads."

The brigade formed into line, and the battle of Port Gibson began in the predawn hours of May 1, 1863. Dunbar related the experience in a letter written on May 8 from the banks of the Big Black River and published in the May 28, 1863, issue of the *Hancock Democrat,* excerpted here:

> . . . After we got in range, the shot and shell came thick and fast booming and bursting on both sides of us and above our heads. The regiment happened to marching left in front; consequently Cos. A and B were longest exposed to the fire and should have suffered more, but fortunately did not lose a man. Ike McGee of our company had his nose skinned by a piece of shell. When the regiment neared the battery, it filed right and went down into a hollow out of direct range but was still followed by the missiles of the infernal guns. After getting into the ravine, we were drawn up on the brow of the hill under cover of which we remained until morning.
>
> At sunrise, we opened on their pickets and skirmishers and the 8th Indiana was assigned its position on the extreme right of the line of battle. The battlefield, and indeed the country, is but a succession of hills, ridges, and ravines. The enemy was, of course, concealed in the timber. Their position was well chosen and strong. Our regiment began the musket fire. We were upon one ridge and the enemy upon another with a deep ravine dividing us. We fought there for some time when we were ordered to charge down into the ravine and up the hill from which the enemy was firing. The charge was executed in fine style and with alacrity notwithstanding the difficulties; cane and grape vines covered the sides of both ridges. Arriving upon the hostile hill, the Rebels were not there but had gone we knew not whither. At this time, the battle was raging furiously on the left and center.
>
> By noon, the Rebels were driven from the first position which was taken and the Rebel battery which had scared us so badly the night before was charged and taken by the 18th Indiana. In the afternoon, General [George F.] McGinnis' brigade was holding a hill upon the right and was engaged by a large force of Rebels. His men being handled very roughly, he came to General Benton very excited and

said he would be compelled to give up the point unless reinforced. The 8th Indiana, tired and weary from constant exertion from early dawn, was at that moment doing nothing and at the command promptly hastened on the double quick to the relief of the suffering.

The hill occupied by the enemy was covered with heavy timber but the side next to us was clear. At its base lay the 29th Wisconsin fighting with vengeance, but its dead and wounded were piled up everywhere. Above and in the rear of them was another hill upon which was the 11th Indiana and 11th Wisconsin. When we came to the ravine with the 29th, we were greeted by a deadly volley of musketry—a melancholy introduction to the work before us. We had, as understood, been sent to the support of the regiment there, but to our surprise, they considered themselves entirely relieved and left us all alone in our glory. Standing at the base of the hill, we were fast promising to be cut to pieces when Lieutenant Colonel Charles S. Parrish drew his sword, took the advance, and ordered a charge up the hill with a yell that reverberated afar. Up we went and poured such a deluge of bullets into them that they broke and ran in the wildest confusion. This was a whole Rebel brigade driven from an advantageous position by the impetuous 8th. Our company fought gloriously. Five men were wounded in less than five minutes; none of these are at all dangerous and all except McGee and Roney are now with the company. Many narrowly escaped; John Underwood's cap box was shot through, Eli Stevens had an oil cloth wrapped around him which caught a bullet, and Wallace Alexander was shot through the haversack. I am proud, now doubly proud of the boys. There is no discount on any of those actually engaged.

At sunset the battle closed and we sank to sleep on the field. In the morning the bird had flown. We immediately began pursuing them through the town of Port Gibson, but by burning the wire suspension bridges over the bayou the Rebels succeeded in getting away, leaving most of their dead and wounded. We went to Grand Gulf which had been hastily evacuated. We are in nearly three miles of the Black River on the opposite side of which the enemy is strongly posted. I presume we are waiting the auspicious moment to pounce upon them. Everything is cheerful here. The prospect seems bright and we are ready and anxious to make the grand trial.[1]

Captain Dunbar survived the Vicksburg campaign but would not survive the war. A student at Greencastle College (now DePauw University), Dunbar had plans of becoming an attorney but the outbreak of the war caused him to lay those plans aside and cast his fortunes with the 8th Indiana Infantry. The regiment saw very active service in the Western theater: Captain Dunbar traveled roughly 10,000 miles during his three years at the front, marching nearly 3,000 of those miles.

Dunbar corresponded regularly with the *Hancock Democrat* newspaper back in his hometown of Greenfield, Indiana, and paid his last visit home in the spring of 1864 when the regiment re-enlisted for an additional three-year term. Dunbar was already in poor health, but he wouldn't think of resigning while the war was not yet won. The 8th Indiana traveled back to Louisiana where, on July 9, 1864, Dunbar died of a congestive chill.

"The regiment being under marching orders for the Army of the Potomac, time could not be had for the preparation necessary to send his remains home, so he was buried at Terre Bonne. It was a sad day for the boys of Co. B to thus part with their best friend and officer," his obituary noted. "No other young man in our community so completely carried with him the respect and admiration of the old and young as he did, and none among the numerous souls have gone down to their graves during the progress of this cruel and unfortunate war whose death is so universally lamented."

Dunbar's remains were brought home to Greenfield in November 1864 and a handsome monument erected at Park Cemetery. A witness to the eulogy remarked that "many an eye glistened with the tear of manly sorrow, as the clouds of the valley closed over the form of him, who in life, was the center of a cluster of warm and devoted friends."[2]

1   Letter from Captain Samuel H. Dunbar, *Hancock Democrat,* May 28, 1863, 1.

2   "Death of Capt. S.H. Dunbar," *Hancock Democrat,* July 28, 1864, 3;
Findagrave: https://www.findagrave.com/memorial/114869504/samuel-hammond-dunbar.

The Stakes of Vicksburg

by Chris Kolakowski

Originally published as a blog post on Emerging Civil War on June 20, 2016

On April 30 and May 1, 1863, Union Maj. Gen. U. S. Grant crossed his Army of the Tennessee over the Mississippi River south of Vicksburg. He then plunged inland to surround the city and defeat the Confederates.[1]

Grant's move has been cited as a great risk, which it certainly was. He had to win or face utter ruin of his army and defeat—the starkest all-or-nothing proposition. With hindsight, we know it worked. But what of occasions where such a bold move doesn't work?

Understanding armies that failed in similar circumstances helps define exactly the stakes of the Vicksburg Campaign in May 1863. Let me provide three examples of such failures.

In March 1862, Confederates under Maj. Gen. Earl Van Dorn attacked Union Maj. Gen. Samuel Curtis's forces at Pea Ridge, Arkansas. Van Dorn, who outnumbered Curtis, aggressively split his army and sent part on a flanking march into the Federal rear. For speed, he left his supply wagons behind. His men straggled and arrived tired and hungry for the battle's opening on March 7. Confederate attacks were piecemeal and not as vigorous as needed. The next day Confederate artillery ran out of ammunition and

---

1 For a good overview beyond what we've offered in this collection, see Christopher Gabel, *The Vicksburg Campaign* (Washington DC: US Army 2013).

Curtis swept the field with a counterattack. Van Dorn's routed and hungry men took a week to reform.[2]

In September 1942, General Kiyotake Kawaguchi led an 8,000-man brigade to dislodge the U.S. Marines beachhead on Guadalcanal. He left most of his supplies and support behind and marched his men through a trackless jungle to launch a converging attack on the Marines' perimeter. Over two days (September 12-13), Kawaguchi's men hammered the Marines with repeated attacks that all failed. Kawaguchi took five days to retrace his steps and another month to ready his brigade for a second try. Reinforced with the 2nd "Sendai" Division under Masao Maruyama, the Japanese tried the same plan again in late October. Movement delays resulted in piecemeal attacks between October 23-26, all of

What do Earl Van Dorn (above) Kiyotake Kawaguchi, and Renya Mutaguchi all have in common? (No, the latter two were not killed by jealous husbands.) *LOC*

which the Marines (reinforced themselves by U.S. Army troops) repulsed. The Sendai Division had lost over 50% of its strength and retreated in an agonizing march back to camp, a diseased and starving group of combat-ineffective men. This was the last Japanese attack against the beachhead.[3]

In March 1944, nearly 100,000 Japanese of the Fifteenth Army plunged into India from Burma. The commander, General Renya Mutaguchi, planned for his men to carry rations and eat whatever they could capture from the British. Mutaguchi's plan counted on capturing the bases at Imphal, Kohima, and Dimapur, using their supplies to sustain the offensive. Unlike other

2 For a good overview, see William Shea and Earl Hess, *Pea Ridge: Civil War Campaign in the West* (Chapel Hill NC: UNC Press 1997).

3 John Toland, *The Rising Sun*, Vol I (New York: Random House 1970), 461-503.

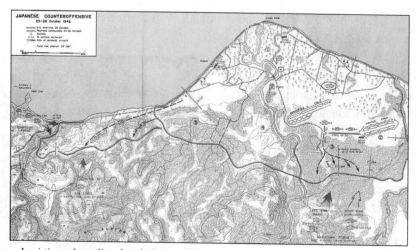

Logistics and supplies played a huge role in the successes and failures of the campaigns by Grant, Van Dorn, Kawaguchi, and Mutaguchi. (And, at Guadalcanal, above, the Marines had a little something to do with it, too.) It's little wonder that Grant, as a former quartermaster, kept such concerns at the forefront. *LOC*

British units before that had succumbed to Japanese attacks, General Sir William Slim's British Fourteenth Army stood firm at Imphal and Kohima for weeks. Air resupply kept Slim's men in fighting trim, whereas lack of supplies withered the Japanese and forced them into desperate attacks (all repulsed). By June, after three months of fighting, Mutaguchi withdrew back to Burma. British pursuers found thousands of emaciated and dead men lining the retreat routes, victims of disease and starvation. Mutaguchi lost over 66% of the men he had led to India, and sustained Japan's greatest single land defeat ever. Conversely, Slim's victory at Imphal and Kohima has been called one of Britain's greatest battles.[4]

Collectively, these examples show the fate that Grant courted in 1863 when he moved against Vicksburg from the south. He risked the Army of the Tennessee in a daring maneuver that succeeded brilliantly, altering the course of the war. That he avoided any of these calamities is a testament to his leadership and the quality of his men as marchers and fighters.

4 For a good overview see Hemat Singh Katoch, *Imphal 1944: The Japanese Invasion of India* (Oxford: Osprey 2018).

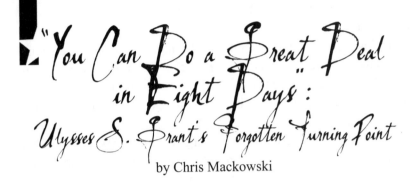

"You Can Do a Great Deal in Eight Days": Ulysses S. Grant's Forgotten Turning Point

by Chris Mackowski

*Originally published as a two-part series on Emerging Civil War
on December 23 & 24, 2020*

Ulysses S. Grant had envisioned his arrival in Grand Gulf, Mississippi, under other circumstances. A week earlier, he had targeted the landing as the ideal spot to cross his army from the west bank of the Mississippi River to the east, and from there, he would launch an overland trek to "the Gibraltar of the Confederacy," Vicksburg, some 35 miles to the north. But on April 29, after a five-hour battle, Federal naval forces proved unable to reduce the Confederate fortifications at Grand Gulf or dislodge the garrison's defenders.

Grant improvised and switched his landing spot to Bruinsburg. The Navy shuttled Grant's army across on April 30 and May 1 and, the very next day, Grant threw his men into combat. By May 3, his forces had advanced far enough inland to outflank the Grand Gulf garrison, which abandoned its post lest the men find themselves trapped. When Grant finally arrived in Grand Gulf, it was by horseback from the east rather than by boat from the west, making a 17-mile ride from an inland crossroads called Hankinson's Ferry.

"I had been in the saddle since we crossed the river, three days before," he later recalled, "and had not had a regular meal or any sleep in that time."[1] And, perhaps worst of all, because he'd been without his baggage "since the 27th of April," he "consequently had had no change of underclothing. . . ."[2]

But his arrival at Grand Gulf on the night of May 3, under trying circumstances large and small, would lead Grant to one of the most consequential decisions of the Civil War—an oft-overlooked turning point that illustrated his determination, resilience, and willingness to take calculated risks.

Grant had been trying to take Vicksburg for months. Six separate attempts had all led to naught, although the resulting operations spread Grant's forces over an arc of more than sixty miles on the Louisiana side of the river. "The division of your army into small expeditions destroys your strength, and, when in the presence of an enemy, is very dangerous," complained Grant's boss, General-in-Chief of the Army Henry Halleck, in early April from his desk in Washington. "What is most desired, and your attention is again called to this object, is that your forces and those of General Banks should be brought into co-operation as early as possible."[3]

Banks, based in Baton Rouge, had been assigned to capture Port Hudson, 25 miles north of the Louisiana capital and, based on at least one estimation by Grant, some 300 river miles south of Vicksburg.[4] Port Hudson, like Vicksburg, was a riverside stronghold that sat atop high bluffs and controlled traffic on the river.

Grant had no desire to join forces with Banks, though, either for a move against Vicksburg or against Port Hudson. Banks, a political general who'd once been speaker of the U.S. House of Representatives, outranked Grant,

---

1   John Russell Young, *Around the World With General Grant* (New York: The American News Company, 1879), Vol. 2, 620.

2   Ulysses S. Grant, *Grant: Memoirs and Selected Letters*, Mary Drake McFeely and William S. McFeely, eds. (New York: Library of America, 1990), 326.

3   United States War Department, *The War of the Rebellion: A Compilation of the Official Records of the Union and Confederate Armies*, 70 vols. in 128 parts (Washington D.C.: Government Printing Office, 1880-1901), Series I, volume 24, part 1, p. 25 (hereafter cited as *O.R.,* I, 24, pt. 1, 25).

4   Grant, *Memoirs*, 328.

so Grant knew any junction of their forces would mean he'd take a back seat to the less-able Banks.

And indeed, Banks had been proving his "less-ableness" for months. Not only had "Commissary Banks" been embarrassed out of Virginia's Shenandoah Valley in the spring of 1862, he'd most recently run into grief in March in a first stab at Port Hudson. Just as Grant looked for ways to bypass Vicksburg, Banks looked for ways to bypass Port Hudson, and in late March began an effort that took him up the Red River. This would prove fortuitous to Grant.

By that point, Grant had begun to develop his next plan for attacking at Vicksburg. He would cross the Mississippi somewhere south of Vicksburg and, subsisting off the land and whatever supply chain he could safely maintain, he would approach the river city from its landward side. But Halleck's pressure to unite with Banks

Nathaniel P. Banks not only out-ranked Grant but out-dandified him, as well. (Epaulets, for instance, do not accessorize well with Mississippi mud.) *LOC*

threatened to undermine the effort. Initially, Grant told his boss he would "send an army corps to Port Hudson to operate with General Banks" in the reduction of Port Hudson, detailing the 19,000 men of Maj. Gen. John McClernand's corps for the task.[5]

Grant promised the detachment by April 25, but by the 19th, he began to equivocate. "This will now be impossible," Grant told Halleck, but added that he would get the men to Banks as soon as possible. "There shall be no unnecessary delay . . . in my movements."[6]

---

5 Ibid.

6 *O.R.,* I, 24, pt. 1, 30.

Grant's relationship with McClernand was certainly fraught, and that no doubt informed his decision to send the difficult subordinate away. McClernand, like Banks, was also a politician-turned-general, and Grant may have felt these two birds of a feather deserved each other. But McClernand did have a credible force and so would be of legitimate assistance. (McClernand had around 19,000 men present for duty; McPherson had around 16,000; Sherman, still defending the Federal supply depot at Milliken's Bend but soon on his way to Grand Gulf, had around 18,000.)

But the more Grant considered the situation on the Mississippi side of the river, the less he wanted to give up any of his men; the more success he met with in his operation, the less he wanted to attend to Port Hudson.

Orders were orders, though. "Up to this time my intention had been to secure Grand Gulf, as a base of supplies, detach McClernand's corps to Banks and co-operate with him in the reduction of Port Hudson," Grant later explained.[7] He rode into Grand Gulf on the evening of May 3 knowing he couldn't put off his obligation to Halleck and Banks any longer.

With an escort of twenty cavalrymen, Grant rode into Grand Gulf. He passed the now-abandoned Confederate forts, Cobun and Wade, and made his way to the river where four ironclads from the U.S. Navy—*Carondelet, Louisville,* and *Mound City*—hunkered on the bank, yards away from the two forts they had unsuccessfully tried to reduce just days earlier. The Navy had heard the sounds of the forts' powder magazines going up, set off by the evacuating Confederates, and had steamed in to investigate.[8] Lieutenant Commander Elias Owen, skipper of the *Louisville*, invited Grant aboard.

Before they got down to business, though, Grant took a bath, borrowed fresh underclothes from a naval officer, and grabbed himself a good meal.[9]

Grant had shared a close working relationship with Porter and his command and, indeed, Grant's success at Vicksburg came in large part because of the navy's cooperation. Although Porter had not been able to initially capture Grand Gulf on the 29th, he had successfully run boats—

7 Grant, *Memoirs,* 327.

8 Michael Ballard, *Vicksburg: The Campaign that Opened the Mississippi* (Chapel Hill, NC: UNC Press, 2004), 247.

9 Grant, *Memoirs,* 326.

twice—past Vicksburg's blockade, and he had ferried Grant's army from Disharoon Plantation to Bruinsburg. Grant trusted him implicitly.

When Grant and Owen consulted on the night of May 3, Owen presented news that changed Grant's situation entirely. Banks had sent a message about his expedition up the Red River, where he'd faced resistance from Confederate Maj. Gen. Richard Taylor. As a result, Banks "could not be at Port Hudson before the 10th of May and then with only 15,000 men."

"To wait for his co-operation would have detained me at least a month," Grant realized.[10]

And then, when he did arrive, Banks would not be able to bring more than 10,000 reinforcements "after deducting casualties and necessary river guards at all high points close to the river for over three hundred miles," Grant figured. Pemberton, meanwhile, would use the month's delay to fortify his position at Vicksburg and bring in more reinforcements than Banks would be able to bring.[11]

If Grant rewrote his plan and moved on Vicksburg rather than on a junction with Banks, he might secure a decisive victory. He had the element of surprise. He had momentum. He had his independence. He faced an under-prepared foe.

And . . . he had a boss back in Washington who would most definitely say "No."

But the operative phrase, Grant knew, was "back in Washington."

To communicate with Halleck, dispatches had to go back across the river and retrace the army's route of march along the west side of the Mississippi back up to Young's Point, near Milliken's Bend, north of Vicksburg. From there, messages then traveled on a dispatch-boat to Cairo, the southernmost tip of Illinois, which was "the nearest point from which they could be telegraphed to Washington."[12]

Even when Grant was still back up at Milliken's Bend in early April, Halleck had reminded him about the difficulties communicating—and that was without the additional legs of the journey now being included in any

10 Ibid., 327.

11 Ibid., 328.

12 Young, 621.

relay. "In regard to your dispatches, it is very probable that many fail to reach here in time," Halleck had warned. He wanted Banks kept in the loop in regards to Grant's plans and reminded Grant "the only way he can get this information is through these headquarters."[13]

As Grant calculated it, a message sent to Halleck and a reply sent to Grant would take eight days to make the full circle.

Eight days.

And that would be without any consultations between Halleck and Banks. Not that Halleck would bother. "I knew well that Halleck's caution would lead him to disapprove of this course," Grant later wrote; "but it was the only one that gave any chance of success."[14]

Grant decided to beg forgiveness rather than ask permission: "I therefore determined to move independently of Banks, cut loose from my base, destroy the rebel force in rear of Vicksburg and invest or capture the city."[15]

Grant wrote a lengthy report to Halleck outlining the details of the campaign thus far.[16] "The move by Bruinsburg undoubtedly took the enemy much by surprise," he said, gearing up for his big reveal. He came to it indirectly, building, talking about the fine "health and spirits" his men enjoyed, how little straggling he witnessed, how nobly they'd all performed thus far. "The country will supply all the forage required for anything like an active campaign, and the necessary fresh beef," he said.

By this point, Halleck, reading along, might have started to wonder, *What "active campaign?"* But Grant plowed on.

"I shall not bring my troops into this place [Grand Gulf]," he finally announced, "but immediately follow the enemy, and, if all promises as favorable hereafter as it does now, not stop until Vicksburg is in our possession."

He sent the letter off, took care of other business—including a second, shorter report that went via Memphis detailing casualties from the fight at Port Gibson—then made the return trip to McPherson's corps at Hankinson's

13 *O.R.,* I, 24, pt. 1, 28.

14 Grant, memoirs, 328.

15 Grant, memoirs, 328.

16 The quotes that follow come from the report, written 3 May 1863 in Grand Gulf, *O.R.,* I, 24, pt. 1, 33.

Ferry. "The time it would take to communicate with Washington and get a reply would be so great that I could not be interfered with until it was demonstrated whether my plan was practicable," he recalled.[17]

Grant now had a window of a little over a week to push toward Vicksburg and either take the city or at least become so deeply involved in operations that it would be impossible to extract himself. Historian Parker Hills correctly summed it up as a "momentous decision to move fast, strike hard, and finish rapidly."[18] It was a turning point not just in the campaign but a turning point for the war itself. Had Grant stuck to script, the Vicksburg campaign would never have unfolded as it did.

Grant soon plunged into the Mississippi interior. By May 10, a letter from Banks, facilitated in a trip upriver by Porter's navy, caught up with him. Banks predicted that cooperation between their two forces should be possible on May 25 and he hoped that, by that time, Grant could send "so many of yours [men] you can spare" to assist in the "instant and certain" fall of Port Hudson.[19] Grant, as he intended, had made it deep into the bosom of Mississippi and was ready to bring on battle. "It was my intention," he explained in a May 10 reply, "on gaining a foothold at Grand Gulf, to have sent a sufficient force to Port Hudson to have insured the fall of that place with your co-operation, or rather to have co-operated with you to secure that end." However, meeting the enemy South of Port Gibson had changed the plan—as though events, not Grant himself, had orchestrated the change. "Many days cannot elapse before the battle will begin which is to decide the fate of Vicksburg . . ." he added. "I would urgently request, therefore, that you join me or send all the force you can spare to co-operate in the great struggle for opening the Mississippi River."[20]

The next day, May 11, marked the end of Grant's original eight-day window. Anticipating the reply from Halleck, the commander of the Army

---

17 Grant, memoirs, 328.

18   J. Parker Hills, "Roads to Raymond," *The Vicksburg Campaign: March 29-May 18, 1863*, Steven E. Woodworth and Charles D. Grear, editors (Carbondale, Illinois: Southern Illinois University Press, 69.

19 *O.R.,* I, 24, pt. 3, 281.

20 Ibid., 288-89.

of the Tennessee sent a preemptive message to buy himself more time: "As I shall communicate with Grand Gulf no more, except it becomes necessary to send a train with heavy escort, you may not hear from me again for several days."[21] Battle at Raymond would erupt the next day.

As Grant prepared to cut communications, Halleck, in Washington, finally sent his reply to Grant's May 3 dispatch. At the time, the battle of Chancellorsville had been demanding most of his attention, so his delay in replying to Grant is understandable, but that delay extended Grant's anticipated eight-day window to fourteen, effectively giving him even more time to get deeper into his overland campaign. As anticipated, he argued strongly against Grant's improvised plan and pushed the original one instead. "If possible, the forces of yourself and of General Banks should be united between Vicksburg and Port Hudson, so as to attack these places separately with the combined forces," the general in chief wrote.[22]

Grant's May 11 communiqué was obviously intended as cover, for he still managed to keep up a stream of almost daily updates to Halleck as the campaign wore on. He never forgot to plant seeds in support of his mission, though. On May 15, writing to announce the capture of the state capital, Jackson, Grant mentioned, "A dispatch from General Banks showed him to be off in Louisiana, not to return to Baton Rouge until May 10. I could not lose the time."[23]

His correspondence dried up shortly after that as he fought his way westward, from Champion Hill to the Big Black River to the outskirts of Vicksburg—and, from there, to an eventual July 4 victory, command of all armies in the West, promotion to Halleck's job as general in chief, Appomattox Court House, and two terms in the White House. In retrospect, the decision he made on the *Louisville* at Grand Gulf could not have come with higher stakes.

"I remember how anxiously I counted the time I had to spare before that response could come," Grant later said. "You can do a great deal in eight days."[24]

21 *O.R.*, I, 24, pt. 1, 36.

22 Ibid.

23 Ibid.

24 Young, 621.

The Battle of Jackson —and Off to Moscow!

by Chris Mackowski

Expanded from a piece, "'Sublime but Dismal Grandeur': The Battle of Jackson, Mississippi" that appeared at Emerging Civil War on May 14, 2021

Samuel C. Miles once described himself, years after the war, as "a high private in the rear rank of the Live Eagle regiment." I don't know what sort of a soldier that made him, but after the war, he seemed quick to take up the pen to refight battles from home. Miles, a veteran of the 8th Wisconsin, deployed colorful hyperbole and an arsenal of adjectives in a series of writings "to present a true narrative of incidents of the soldier's life in camp and field, on the fatiguing march, the chilling bivouac and lonely picket, the lively skirmish, and the fierce and sanguinary battlefield. . . ."[1]

Originally from Springdale, Wisconsin, Miles mustered into Company E on August 18, 1861, one of 72 men to serve in the company. He was briefly taken prisoner on September 15, 1862, during the Iuka campaign but released in time to rejoin the regiment for the battle of Corinth in October. He continued to serve until mustering out on September 16, 1864. After the

---

1 S. C. Miles, *An Epic on "Old Abe," The War Eagle* (Stetsonville, WI: The War Eagle Book Association, 1894), 5. A fragment of the manuscript exists in the Wisconsin Historical Society online collection. (https://content.wisconsinhistory.org/digital/collection/quiner/id/41362)

war, he retired to the hat-sounding Stetsonville, Wisconsin.[2]

Between 1893 and 1897, Miles took up his pen no fewer than 15 times to correspond with *The National Tribune*'s "Fighting Them Over" section.[3] He also wrote *An Epic on "Old Abe," The War Eagle* and collected his work in *A Prospectus of The Eagle Regiment*, creating The War Eagle Book Association to solicit funds from veterans to fund his work.[4] "[I]f not recorded by the actor or participator while living, [it] will leave a vacant page in our great nation's history to be filled by the less desirable article of fiction," he exhorted.[5]

Miles's "true narrative," he promised, required "no coloring of imagination or romance to satisfy the taste of the reader for the romantic or heroic phases of life.

S. C. Miles as sketched for his own book— which made him kind of sketchy. *An Epic on "Old Abe"*

Romance could not exceed the reality. . . ."[6] Yet his writing often has that same delightfully over-the-top quality that John Brown Gordon's memoir has: not only was Gordon going to successfully lead counterattacks across the interior of the Mule Shoe at Spotsylvania, he was going to out-Blitzkrieg

2 *Roster of Wisconsin Volunteers, War of the Rebellion, 1861-1865* (Madison, WI: Democrat Printing Company, 1886), 589; George W. Drigg, *Opening of the Mississippi: or, Two Years Campaigning in the South-West* (Madison, WI: Wm. J. Park & Co., 1864), 11.

3 Richard A. Sauers, ed., *The* National Tribune *Civil War Index: A Guide to the Weekly Newspaper Dedicated to Civil War Veterans, 1877-1943*, vol. 3, (El Dorado Hills: Savas Beatie, 2017), 206.

4 Miles, "The War Eagle Book Association," *Epic*, 53.

5 Miles, *Epic*, 5.

6 Miles, *Epic*, 6.

the German Blitzkrieg and defeat their panzer divisions while successfully driving all the way to Moscow in the dead of winter while saving Francis Barlow as he did it. Boom!

Miles's recollections feel a little like that, too. Case in point: his account of the "Live Eagle" Brigade's involvement in the battle of Jackson, Mississippi. To read Miles's rendering, which appears in two installments in *The National Tribune* on July 27 and August 3, 1893, his brigade seems to have captured the state capital almost single-handedly. "There are some slight errors in history in regard to the capture of Jackson, which I will take opportunity to correct," he declared in his opening column, staking his credibility on the fact he was "in the habit of taking notes of such matters as appeared to us of interest worthy of remembering. . . ."[7] (Note his revealing decision to speak of himself in the third-person plural: "us"!)

Miles's regiment, the 8th Wisconsin, served in Brig. Gen. Joseph Mower's Second Brigade in Brig. Gen. James Tuttle's Third Division in Maj. Gen. William T. Sherman's XV Corps. The regiment had as its mascot a live bald eagle named "Old Abe," named after the president of the United States, which gave the regiment and the brigade its "Live Eagle" nickname. With "lightning playing on his pinions," Old Abe went into battle with the brigade, one member of the regiment said.[8] Miles described the eagle as a "fine specimen of our national emblem . . . [who] so grandly shared all the privations, exposures and perils of the grand and triumphant campaigns and over thirty battles. . . ."[9]

On the night of May 13, Sherman's corps advanced northeast from Mississippi Springs, toward the state capital—"Fighting Joe Mower's invincible Second (Live Eagle) Brigade in the lead, skirmishing with the enemy and steadily driving them toward Jackson," crowed Miles. To the north, Maj. Gen. James McPherson advanced on Jackson from the northwest. The two wings of the army had coordinated closely to time their arrival in Jackson as simultaneously as possible.

7　S.C. Miles, "Capture of Jackson," 27 July 1893, *The National Tribune*, 3, (https://chroniclingamerica.loc.gov/lccn/sn82016187/1893-07-27/ed-1/seq-3/).

8　Frank Abial Flower, *Old Abe, the Eighth Wisconsin War Eagle. A Full Account of His Capture and Enlistment, Exploits in War and Honorable as well as Useful Career in Peace* (Madison, WI: Curran and Bowen, 1885), 38-39.

9　Miles, *Epic*, 6.

Awaiting them were about 6,000 Confederates under the titular command of Gen. Joseph E. Johnston, recently arrived from his headquarters in Tennessee. But no sooner had Johnston disembarked from his train than he took one look at the situation and declared "I am too late," then immediately set to work on plans to evacuate the city. Doing so left his chief subordinate, Lt. Gen. John Pemberton, isolated and unsupported even as a vast Union host under Ulysses S. Grant stalked the Mississippi interior. Neither Pemberton nor Johnston could get reliable information on what Grant was up to.

In part, the confusion stemmed from Grant's victory at Raymond on May 12. From there, he sent McPherson north to sever the Confederate rail line in Clinton, cutting off Pemberton in Vicksburg from his main supply and reinforcement route. To ensure Pemberton remained cut off and crippled, Grant decided on the spur of the moment to capture Jackson and, if possible, flush out any Confederate forces there so as to eliminate any threat to his rear once he finally did advance on Vicksburg.

As Johnston packed up the huge quantity of supplies stored in the city's warehouses and sent them via wagon train to the northeast toward Canton, he appointed Brig. Gen. John Gregg to nominal command of the defenses. Gregg was to buy as much time as possible for Johnston and the supplies to make their escape.

Gregg's 3,300-man brigade of Texans and Tennesseans had arrived as reinforcements from Port Hudson, Louisiana, just in time to run into the Federal army in Raymond on May 12. Gregg acquitted himself well, but his men had been roughly handled. Now he had to deploy them again for battle, along with a few other reinforcements that had begun to arrive in the city. Along with Gregg's brigade, a scant garrison under Brig. Gen. John Adams, and local militia, the city's defenders included six companies of the 3rd Kentucky Mounted Infantry and one battery—about 1,200 men—under Brig. Gen. W. H. T. Walker, recently arrived from Savannah, Georgia, as well as portions of a brigade under Col. Peyton Colquitt sent from Charleston, South Carolina. Thousands of other reinforcements were en route to the Mississippi capital, as well, but Johnston began redirecting them so as to not entangle them in a fight he did not want to engage in.[10]

---

10 As historian Michael Ballard once wrote, "Johnston seldom fought if retreat was possible." Michael B. Ballard, *Vicksburg: The Campaign that Opened the Mississippi* (Chapel Hill, NC: University of North Carolina Press, 2004), 158.

Gregg posted Colquitt's force as well as his own, plus two batteries, to the northwest of the city to block the road coming down from Clinton. He sent the Kentuckians, a battalion of sharpshooters, and a single battery to the southwest to block the road coming up from Raymond. Adams, meanwhile, oversaw the evacuation of the wagon train. Militia filed into the earthen defenses that ringed the city.

Joe Johnston set his evacuation plan into motion at 3:30 a.m.—about the same time the two Federal columns began their advances on the city. Rain, which began sometime overnight, caught both columns on the march and became so heavy that roads turned to mires and streams flooded. But they plodded and sloshed on, closing in on the capital in a perfectly executed pincer movement. Confederate horsemen could only harass but not delay either force. "[T]he steadily-advancing skirmish-line develops each hidden stand of the enemy," wrote S. C. Miles of the advance from Raymond, "and a charge of the advance regiment of the brigade soon routs them from cover, so that there is no halt or delay in the onward march of the Fifteenth Corps. . . ."

Battle finally opened in earnest just after dawn. The day's heaviest fighting would occur on McPherson's front, but to read Miles's account—told in a voice that would make later pulp novelists proud—Sherman's men experienced the full drama and trauma of war. Just after dawn, the men in Sherman's column could hear "the heavy booming of cannon away to the left, where McPherson was engaging the enemy," Miles wrote, "with the shells bursting around us, the rapid fire of musktey [sic] and a storm of leaden hail sweeping by, blending with the almost incessant lightning and thunder crash of heaven's artillery, with the down-pouring torrents from the clouds—all combine to make a scene of sublime but rather dismal grandeur."[11]

The Kentuckians made a smart defense along a rain-swollen creek Sherman's men could not cross, forcing a bottleneck at the bridge where the road crossed the stream. Sherman's troops forced passage when the Kentuckians failed to torch the bridge, perhaps because the wood was too drenched from the storm. As Federals flooded across the span, the Confederates fell back to the works at the edge of town. A number of artillery pieces bolstered the works, manned by eager if slightly trained citizen volunteers.

---

11   Miles, "Capture of Jackson," *The National Tribune,* 3 August 1893, 3, (https://chroniclingamerica.loc.gov/lccn/sn82016187/1893-08-03/ed-1/seq-3/) Hereafter, all quotes from Miles about the battle come from this article.

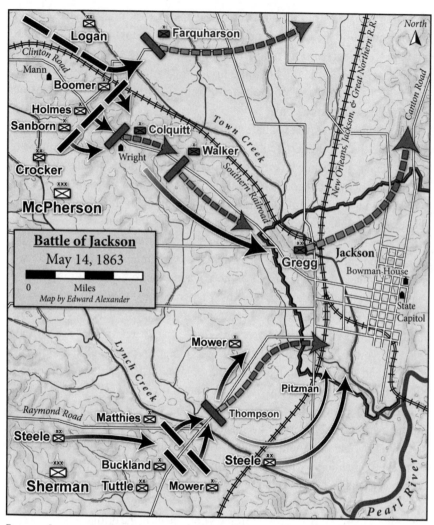

BATTLE OF JACKSON—McPherson's corps approached the capital of Mississippi from the northwest while Sherman's corps approached from the southwest. Close communication overnight ensured the columns reached Jackson almost simultaneously. Confederate commander Joseph E. Johnston ordered just enough defense to hold Federals off long enough to evacuate Confederate forces and supplies from the city.

From a distance, the Confederate fortifications around the town looked formidable. Although he deployed the brigades of Mower and Brig. Gen. Charles Matthies, joined later by the brigade of Brig. Gen. Ralph Buckland, Sherman thought twice about actually sending them forward for an all-out frontal assault. Instead, he called for Capt. Julius Pitzman, the XV Corps' acting chief engineer, and told him to scout around to the Confederate left and see if he could find a weak spot in the line anywhere. Sherman assigned the 95th Ohio Infantry to accompany the engineer, doubling as protection and a strike force.

Pitzman's reconnaissance eventually discovered a way into the city along the New Orleans, Jackson, and Great Northern Railroad, which ran northward through the Confederate works and straight into the city. As the expedition advanced, they found the works deserted. The 95th advanced into the breach even as the engineer returned to Sherman to report his discovery. Sherman immediately ordered Maj. Gen. Frederick Steele's entire division to follow in the Ohioans' footsteps and secure the way into the city.

At about this time, the skies began to clear, and the situation in front of Tuttle's division looked clearer, too. "The rain is now over, and the bright sun begins to pierce the fast-fleeting clouds and cheer the thoroughly-drenched soldiers with his bright rays," wrote Miles, apparently ebullient that his Vitamin D deficiency would soon be alleviated.

Confederate artillery from the earthworks played against the Federals, but Mower, at the center of the Federal line, began to suspect that not all was as it appeared before him. Then came the sound of cheering from somewhere in the Confederate position—the huzzahs of the 95th Ohio as they began to capture Confederate artillery positions from the rear. Tuttle decided to send Mower, Matthies, and Buckland forward.

"We meet the heavy artillery fire from the enemy's line of city defenses along the ridges and high ground across the open fields," Miles wrote, using present tense to underscore the immediacy of the action:

> but without delay Fighting Joe issues orders to his regimental commanders to deploy in line as they advance under cover of the timbered ridges along the open fields. Above the battle's din of booming cannons' roar and bursting shell the command rings forth along the line, 'Attention! Fix bayonets—Forward—Double-quick—Now, steady, boys! Keep your alignment—March!' And now out upon the open field sweeps that invincible line of loyal blue and vengeful glistening steel . . . [toward] the unquailing, even line of valiant defenders. . . .

Mower's four regiments made up the center of the attack. "[B]eneath one of those four stands of proudly-waving regimental banners," recalled Miles, "the War Eagle Old Abe's valiant form and spreading wings proclaim to that line of rebel gray that they are vainly resisting a foe who never knew defeat." One of Old Abe's biographers (and there were a few, Miles among them) later described the eagle as "all spirit and fire. He flapped his pinions and sent his powerful scream high above the din of battle."[12]

In his account, Miles hits his stride during the sprint to the Confederate earthworks:

> On sweeps the irresistible line of blue, undismayed and unchecked by the terrible storm of lead and iron which thins their ranks and strews the field with mangled slain. With their thundering Union cheer pealing clear above the battle's horrid din, as their undaunted line sweeps up that last homestretch of bristling trench and parapet-crowned hights [sic], is it any wonder that when they leap over those defenses they find most of that chivalrous line in full flight for safer localities, while those brave men who choose to stay, either too brave to run away, that they may fight another day, or dare not leave the shelter of their trenches to turn their backs toward the charging foe, are gobbled within their defenses?

In fact, Confederates had largely abandoned the works already on Gregg's orders. Gregg had received word from Johnston that the evacuation of supplies had been completed and so Gregg no longer needed to hold off the Yankees. "I immediately ordered the entire force to withdraw," Gregg wrote in his official report, "which was done in excellent order, our troops not having permitted the enemy to press them back at any point until the order was given."[13] That wasn't quite true because, on the northwest front along the Clinton Road, McPherson's corps had pressed Confederates quite

---

12   Flower, 38-39.

13   United States War Department, *The War of the Rebellion: A Compilation of the Official Records of theUnion and Confederate Armies*, 70 vols. in 128 parts (Washington D.C.: Government Printing Office,1880-1901), Series I, volume 24, part 1, p. 786 (hereafter cited as *O.R.*, I, 24, pt. 1, 786).

convincingly. Nonetheless, Gregg had done the job assigned to him and done it well, and by 2:00 p.m.—the same time the rain cleared—he began his withdrawal, pulling his forces to the northeast and the road Johnston had taken toward Canton.

This is where Miles's account really inflates with off-to-Moscow, Gordon-like flair. "Having cleared and captured the defenses of Jackson on the southwest," Miles reported, "the Live Eagle Brigade pursues the retreating Confederates through the streets to the north . . . covering the Clinton road, thereby compelling their hurried vacation by the enemy to avoid capture, and the whole Confederate force is immediately in hasty retreat in the direction of Canton. . . ." By his account, the thundering success of Sherman's assault, not Gregg's orders, "compelled the hasty evacuation of those in front of McPherson's Corps on the Clinton road. . . ." Miles here may have taken a page out of Gregg's official report (and Gordon's playbook!) for advantageously exaggerating events.

The regiment's route of march brought them to the Mississippi statehouse "where the Confederate flag is arrogantly waving above the State capitol dome," Miles snarled. "It does not take the Color Guard of the Live Eagle regiment many minutes to enter the building and haul down the Secession rag, and . . . the Stars and Stripes of the 8th Wis. are proudly waving in its place."

This incident, over time, became a source of great tension among veterans of the Army of the Tennessee. Members of the 59th Indiana of Col. John B. Sanborn's brigade—part of McPherson's force—claimed the honor of flying their colors over the statehouse. "They were the first and only colors planted on the capitol of Jackson," Alexander bragged in his official report, written soon after the battle, "and they remained above the capitol dome until the regiment moved out the following day."[14]

Miles, writing thirty years later, nonetheless asserted the Wisconsinites' claim—indeed, this seems to be what inspired him to begin his writing crusade in the first place as a responding salvo against an account about the flag published in the *Tribune*. "[A] capture of a State Capitol and a Confederate flag floating thereon was not a matter of such common

14 *O.R.*, I, 24, pt. 1, 772, 730.

The Mississippi state house became the hub of the Federal occupation. *Harper's Weekly*

occurrence as to be considered unworthy of record," he insisted.[15] Several other members of the regiment, in their own writings, corroborated Miles's assertion, but no definitive proof has ever emerged.

With Gregg's men gone and the local citizen volunteers flushed out of the trenches and back into their homes, Sherman's XV Corps filed into the city from the southwest, McPherson's XVII Corps filed in from the northwest, and Union troops made their camps everywhere in the city. Grant, traveling with Sherman, made his headquarters at the Bowman House Hotel, taking the same room Joe Johnston had taken the night before. Sherman and his staff occupied a nearby "magnificent dwelling near the center of the city," Miles reported, before then cataloging the lodging for the rest of his order of battle: "Gen. Tuttle . . . finds neat and comfortable quarters in the suburbs of the city. Gen. Mower . . . occupies the Supreme Court room in the capital. Col Robbins, in command of the 8th Wis., temporarily fills the office of the Judges of Errors and Appeals. Col Webber, of the 11th Mo. . . . fills the office of Secretary of State. Col. Hubbard, of the 5th Minn., takes the Attorney-General's Office, and Col. Cromwell, 47th Ill., usurpes [sic] the office of the State Librarian."

Lieutenant Colonel John Jefferson of the 8th Wisconsin, assigned the role of provost-marshal, took up duties in the State Treasurer's Office, which was, groused Miles, "crowded day and night with citizens and refugees seeking protection from the military officers of the Government they have outraged, defied, and insulted." The 8th, encamped in and around the capitol, came into contact with a number of captive Confederates because of their lieutenant colonel's policing duties. "The legislative halls

15   Miles, 27 July 1893.

are occupied by prisoners of war who are present at all hours with a full quorum," Miles wrote, "and no filibustering is indulged in to defeat or delay business, but all are alert to devise the best means of bettering their deplorably-degenerate seceded State."

Early the next morning, Grant directed McPherson back to the west to link up with John McClernand's XIII Corps, then guarding the army's Vicksburg-facing flank. By then, Pemberton had sallied forth from the Gibraltar of the Confederacy and, under confusing orders from Joe Johnston, was bumbling through the Mississippi countryside. A clash at Champion Hill was only a day away.

Grant followed McPherson out of town but left Sherman's XV Corps in Jackson to destroy anything of military value that remained. Grant did not want Johnston or any other Confederate reinforcements to slip into his rear and find the city a convenient base for launching operations against him. "On the 15th, the ruthless hand of destruction and devastation has full sway," Miles wrote, "and immense amounts of Confederate property, military manufactories and stories are destroyed." Grant later commended Sherman, saying, "He did the work most effectually."[16] Following their day of destruction, the corps pulled out at about 11 a.m. on May 16 "with the rebel cavalry at its heels," Miles reported, taking an opportunity for one final swipe at his opponents: "as is usual with that kind of beast, ready to follow and hiss out their spite like a goose when one's back is turned, and still more ready to run when turned upon."

As any soldier who has only a glimpse of the action on his immediate front, Miles's account of the battle of Jackson gives great weight to the fighting by Mower's brigade, even to the short shrift of other brigades in the division (Buckland's brigade, for instance, sustained heavy, straight-on artillery fire). However, McPherson's corps, fighting along the Clinton road, bore the greatest brunt of the battle. The Federals suffered exactly 300 casualties, with 265 of them on McPherson's front. The 17th Iowa, raked by flanking artillery fire during a charge against the Confederate line, accounted for most of those: 16 killed, 60 wounded, 1 disabled by a shell,

---

16 Ulysses S. Grant, *Grant: Memoirs and Selected Letters*, Mary Drake and William S. McFeely, eds. (New York: Library of America, 1990), 338.

and 3 missing; their 80 casualties out of 350 men engaged accounted for 23 percent of the regiment and 27 percent of Grant's total losses.[17]

The Confederates, meanwhile, suffered some 845 casualties and the stinging loss of 17 guns, most of which were captured by Tuttle's division as it swept into the works following Gregg's withdrawal. Thinly defended by local volunteers or not, though, the captured cannons made a fantastic prize by any Federal standard—and a sore loss for the Confederates. Gregg, writing in a pique of denial that might have made Miles envious, completely ignored the lost artillery in his official report, instead focusing on the "excellent order" his force maintained when ordered to withdraw, "our troops not having permitted the enemy to press them back at any point until the order was given."[18] Again, on McPherson's front in particular, the Federals did plenty of pressing back, but overall, Gregg's men performed admirably against a *much* larger force.

Joe Johnston, after teasing Pemberton on to ruin at Champion Hill, would come creeping back to Jackson enough to worry Grant during his siege of Vicksburg, but ultimately Johnston would do nothing. Grant would finally shoo him away in mid-July, after the fall of the beleaguered city, by sending Sherman back to Jackson one more time. Sherman would return again in February 1864 during the Meridian campaign.

Although the May battle of Jackson was not as pivotal as, say, Port Gibson or Champion Hill, it provided Grant with much-needed breathing room by dispersing Johnston's potential threat in the Federal rear. It also hampered the Confederacy's ability to reinforce or resupply Pemberton's men in Vicksburg by cutting one of the necessary rail lines for moving in troops or supplies. Finally, the fall of the state capital—the third to fall in the war—provided a shocking blow to morale throughout the South.

"[T]he city still stands," Miles wrote in 1893, capturing in present tense the moment of his brigade's departure in 1863 but reflecting, through his sense of drama, something larger, too, "and her magnificent capitol, with all its valuable records, where foul treason was first ordained, is left unharmed, as a monument of their outraged country's forbearance and the generosity of their hated Yankees and conquerors, a monument to their shame. . . ."

---

17 *O.R.*, I, 24, pt. 1, 779.

18 Ibid., 786.

"Our Army Was Thoroughly Beaten": An English Rebel Remembers Champion Hill

by Daniel A. Masters

Originally published as a blog post on Emerging Civil War on May 16, 2021

This extraordinary letter, written by former English army officer Stephen Edward Monaghan Underhill to his mother in Coldstream, Scotland, in the waning days of the siege of Vicksburg, gives us an account of Underhill's experiences during the campaign. At the time, Underhill was serving as an aide-de-camp to Confederate Brig. Gen. Stephen D. Lee. The 21-year-old Underhill had resigned his commission in the British army and entered the Confederacy through the blockade at Charleston, South Carolina, in January 1863. From there, he journeyed to Mississippi and gained an appointment to Lee's staff. Underhill gained favorable notice from Lee for his "gallantry and efficient service" during the Vicksburg campaign.

The letter had a rather twisted path to publication in the *Guernsey Times* of Cambridge, Ohio. Underhill wrote that he had entrusted the letter to a civilian in Vicksburg because he anticipated that the city would soon be captured and that his private communications would be limited. Underhill's letter was evidently either found or intercepted by Lt. John C. Douglass of the 78th Ohio Volunteer Infantry, who was then serving as assistant adjutant general on Brig. Gen. Mortimer Leggett's staff (Second Brigade, Third

Division, XVII Army Corps). Douglass sent the letter home to Ohio, and the *Guernsey Times* ran Underhill's letter in their August 20, 1863, issue.

The letter is dated "Sunday, June 28, 1863, 11 a.m. to 4 p.m., the 42nd day of the siege" from "Trenches, Vicksburg, Mississippi." "It is with feelings of great doubt and uncertainty that I sit down to write this," Monaghan began before recounting events of the campaign. Stationed in Vicksburg itself as Grant's army moved across the countryside, Pemberton's forces finally "heard that reinforcements were on their way from Charleston, South Carolina, and Port Hudson, Mississippi, to our relief and that General Joe Johnston himself was about to command us in person," Monaghan wrote. Pemberton responded to Johnston's orders by moving to the east bank of the Big Black River, where he then bogged down with indecisiveness.

> The two days we lay in line of battle in strong position near Edward's Depot awaiting the enemy. On the evening of the 15th we started toward Clinton where we heard the enemy had last been seen. Our division being in advance, General Loring's division (Buford and Tilghman's brigades) 5,000 strong came next, and then came Bowen's and Green's Missouri brigades. Smith's division remained behind to guard. Lieutenant General [John C.] Pemberton now took command we brought our forced march of Friday evening May 15th to a close on Saturday about 2 a.m. when we bivouacked in an open field. We had no wagons with us, but the men were so exhausted that they soon forgot their hunger in sleep. By 4:30 next morning, a courier arrived from General [Joseph E.] Johnston directing us at once to make a junction with him and immediately afterward a scout came in to say the enemy was making a forced march to get in our rear and between us and Vicksburg. General Pemberton at once ordered a retreat. Our wagons, ordnance, hospital, trains, etc. were all sent off on the Vicksburg road while the troops after a five-mile march formed line of battle on a strong position near Baker's Creek and Edward's Depot on the Raymond and Clinton road, and there awaited the approach of the enemy.
>
> It was now about 7 a.m. The men were completely broken down by hard marching and none had had anything to eat for nearly 36

hours. Under these auspices we awaited battle on a glorious May morning. General Loring's division was on the right; Stevenson's on the left extending nearly to Baker's Creek and our brigade (Lee's) was on the extreme left of our division (Stevenson's). General Bowen's division was in reserve and General Pemberton commanded in person. The battle commenced about 7:30 with heavy skirmishing on the right. It gradually rolled round to the left, however, and came to us, ceasing on the right entirely. By 9 o'clock the enemy had massed large bodies of troops in our front and Cumming's on our right. General Lee had, six different times, moved his brigade that it might not be outflanked by the overwhelming numbers of the enemy. Five separate times did I gallop at top speed upward of a mile and back bearing the same message from General Lee to General [Carter L.] Stevenson to the effect the enemy were outflanking him. Five times did I bring the reply, "Tell General Lee I know it and am moving my division accordingly." Five times did we take a new position on our left, but the cry was "still they come."

At this time the enemy seemed to have completed their arrangements for they made a simultaneous and vigorous attack along our lines. They advanced in three lines and to each of our little brigades they opposed at least a division. We could only bring two brigades into the fight at this time for the others were guarding and holding important positions. At first our men stood up to the work gallantly and vigorously returned the deadly fire that thinned their ranks. They went down by dozens before the Yankee artillery and musketry, but many a Yankee bit the dust. There were two distinct lines respectively of blue and brown, marking where the dead of either army lay where they had fallen when the fray began. This unequal contest lasted several hours but though wearied almost to death and though pressed by overwhelming odds, the Second Brigade still held out, patiently awaiting the arrival and aid of our other two brigades or those of Loring or Bowen. It did not come, however, and one of Cumming's Georgia regiments being hard pushed broke and took shelter in the woods. It was like a bank crumbling away before the action of a torrent to watch our lines at this juncture. The panic seemed contagious and as it ran down the lines, regiment after regiment caught it till both brigades were in full retreat, leaving all their artillery and all dead and wounded in the enemy's hands.

With some trouble the fugitives were rallied on the crest of a hill and again faced the now victoriously advancing enemy. Once more the men from Alabama and Georgia sent their missiles into the ranks of Indiana, Wisconsin, Illinois, and Ohio, and the death yell of the Western men rang loudly out under the luxuriant magnolia groves in which they fought. Again, the Southern troops showed signs of wavering and General Lee, seizing the banner of the 30th Alabama and followed by his staff, rode down the line and led it to the charge. New life seemed to have been infused into the Southern troops. They rushed on with leveled bayonets, cheering wildly. The Northerners rapidly though steadily retiring and pouring volley after volley into their pursuers. At length a shout announced some triumph for the enemy who in a moment rallied and halted, as did also our men, and sure enough there lay General Lee upon the ground. Before any of us could reach him he had disengaged himself from his dead horse and mounting another once more led the charge. We were now passing over our old position when once more did Lee's horse fall dead, amidst a triumphant shout from the enemy. This time our troops fairly broke and ran notwithstanding every effort and all example. General Lee stood for a moment in despair. A ball, and then a second, both fortunately spent, struck his left sleeve, penetrating it and bruising his arm but doing no further damage. Captain Elliott of our staff had his horse shot and a ball broke his sword. I escaped.

General Lee now mounted a third horse and followed his brigade which was once more formed in the magnolia wood upon the hill. He sent me to General Barton to ask for reinforcements. I took a short cut and the first thing I knew I was amongst a number of Yankee sharpshooters who demanded my surrender. I declined, and spurring my horse in another direction, some of them fired and killed my horse. I then jumped into a ravine. At the bottom

I met a wounded Federal officer who when I wouldn't yield, fired three shots of his Colt at me but would not face me with his sword. I got into a rye field and ran up it. Some of our men were at the top and fired several shots at me ere they discovered their mistake. When I got up to the road I caught and mounted a loose horse (which by the way died last week of the sixth shot, five balls having failed even to maim him), saw several aides riding about who all told me the day was lost. Barton's brigade had been demolished and Green's wild Missourians, after having completely routed one Yankee division, retaken all our artillery and made 560 Yankees prisoners, had been surrounded by two other divisions and had only cut its way out with frightful loss. General Tilghman had been killed by a chance shot and General Pemberton had ordered a retreat to Big Black Bridge. I tried to get back to General Lee but the Yankees intervened. I tried to get around them, lost myself in a wood, got fired at again, and finally escaped by swimming Baker's Creek.

I was so hot, hungry, and tired to death that life was hardly endurable, but I rode sadly on with the tide of wagons and fugitives that poured along the road. At last, I came up with our headquarters wagon, hauled it on one side, and enjoyed a wash and some flour scorees and a drink of water. I now asked if it was near noon and was thunderstruck to find it was past six. At Big Black Bridge I saw General Pemberton, but he could tell me nothing. I heard General Lee was killed and his brigade taken and was in despair. From a gentle eminence I could see Edwards' Depot and the fine plantations and country seats in a blaze, showing too plainly the advance of the pursuing foe. I had nothing to do at the bridge, so I rode on to Vicksburg, got there at midnight, and put up at our own headquarters. So ended the battle day.

Our army was thoroughly beaten. Our junction with Johnston was prevented and we lost 18 guns and several thousand stand of small arms and some 5,000 killed, wounded, and prisoners. Our own brigade suffered frightfully. Naturally Vicksburg was in great alarm. I heard that General Lee had been surrounded, lost one regiment, and had cut his way out with the remainder of his brigade; that our whole army, except Loring's division, had crossed to this side and we held the Yankees at bay at our breastworks on the other side until 8 o'clock, though there was some very severe fighting when Vaughn's brigade broke and run. Upwards of 2,000 of them were taken as well as a number of Missourians who could not get away. The enemy took 21 more guns, making our two days' loss in artillery amount to some 39 pieces. We were obliged to burn the bridge, a very fine one, which with its trestlework extended nearly a mile.

I wrote you on Friday by a Federal prisoner going out and I hope you will get it soon. I will write you as soon as I can. I am naturally down spirited, so you must not expect me to say more. Before this reaches you the papers will have told you whether my hopes or fears will have been realized. . . .[1]

Lieutenant Underhill did get an account of the Vicksburg campaign into the hands of his family. A similar missive to the one captured by Lieutenant Douglass appeared in an August issue of the *Edinburgh Scotsman* in Scotland, which was later picked up and re-published by the *New York Evening Post* on September 7, 1863. Following his parole at Vicksburg, Underhill was commissioned as a first lieutenant of cavalry and eventually became colonel of the 65th Alabama Infantry, serving in the defenses of Mobile until the end of the war. Underhill elected to remain in the United States, becoming a resident of Mobile and serving for a time as the city's chief of police. He later moved to Austin, Texas where he died on February 6, 1904, at age 62.

---

1   Stephen Edward Monaghan Underhill to Mrs. Underhill, Letter, in *Guernsey Times*, August 20, 1863.

Old Abe, the 8th Wisconsin War Eagle: A Short Account of His Exploits in War and Honorable—as well as Useful—Career in Peace, with Emphasis on the Vicksburg Campaign

by Meg Groeling and Chris Mackowski

It was noisy and confusing to Old Abe, the famed War Eagle of the 8th Wisconsin, but his boys were "going in," and he was ready as well. The morning's storm had roused him, with "lightning playing on his pinions," said one member of the regiment, adding "a revelry of delight to the wild and stormy spirit of an eagle."[1]

Old Abe was no stranger to battle. The fearful noise and running soldiers were well known to this eagle, who had "seen the elephant" before. This time—May 14, 1863—he and the men of the 8th found themselves, with the rest of Joseph Mower's brigade, at the forefront of the attack on the fortifications surrounding Jackson, Mississippi. "Beneath one of those four stands of proudly-waving regimental banners," wrote Samuel C. Miles for the *National Tribune*, "the War Eagle Old Abe's valiant form and spreading

---

1 The quote, as well as the inspiration for the title of this piece, come from Frank Abial Flower, *Old Abe, the Eighth Wisconsin War Eagle. A Full Account of His Capture and Enlistment, Exploits in War and Honorable as well as Useful Career in Peace* (Madison, WI: Curran and Bowen, 1885), 38-39.

wings proclaim to that line of rebel gray that they are vainly resisting a foe who never knew defeat."[2]

Shortly after 2:00 p.m., the Federals charged forward. "Abe was all spirit and fire," wrote one of the Wisconsinites. "He flapped his pinions and sent his powerful scream high above the din of battle."[3]

"He was . . ." said another, "the embodiment of a sublime fury."[4]

*   *   *

The Roman legions carried their eagles freely, and fearlessly. Napoleon chose the eagle as the symbol of the French Empire, proudly displayed, addorsed and inverted, with the thunderbolts of Jupiter in his talons. On June 20, 1782, Congress chose the eagle as the symbol on America's Great Seal. The escutcheon on the breast of the American Bald Eagle identifies him as ours. In his dexter talon, he holds an olive branch, in his sinister claw a bundle of thirteen arrows, and in his beak, a scroll inscribed with the motto, *E Pluribus Unum.* The olive branch signifies peace, the arrows themselves war, while their number, thirteen, represents the original thirteen colonies. From this device on the Great Seal of the United States, Americans acknowledge the eagle as their national emblem, in peace and war.[5]

In particular, one eagle has become associated with the Civil War and with the Union soldiers of the 8th Wisconsin. Originally purchased from a Native American in trade for a bushel of corn, he belonged to a saloon owner who then donated the eagle to Capt. John E. Perkins—who was organizing a volunteer infantry company at Eau Claire for the Wisconsin 8th Regiment—as a show of support.[6] The beautiful young eagle was sworn in by putting red, white, and blue ribbons around his neck. He wore a rosette

---

2 Samuel C. Miles, "Capture of Jackson," *National Tribune* (Washington, D.C.) August 3, 1893, 3.

3 Flower, 39.

4 John Melvin Williams, *The "Eagle Regiment,": 8th Wis. Inf'ty. Vols.* (Belleville, WI: Recorder Print, 1890), 58.

5 Charles Thomson, "Remarks and Explanation," June 20, 1782, http://greatseal.com/symbols/explanation.html.

6 Flower, 11.

of the same colors on his chest. Thus caparisoned, the eagle then became the charge of Pvt. James McGinnis, who was given the privilege of being his keeper. In a few days, McGinnis produced a perch with a shield attached to the vertical wooden handle. Two patriotic ladies made little flags to be carried on either side of him when on the march.

On September 6, 1861, with bands playing, banners flying, and people cheering, the Eau Claire Eagles marched from camp down to the Chippewa River, on their way to Camp Randall, near Madison, where they were to be mustered in. Old Abe was perched proudly on his shield between the flags presented by the Ladies' Aid Society, his smooth, graceful neck encircled with those ribbons of red, white, and blue.[7] The

Old Abe had his own carte de visite, which he would "sign" by biting it. *LOC*

enthusiasm of the men of Company C was so infectious that the entire 8th Regiment took the name "The Eagle Regiment."[8]

As Old Abe's fame spread, he acquired a new perch. The shield was heart-shaped and proudly bore the stars and stripes and the words "8th Reg. W. V." painted along its base.[9] Wherever the 8th Wisconsin fought, Old Abe was there. On November 2, 1862, the 8th Wisconsin joined Gen. U. S. Grant's forces in the first attempt to take Vicksburg, Mississippi. Grant met up with Gen. William T. Sherman at Grand Junction, Tennessee. They moved the armies down the Mississippi Central Railroad to the north of

7   Ibid., 13-14.

8   Ibid., 17.

9   Ibid., 17-18.

Abbeville, near the Tallahatchie Bridge. The Confederates attempted a defense but Grant flanked them. The 8th was in the thick of things during this push down the railroad past Oxford, Water Valley, Coffeeville, and on to Oakland, where the Federal advance stalled.[10]

In Oxford, the regiment was accosted by a Confederate belle who scornfully exclaimed: "Oh! See that *Yankee Buzzard.*" This angered the soldiers of the 8th so much they hollered back at her, using a few ungentlemanly epithets, which caused the "belle" to retreat hastily to her own home. Old Abe was never hurt by any Rebel ammunition or words.[11]

In March, the 8th joined the second brigade of the third division of Sherman's XV Corps, under the command of recently promoted Brig. Gen. Joseph A. Mower. The last of Grant's corps to cross the Mississippi River for the overland march to Vicksburg, they caught up to Grant just before the battle of Raymond on May 12. The next day, the corps marched overnight in a torrential downpour to reach Jackson on May 14, intent on capturing the state capital.

As Sherman aligned his forces, Mower's brigade found itself at the center of the assault formation. "Gazing at the heavens, the eyes of the Eagle seemed as lightning . . ." wrote one hyperbolic Abe admirer. "[W]hen he stretched [his pinions] forth and dashed the electric drops of rain upon the soldiers, they were inspired with an inexpressible enthusiasm."[12]

That enthusiasm helped Mower's brigade sweep into the city, driving its few Confederate defenders before them. "The federals won," wrote Frank Flower, a regimental historian, "and Old Abe . . . entered the capital of Mississippi at the head of the victorious army."[13]

The 8th made its headquarters near the state capitol. "The Confederate flag was soon hauled down and the Union colors hoisted in its stead," Flower continued, "and Old Abe, the living emblem of our free and undivided country, perched on his shield of stars and stripes, was placed in

10   Carter, Alden, ed. *Brother to the Eagle: The Civil War Journal of Sergeant Ambrose Armitage, 8th Wisconsin Infantry* (booklocker.com, 2006), 327.

11   George W. Driggs, *Opening of the Mississippi: or Two years' campaigning in the Southwest* (Madison, WI: William J. Park & Company, 1864), 48.

12   Williams, 58.

13   Flower, 39.

the beautiful park in front of the steps of the beautiful capitol building, on which, in other days, hundreds of human beings had been sold at auction in hopeless slavery. What a contrast!"

Grant's objectives were further consolidated when his army prevailed at the battle of Champion Hill on May 16, and at the battle of Big Black River Bridge on May 17. On May 19 and 22, Mower's brigade took part in the assaults against Vicksburg. On the 22nd, Sherman sent Mower's brigade from Graveyard Road toward Stockade Redan, and Ole Abe had a near-miss.

During the assault, Abe's loyal caretaker, Edward Homaston, tripped—just in time to put his feathered charge in the way of a minié ball, which "struck Abe a glancing blow." The projectile slightly clipped the eagle's breast, doing no damage but frightening both bird and bearer. Abe flapped his wings, dragging Homaston a few feet—a moment of panic that proved fortuitous to both man and bird. "Although both were somewhat injured by the mishap, the wonderful strength of the bird saved Homaston's [sic] life," wrote the regimental historian; "for as Abe dragged him along a bullet struck the spot he had that instant vacated."[14]

The sequence of mishaps caught the attention of a lieutenant, who in turn ordered a sergeant to keep an eye on Homaston. Should the private get killed, the lieutenant said, "secure Abe at all hazards."[15]

Once Homaston collected himself and rejoined the regiment, he carefully placed Abe and his perch next to the regimental colors, under a tree and in plain view of the enemy, about 550 yards distant. Of course, the Confederates noticed the red, white, and blue, and saw, as well, the glossy brown and white eagle nestled among the brighter hues. Shots were fired. One struck the tree, sending a deadly scattering of wood and bark into the flags and killing several infantrymen and two officers. "The eagle sprung for flight again, but was held fast," wrote Flowers.[16]

Homaston and the color guard lowered the colors and their eagle and hunkered beneath "the shivered tree expecting annihiliation [sic]." As

14   Ibid., 40.

15   Ibid.

16   Ibid., 41.

Going into battle with a national flag and a live bald eagle—if that doesn't say "America!" what does? *ECW*

Federals traded a brisk fire with Confederates, "an adjutant rode briskly to the spot and announced the order to, 'go forward into the ravine and avoid the slaughter.'"[17] The ravine, to the regiment's right, had bedeviled the Federals during the May 19 assaults but now offered a perfect refuge for the grateful men of the 8th Wisconsin—if they could get there. "The regiment recoiled over swaths of the slain, receiving an appalling storm of shot," Flower wrote. "Many fell, but Old Abe and his bearer came out without a scratch." As another Abe biographer, Joseph Barrett, characterized it, "It was indeed an *eagle* leap from a maelstrom of consuming fire."[18]

In the ravine, one of the men caught a live rabbit to soothe the agitated bird. "Here, Abe," he said, tossing the rabbit to Abe's perch. "You've earned this fellow." The eagle caught it with his claws and, according to another soldier, "There, admidst [sic] the rage of battle, as shell and

17 Ibid.

18 Joseph O. Barrett, *The Soldier Bird: "Old Abe": the Live War Eagle of Wisconsin, that Served a Three Years' Campaign in the Great Rebellion* (Madison, Wisconsin: Atwood & Culver, 1876), 64.

cannon were playing freely overhead, he devoured his prey, heedless of noise and excitement."[19]

Homaston took some time to fill canteens for himself and several comrades, then returned to his charge to conduct an examination. As Barrett tells it, Homaston concluded Abe had probably been hit with a spent Minie ball.

The ball passed down his neck and breast, cutting off the feathers in its track. Had it glanced the other way, the proud bird would have fallen; but being shot in the direction of the lay of feathers, as he faced the foe, they saved his life. Another ball passed through the web of his left wing, making a round hole in it. He is a scarred veteran to this day.[20]

The May 22 assaults failed, and a siege ensued. It was a time, for both armies, of struggle and peril—and, for Confederates, slow starvation—but Abe endured it all. "[T]he soldiers often forgot themselves, but never forgot Abe," wrote Flower, "their playmate in camp and their companion and emblem of victory in battle."[21] "[A]ny day, the whole regiment would have fought for him," Barrett added. "Sharing alike the dangers of march and battle, the Eagle was companion and warrior, sign and seal of victory." Soldiers held "undying attachment and devotion to the liberty which the noble bird so grandly emblemized."[22]

Vicksburg surrendered on July 4, 1863. Maj. Gen. John A. Logan—the Black Eagle of Illinois—entered the besieged city at the head of the victorious Union Army of the Tennessee. At his left rode Old Abe, the proud symbol of the 8th Wisconsin. The trumpets rang out, the soldiers cheered, General Logan swept his hat from his head, while the eagle was "all fire and spirit."[23] He flapped his wings and sent his war scream high above the roar of victory.

19 Flower, 40-41.

20 Barrett, 65.

21 Flower, 42.

22 Barrett, 65.

23 Flower, 39.

"The Forlorn Hope"

by Andrew Miller

*Originally published as a blog post on Emerging Civil War
on May 22, 2018, in commemoration of Memorial Day*

As Memorial Day weekend approaches, I cannot help but reflect about the great sacrifices our men and women have made for our great country. Like many of the followers of Emerging Civil War, the great contest for our nation's survival is always on my mind, although these days a career change and lateral movement to Vicksburg National Military Park now consumes my every thought. Today, as I began to pack my uniform items away and clear out my locker, I realized it is the 22nd of May.

One hundred and fifty-five years ago, Ulysses S. Grant's Army of the Tennessee was unleashing an all-out assault along a three-mile front of Confederate entrenchments surrounding Vicksburg, Mississippi.

A previous assault by elements of William T. Sherman's XV Corps had failed in a bloody repulse three days prior, and Grant was not going to be so shortsighted this next time.

As part of the prepared assault, regimental commanders in Frank P. Blair's second division of Sherman's corps, asked for volunteers to come forward and organize into a vanguard force carrying cane bundles called fascines, planks, and ladders for scaling the rebel works. One hundred and fifty men stepped forward and were told this mission was an important one, but a "forlorn hope." The term meant it would be a disaster for them, a sacrifice of their lives for the greater good.

On May 22, 1863, as thousands of Federal soldiers physically and

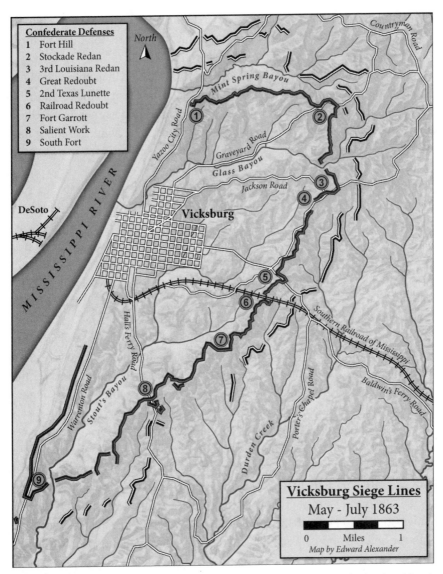

Confederate Defenses
1 Fort Hill
2 Stockade Redan
3 3rd Louisiana Redan
4 Great Redoubt
5 2nd Texas Lunette
6 Railroad Redoubt
7 Fort Garrott
8 Salient Work
9 South Fort

VICKSBURG SIEGE LINES—Confederate defenders had months to prepare defenses for the city, although most efforts assumed an assault from the river. Grant ultimately approached from the east, but still found himself facing formidable obstacles. His May 19 assaults, rushed, underestimated the strength of the defenses; his May 22 assaults, better planned out, still weren't enough.

mentally prepared for the task at hand, the "Forlorn Hope" grabbed their ladders and planks for their part in this attack. In their book *Deeds of Valor*, W. F. Beyer and O. F. Keydel described the assigment of these brave soldiers:

"The advance party was to carry . . . logs, two men to each log, make a dash for the enemy's entrenchments and throw the logs across the ditch to form the ground work of a bridge."[1] *(See map on page 172.)*

At 10 a.m., the "Forlorn Hope" raced out from behind their entrenchments where they were almost immediately shrouded in enemy smoke and rifle fire. Logs, ladders, and planks dropped by the wayside as men were killed and wounded. Somehow, Pvt. Howell G. Trogden, carrying a guiding flag of the storming party, planted it on Stockade Redan's parapet, marking the location for the assault.

One member of the "Forlorn Hope," Pvt. William Archinal, carried a log with another Federal soldier, and when his comrade was killed, the log dropped, throwing Archinal to the ground and knocking him senseless. When awoken, he was brought into the Rebel lines where he was questioned by an officer. The astonished officer asked, "Didn't you know it was certain death" to attack the works, to which Archinal replied, "Well, I don't know, I am still living." The Rebel officer responded boldly, "Yes, you are living, but I can assure you that very few of your comrades are!"[2]

Tragically, the supporting Union regiments did not receive the orders to follow and, subsequently, the eventual assaults were unsuccessful in storming the works. Sherman was furious. Grant's second assault on the entrenchments surrounding Vicksburg failed, and he settled into besieging the city, which ultimately capitulated on July 4, 1863.

Examples of selfless acts like those of the "Forlorn Hope" are why we observe the sacrifices of our American soldiers on Memorial Day. These volunteers who gave "the last full measure of devotion" in charging against Stockade Redan on that sweltering May 22, with ladders in hand, home on their minds, and family in their hearts, moved up the appropriately named Graveyard Road and into the annals of military history. To their memory, we stand in solemn appreciation, never forgetting their valiant deeds.

---

1 W.F Beyer, "The 'Forlorn Hope' at Vicksburg," in *Deeds of Valor: How America's heroes won the Medal of Honor. A history of our country's recent wars in personal reminiscences and records of officers and enlisted men who were rewarded by Congress for most conspicuous acts of bravery on the battle-field, on the high seas and in arctic explorations.* Vol. I, (Detroit, MI: The Perrien-Keydel, 1905), 191.

2 Ibid, 194.

The Forlorn Hope at Vicksburg

by Chris Mackowski

Originally published as a blog post at Emerging Civil War
on December 18, 2020

Google "Forlorn Hope" + "Civil War," and several desperate actions show up. "A forlorn hope," says the Wikipedia entry, which appears first, "is a band of soldiers or other combatants chosen to take the vanguard in a military operation, such as a suicidal assault through the kill zone of a defended position, where the risk of casualties is high." A military dictionary of the day defined a forlorn hope as "Officers and soldiers who generally volunteer for enterprises of great danger, such as leading the attack when storming a fortress."[1]

Additional search results that follow the Wikipedia definition provide several examples that any Civil War buff would find chilling.

Maine Public media features a 26-minute documentary about the charge of the 1st Maine Heavy Artillery at Petersburg on June 18, 1864. The Library of Congress offers an image of the 7th Michigan and 19th Massachusetts

1   See also Henry Lee Scott, *Military Dictionary: Comprising Technical Definitions; Information on Raising and Keeping Troops; Actual Service, Including Makeshift and Improvised Matériel; and Law, Government, Regulations, and Administration Relating to Land Forces* (New York, D. Van Nostrand, 1861), 310.

storming up the bank of the Confederate side of the Rappahannock at Fredericksburg on December 11, 1862.[2]

But the one that seems to have the most notorious claim to the capital letters—"The Forlorn Hope," as in "The Peach Orchard" or The Cornfield"— occurred at Vicksburg on May 22, 1863.

Grant's initial attempt to take Vicksburg on May 19 ended in a series of bloody repulses. He knew he could settle into a siege and starve the Confederates into submission, but he also faced a possible threat in his rear from Gen. Joseph E. Johnston. Johnston could potentially pin Grant's army against the exterior of the Vicksburg defenses, where they would be subject to fire from John Pemberton's forces in the beleaguered city even as Johnston assaulted the Federals from behind.

As it happened, the threat from Johnston never materialized, but Grant had no way of knowing that at the time. Instead, he chose to take one more swing at Vicksburg in the hope of smashing through, thus eliminating the anvil for Johnston's looming hammer.

Grant planned attacks by all three of his corps commanders, John McClernand, James McPherson, and William Sherman. Sherman felt particularly battered after the May 19 assaults. His men had advanced across more than 150 yards of open ground, navigating a troublesome abatis-filled ravine and dealing with several fences—all while heading straight at a massive redan that protected one of the main roads into the city.

Stockade Redan, as it was called, had a seventeen-foot-tall exterior wall fronted by a six-foot-deep ditch. The crest of the wall was sixteen feet wide, and behind it, on firing platforms, stood Mississippi and Missouri troops from Brig. Gen. Louis Hébert's and Brig. Gen. Francis Cockrell's brigades. The 36th Mississippi manned the wall while elements of the 1st and 5th Missouri stood inside the redan as reinforcements and to protect its flanks. Graveyard Road, one of the main avenues in Vicksburg, ran along the ditch on the redan's front face. The redan had been built specifically to protect the road.[3]

For the May 22 attack, Sherman changed his route of approach. Rather

---

2 *Forlorn Hope* documentary on Maine Public: https://www.mainepublic.org/post/forlorn-hope

3 Terrence J. Winschel, *Triumph & Defeat: The Vicksburg Campaign* (Mason City, IA: Savas, 1999), 121.

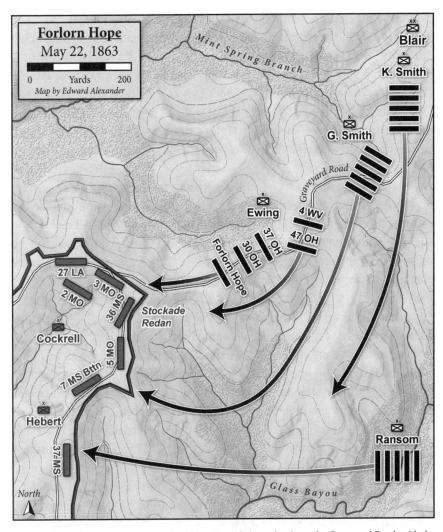

FORLORN HOPE—The volunteers of the "Forlorn Hope" led a sprint down the Graveyard Road, with the 30th and 37th Ohio close behind. The Ohioans caved under intense fire, though, blocking the road and forcing subsequent reinforcements to move farther and farther around the left; days earlier, assaulting Federals had tried assaulting from the right, through ravines created by tributaries of Mint Spring Branch, leading them to grief.

than cross the open ground, he would advance down the Graveyard Road itself—a route that would take him not at the wide open front of the redan but toward a sharp angle in its construction. The redan was shaped like a wide "V," and Graveyard Road ran straight at the exterior tip of the "V" before veering toward the right and running parallel to the redan's formidable exterior wall. Because Confederates occupied the interior of this "V," they would not be able to bring as much firepower to bear on any force advancing directly down the road.

Sherman chose Maj. Gen. Frank Blair's division to spearhead his assault. He stacked Blair's brigades three deep: Brig. Gen. Hugh Ewing first, then Cols. Giles A. Smith and Thomas Kilby Smith. They would be followed by the brigades of Brig. Gen. James Tuttle's division stacked similarly. With Graveyard Road as their axis of advance, the massive column would charge the Confederate defenses.

In the vanguard, Blair assembled a squad of 150 volunteers "consisting of 2 officers and 50 men from each brigade of the division" under the command of Capt. John H. Groce and Lt. George O'Neal.[4] They would advance not with rifles but with lumber. The first fifty would carry heavy timbers to be placed across the ditch, while the second fifty would carry planking to lay across the timbers. Thus, instant bridges would be made. The third fifty would carry ladders so invaders could more easily scale the redan's exterior wall. None of the volunteers carried rifles. The squad consisted only of single men because all expected a high casualty rate.

Preparations went smoothly. "All our field batteries were put in position, and were covered by good epaulements; the troops were brought forward, in easy support, concealed by the shape of the ground," Sherman wrote.[5] He opened the morning with a bombardment to soften the Confederate line. It was "a most furious fire . . . of shell, grape, and canister," wrote Cockrell, commanding the defenders. "The air was literally burdened with hissing missiles of death."[6]

Blair massed his division to the left of the Graveyard road. At 10:00, he started his infantry forward. Sherman, watching from 200 yards away, noted the group of grim volunteers in the lead. "A small party, that might be called a forlorn hope, provided with plank to cross the ditch, advanced at a run, up to the very ditch," he wrote; "the lines of infantry sprang from cover, and advanced rapidly in line of battle."

---

4   This and all Blair quotes come from Francis Blair, O.R., XXIV, Pt. 2, 254.

5   William T. Sherman, *Personal Memoirs of Gen. W. T. Sherman* (New York: Charles L. Webster & Co., 1890), 354.

6   This and all Cockrell quotes come from Francis Cockrell, O.R. XXIV, Pt. 2, 414.

The volunteers initially benefited from the cover of the terrain, but at last Graveyard Road rose from a swale, cut through a low ridge, and arrowed across 150 yards of open ground directly at the "V" of the redan. The road—"a narrow, deep-cut road," as Ewing described it—offered protection as the men double-timed through the ridge.[7] Beyond, they spilled out into the open and began a mad sprint forward with their bridging materials.

At first, "The rebel line, concealed by the parapet, showed no sign of unusual activity," Sherman recounted, "but as our troops came in fair view, the enemy rose behind their parapet and poured a furious fire upon our lines."[8] Cockrell called it "a most desperate and protracted effort to carry our lines by assault," which his men met "with defiant shouts and a deliberately aimed fire."

Many of the volunteers fell. Others dropped their loads and fled. Some made it all the way to the ditch, where they hunkered against the embankment in an effort to stay beneath the depressed barrels of the Confederate muskets.

Meanwhile, the lead regiment of Blair's lead brigade, the 30th Ohio, rushed forward on the heels of the storming party. They advanced, said Blair, "with equal impetuosity and gallantry," but then trouble began. Casualties from the storming party littered the road and, as casualties from the 30th Ohio fell alongside them, the road became littered with obstacles. The 30th Ohio "moved close upon the storming party," Ewing said, "until their progress was arrested by a front and double flank fire, and the dead and wounded which blocked the defile."

As a result of the litter of dead and wounded, the next regiment, the 37th Ohio, lost all momentum as soon as it reached the open ground. The column "faltered and gave way under fire of the enemy," dispersing and going to ground. "After the check, a few passed on, but were mostly shot," Ewing said.

In his report, Blair could hardly contain his frustration. "The men lay down in the road and behind every inequality of ground which afforded them shelter, and every effort . . . to rally them and urge them forward proved of no avail . . ." he wrote. "They refused to move, and remained in the road, blocking the way."

---

7 This and all Ewing quotes come from Hugh Ewing, O.R. XXIV, Pt. 2, 282.

8 Sherman, *Memoirs*, 354.

The Forlorn Hope charged along the Graveyard Road straight at Stockade Redan. Imagine being shot at the entire time you ran across this exposed ground. *Kris White*

The 47th Ohio and 4th West Virginia, finding their advance blocked by the Buckeyes, left the road and ascended a small rise, advancing with what Blair described as "commendable spirit and alacrity." From their new position, they laid down covering fire so the men trapped in the road could withdraw.

The volunteers from the Forlorn Hope found themselves trapped in the worst position of all, pinned between the redan and the fire coming from Ewing's brigade. Some Confederates even lobbed make-shift hand grenades over the works, throwing them into the ditch.

In the midst of the melee, the storming party's color-bearer, Private Howell G. Trogden of the 8th Missouri, managed to climb to the top of the redan and plant his flag, which the Confederates tried, unsuccessfully, to capture several times. "He carried his regiment's flag and tried to borrow a gun to defend it," a later Medal of Honor citation would laud. Groce, too, made it as far as the parapet, but he, like O'Neal, fell wounded.

While the storming party writhed on the face of the redan, Blair looked for ways to come to their relief and continue the assault. With the road heavily bottlenecked, he tried improvising by going around, but the new approach proved just as problematic. "[T]his route, while it was better covered from the fire of the enemy, led through ravines made almost

Monuments on the face of Stockade Redan mark the points of farthest advance by the storming party. *Kris White*

impassable with abatis of fallen timber, and did not admit of anything like a charge," Blair conceded.

Sherman, too, later conceded the futility of the operation. "[F]or about two hours, we had a severe and bloody battle, but at every point we were repulsed," he wrote. According to historians Leonard Fullenkamp, Stephen Bowman, and Jay Luvaas, "Less than 1,000 of Sherman's 15,000 men had been committed to the attack, since there was no good avenue to push the remainder into the battle."[9]

Sherman's men did take part in another attack late in the day, meant as a diversion while McClernand tried to exploit a supposed opportunity. Even with a brigade of reinforcements from McPherson's corps to add extra weight, Sherman's men made minimal gains. "[I]ts failure only served to prove that it is impossible to carry this position by storm," Blair said. Survivors had to wait until nightfall before they could withdraw to safety.

Sherman's account gave the action its name, "a forlorn hope," although he did not use capital letters in describing it. Those would come later as the

---

9 Leonard Fullenkamp, Stephen Bowman, and Jay Luvaas, editors, *Guide to the Vicksburg Campaign* (Lawrence, KS: University of Kansas Press, 1998), 430.

bravery of the men became enshrined in Vicksburg's larger story over time. Of the 150 men who rushed forward as the Forlorn Hope, 19 were killed and 34 were wounded.

In his after-action report, Blair recommended "that the medal of honor voted by Congress be presented . . . to all the noncommissioned officers and privates composing the storming party on the 22d." Sherman agreed, and then some: "[T]he storming party that volunteered to scale the works, and did do so, and remain on the exterior slope amid that fierce conflict, merit not only the medal of honor, but more substantial reward."[10] Of the survivors, 78 later received the Medal Honor for their heroism, cited specifically for "Gallantry in the charge of the 'volunteer storming party.'"[11]

The men of the storming party certainly had an inkling of what they were getting themselves into. "[I]t was a solemn thing and almost sure death," said one soldier. But, as another stoically observed, "Somebody had to go, I thought, so I volunteered."[12]

Somebody had to go . . . .

I think of that in the context of the other "forlorn hopes" brought up by my Google search, inspired by a recent trip to Petersburg and further informed by the recent anniversary of the battle of Fredericksburg.

At Fredericksburg, on December 11, 1862, Maj. Gen. Ambrose Burnside looked for volunteers to clear Confederates from the far bank of the Rappahannock so Federal engineers could complete their pontoon bridges in safety. "[T]he effort meant death to most of those who should undertake the voyage," he proclaimed. Colonel Norman Hall of the 7th Michigan nonetheless responded with vigor. "My soldiers are ready to cross the river and drive out the Confederates," he said, and his men responded with three cheers.[13]

---

10 Sherman endorsement of Blair's report, *O.R.* XXIV, pt. 2, 261.

11 For a list of the 120 Medal of Honor recipients from the action at Vicksburg: https://www.nps.gov/vick/learn/historyculture/vicksburg-medal-of-honor-recipients.htm

12 Quotes come from Andrew McCormack of Illinois and John O'Dea of Missouri, quoted by Tim Smith in *The Union Assaults at Vicksburg: Grant Attacks Pemberton, May 17-22, 1863* (Lawrence, KS: University of Kansas Press, 2020), 158.

13 H. H. Ring, "Under Heavy Fire: Crossing the Rappahannock with the 7th Mich.," *National Tribune*, 29 April 1897, 3.

The crossing party, which numbered between 60 and 70 men, lost one man killed and several wounded, including their lieutenant colonel, Henry Baxter, on their way across the river.[14] Artist Henri Lovie's sketch captures the survivors scrambling out of their boats and up the embankment, "each man to make the best fight he could," as one Michigander said.[15]

At Petersburg, the 1st Maine Heavy Artillery was ordered forward as part of an assault on June 18, 1864, against fortified Confederate works. The Mainers were relatively new to the army, having just arrived a month earlier. They charged forward, as ordered, with enthusiasm, but the veteran units around them understood how formidable the works looked and refused to go, leaving the Mainers to make their headlong rush alone. The 900-man regiment, with all Confederate rifles turned on them and only them, sustained 67 percent casualties in 10 minutes: 115 men killed, 489 wounded, and 28 missing.[16] No other army unit sustained a higher casualty rate during the war.[17] A Park Service wayside at the location of the assault describes it as "a forlorn hope."

I've even heard the argument that "forlorn hope" is applicable only to the Confederate defenders at Vicksburg, not to the Federal attackers. Pemberton's forces held out against Grant's siege in the hope that relief would come—in the end, a forlorn hope, indeed.

It would be a grim contest for us to try and weigh these competing claims against one another to determine who has earned the title by being assigned to the most forlorn, the most hopeless mission. We have a comfortable perch from which to make such assessments. But in the midst of battle, in the crucible of the moment, facing "almost sure death," someone had to go. Against all hope, consider how many went.

---

14   Norman Hall, O.R., XXI, 282.

15   Ring, "Under Heavy Fire," 3; "The Forlorn Hope" sketch by Henri Lovie in *Frank Leslie's Illustrated Weekly,* from the Library of Congress collection: https://www.loc.gov/resource/cph.3c19620/

16   http://www.maine.gov/sos/arc/archives/military/civilwar/1meha.htm

17   For more on the 1st Maine Heavies, see Chris Mackowski, "The 1st Maine Heavy Artillery at the Battle of Harris Farm: The Hometown Press Reports Their Baptism of Fire," *Blue & Gray*, issue 6, 2011.

Reconstructed earthworks at Vicksburg National Military Park offer a small glimpse of what Confederate defenses looked like in 1863. Earthen mounds fortified wooden walls made of planks or logs. Firing ports provided openings for artillery. *Cheval de frise*—logs with protruding spikes—served as obstructions against infantry charges. Woven baskets filled with dirt, then tipped over, could serve as barricades; they could also be placed at the head of a trench and rolled forward as shovelers extended the trench. *Chris Mackowski*

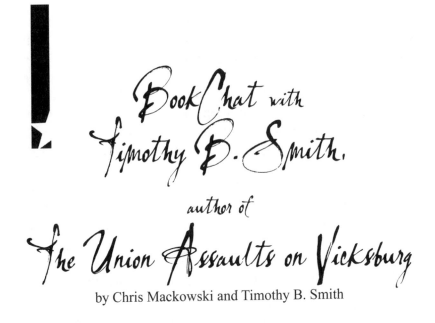

Book Chat with Timothy B. Smith,

author of

The Union Assaults on Vicksburg

by Chris Mackowski and Timothy B. Smith

Originally published as a blog post at Emerging Civil War on January 5, 2021

Timothy B. Smith is the author of *The Union Assaults on Vicksburg: Grant Attacks Pemberton, May 17-22, 1863*, published by the University Press of Kansas. The author of numerous books on the Civil War, Smith teaches history at the University of Tennessee at Martin. In 2017, his book *Grant Invades Tennessee: The 1862 Battles for Forts Henry and Donelson* won the inaugural ECW Book Award.

Chris Mackowski: You've been slowly working your way through the Vicksburg Campaign in your work. Was there anything in particular you were looking forward to when you started working on this volume?

Timothy B. Smith: Yes, exploring the assaults in more detail. In fact, that's the goal in more than just this volume. That might sound odd considering there is already a massive three volume set on Vicksburg by Ed Bearss and other large one volume studies, but the Union effort to capture Vicksburg lasted more than thirteen months and the campaign proper more than eight months, so there is a lot of material to cover. Some aspects of the campaign have been barely treated, in particular the May assaults. The siege is also sometimes short shafted, as has been the fall/winter 1862 Mississippi Central/Chickasaw Bayou efforts. This will likely turn into a large five-volume series before it's done, with volumes also dedicated particularly to the siege and those 1862 efforts.

CM: The assaults on Vicksburg tend to get forgotten about in the popular imagination; people mostly think of "the siege" of Vicksburg. Why do you think that is?

TS: It is odd. Obviously, the siege lasted a lot longer than the assaults. But both the assaults and siege "battlefields," if you will, are contained in the Vicksburg National Military Park. But most people tend to gloss over the assaults phase and focus in on the weeks and weeks of siege. Likewise, before that came the monumental land campaign wherein Grant defeated the enemy five times in seventeen days. The assaults get kind of sandwiched in between these two "major" efforts, but it was the largest battle of the campaign in terms of numbers engaged.

CM: You're well-steeped in the history of this battle. Was there something new that you learned or that surprised you as you worked on this book?

TS: Certainly, mainly again in the detail. Exactly how defensible Vicksburg truly was both by nature and human engineering was surprising, as was the sheer courage of the Union troops to attack across that terrain. Perhaps most of all was just how difficult the terrain was. You get some sense of it riding around or even walking or jogging the tour route, but to really understand it you have to get out into the woods and ravines themselves.

CM: What differentiated the assaults of the 19th from the assaults of the 22nd?

TS: Scope, size, and preparation. Blair's attempt on May 19 was hurried and limited, Grant hoping to score a quick victory against a reeling opponent.

Given all Grant knew at the time, it made sense. The May 22 assault was much better planned and equipped, but likewise failed due largely to the terrain and the stout Confederate defense.

CM: Is there a particular assault or a particular front you found especially interesting?

TS: I've always liked the Stockade Redan action, because it had major efforts both days and was until the last decade or so the only real place at the park you could get a sense of what it might have looked like, many of the trees being cleared there. Fortunately now, much more of the ground cover has been removed and you can see the terrain in other places as well. Mostly, though, it comes from the fact that I had two direct great-great-grandfathers (their children married each other long after the war) in the same company of the 36th Mississippi defending the redan during both days of the assaults. I had two other direct great-great-great grandfathers inside Vicksburg as well (and another marched away with Loring at Champion Hill), but neither were in the thick of the fighting like these two.

CM: How do you think Grant's relationship with McClernand affected the operations on the 19th and 22nd?

TS: I'm not sure the previous relationship affected it much in terms of where or when to assault. All three corps were supposed to move forward on both days. As it turned out, only one division did on May 19 but all attacked on May 22. McClernand in fact gave it the best effort of all three corps commanders on May 22. The previous relationship of mistrust Grant had for McClernand if anything almost stopped the renewed assaults later that afternoon when McClernand called for help. Grant did not believe McClernand's dispatches but Sherman talked him into trying again. Obviously, the problems emanating from the May 22 assaults had a much larger impact on the Grant/McClernand relationship than going into them.

CM: While the book's title touts a focus on the *Union* assaults, the Confederate defense played a role in events. What do you think they did well during the battles? Did that help or hurt them in the long term?

TS: They just had to hold their defenses and shoot down the enemy, so there was not a lot of decision making or tactical movements on the Confederates' part. In fact, that was a problem I ran into, desiring to give both sides equal coverage. There are only so many ways you can say the Confederates held their earthworks and shot at the enemy columns. It gets repetitious after a while.

On the other hand, there was a lot of decision making and tactical movements and maneuver on the Union side to cover. If the book is tilted a little toward Union coverage, it was certainly not intended but more the result of who was doing more moving during the time. Plus, there are fewer comparative sources for the Confederate side whether its reports or letters or diaries. But that is something every historian of the war faces. But back to the question, the Confederates did well amid tough circumstances as well, although better off than the Federals. It definitely helped their continued defense in shoring up morale for the siege.

CM: You open the book by raising the tantalizing possibility of reinforcements from Lee's Army of Northern Virginia coming to Mississippi. Of course, Confederate officials decided on an invasion of the north instead. Simply for the sake of fun, let's consider the "What If" question you raise: what if Confederate forces from the east shifted to the west to relieve pressure on Vicksburg? Would it have made any difference?

TS: It's hard to say what would have occurred on anything, but I'm not sure it would have made much difference. One, the distance involved was much farther than what Longstreet even did at Chickamauga. And getting equipment and wagons and horses and all to Mississippi would have been a mammoth undertaking. Then, these troops would not have gone directly into Vicksburg but would have been out under Joseph E. Johnston's command in an effort to relieve the city. I'm not sure Johnston would have done anything even if he had huge numbers.

CM: Why is that?

TS: While not necessarily dealing with the assaults book, in writing the siege volume [his current project], I have become convinced that Johnston had made up his mind Vicksburg was doomed, probably because Pemberton had not taken his advice in getting out of the trap. He had a very timid outlook the whole time, never taking control of the situation but quickly starting to lay the groundwork for blame for the surrender on Pemberton, Davis, the trans-Mississippi Confederates, and anyone else he could think of. And he did only enough to make it look like he was trying, but my guess is he never intended to do anything to save Vicksburg.

It is interesting that when Pemberton twice gave Johnston the max time he could hold out, which turned out to be very accurate–within a day or two of the real surrender date–Johnston only started to move just a few days prior to that, stopped the advance to reconnoiter for two full days, and then set his timetable of attack on July 7, which was after both days Pemberton had said he could only hold out to. I think this was a crisis that deserved a long-shot gamble, and I compare it to Albert Sidney Johnston at Shiloh, who took the gamble. Joe Johnston never did. I've never been a Joe Johnston fan, and researching his activity in the Vicksburg "Army of Relief" had lowered my estimation of him considerably.

CM: I love the converse idea you also pose, by the way: If Grant took Vicksburg, would Davis have allowed Lee's campaign northward?

TS: Yeah, it's a little-used reverse thought, I guess, but it does show the strategic importance even of the isolated assaults themselves. Their effect went far beyond Mississippi.

CM: What was your favorite source you worked with while writing the book?

TS: I love them all, including the often-maligned, boring *Official Record* reports. The letters and diaries are also fascinating, for their material but also I guess in the connection of how they are found and used. Most of the time it involves travel which I enjoy, and it's almost like a treasure hunt. If I had to pick just one, though, it would be a memoir of a member of the aforementioned 36th Mississippi. It gives a good idea of what my folks would have seen.

CM: Who, among the book's cast of characters, did you come to appreciate better?

TS: Probably above all the common soldier on both sides. There were no real eye-popping tactical movements or flank marches or anything like that, just common soldiers slugging it out on perhaps some of the worst terrain imaginable. The terrain at Vicksburg makes Gettysburg look like a pancake.

CM: What modern location do you like to visit that is associated with events in the book?

TS: The entire battlefield as contained in the national park, but again I always make a point to go by the Stockade Redan anytime I'm there.

The terrain in front of Stockade Redan proved as difficult to assault across on May 19 as the redan itself was to assault against. The view into this ravine was taken from Graveyard Road—the road the Forlorn Hope charged down on May 22 as it charged the redan. The redan is behind the camera. *Kris White*

The Falling Out Between McClernand and Grant

by Sean Michael Chick

Originally published as a blog post at Emerging Civil War on March 31, 2016

Butler, Banks, Sigel, McClernand. These are often thought of as the most infamous "political generals" of the American Civil War. The four named here are usually considered military incompetents, their victories considered aberrations in an otherwise consistent record of failure. To be fair, some of these men fit the mold well, in particular Maj. Gen. Nathaniel Banks, but with Maj. Gen. John McClernand, the story is much more complicated.

McClernand was among the most powerful Democrats of his era and nearly became Speaker of the House of Representatives. His support for the Union war effort was considered crucial, particularly since southern Illinois—McClernand's home region—had some sympathy with the Confederacy. Although not friends with President Abraham Lincoln, the two had mutual respect for each other, even if they were from opposite political parties. They had even worked together on a court case.[1]

McClernand's fate would end up being tied to Maj. Gen. Ulysses S.

---

1 Richard L. Kiper, *Major General John Alexander McClernand: Politician in Uniform* (Kent: Kent State University Press, 1999).

Grant, a fellow Democrat. Grant voted for Stephen Douglas in 1860, but was otherwise not very active in politics. In 1861, Grant was lucky insofar as he had West Point training, a good record in the Mexican-American War, and the patronage of Congressman Elihu B. Washburne and Gov. Richard Yates, powerful Republicans with Lincoln's ear. At the same time, Grant cultivated a friendship with Illinois Democrats such as McClernand and John A. Logan. Grant allowed both to address Illinois state troops who were considering not enlisting in the national army. At Cairo, Illinois, McClernand was Grant's chief subordinate. It is possible that Grant favored McClernand because of his political connections. Such a man could take Grant far.[2]

At first all was well. McClernand took his job seriously. He trained his men well and was personally brave. The friendship seemed to be cemented at the battle of Belmont on November 7, 1861. McClernand was at the front, directing troops under fire and leading the retreat. After the battle concluded, Grant praised McClernand and treated him as his right-hand man. However, Lincoln congratulated McClernand and not Grant, which likely planted the seeds of the feud.[3]

Whatever his personal morals, Grant was susceptible to cronyism. As examples, at Cairo Grant allowed an acquaintance, George Graham of Galena, Illinois, to manage water transport for the growing army. Graham was shamelessly corrupt. Making matters worse was quartermaster Reuben Hatch, whose brother was Lincoln's secretary. Hatch was not only corrupt, but also lazy and duplicitous. Grant used his influence to shield Hatch and enlisted the aid of Washburne and Yates. Hatch managed to stay in Federal service throughout the war.[4]

In contrast to his support for Graham and Hatch, Grant disliked Capt. William Kountz, who oversaw river transportation once Graham proved inadequate. Kountz reported first to McClernand and not Grant, which drew Grant's ire. McClernand liked Kountz, though, and supported his reforms

---

2   Ulysses S. Grant, *Personal Memoirs of U. S. Grant*, Vol. 1, (New York: The De Vinne Press, 1885), 196-197.

3   Nathaniel Cheairs Hughes Jr., *The Battle of Belmont* (Chapel Hill: University of North Carolina Press, 1991), 195-196.

4   Joseph A. Rose, *Grant Under Fire* (New York: Alderhanna Publishing, 2015), 58-66.

and attempts to weed out corruption. Kountz appears to have been given to vindictiveness; the boatmen did not like him and soon newspapers were printing negative stories. In January 1862, Grant had Kountz arrested, but pressed no charges, preferring to merely transfer him. This was likely because Kountz had a powerful ally in Maj. Gen. George McClellan, the general in chief of the Union Army. At any rate, Kountz ended up accusing Grant of drunkenness.[5]

McClernand still supported Kountz, so Grant personally explained to him the reasons for the arrest. At this point, the relationship began to strain. Regardless, Grant still relied on McClernand in his drive to capture Fort Henry and Fort Donelson. McClernand's division led the way.[6]

Fort Donelson ruined what might have been a fruitful partnership. A morning attack battered McClernand's division. Grant, who was conferring with the Navy, returned to the field and met McClernand and Lewis "Lew" Wallace. In one account, McClernand grumbled, "This army wants a head." Grant replied, "It seems so. Gentlemen, the position on the right must be retaken." The attacks were made and the battle was won, but for the Grant–McClernand partnership the damage was done.[7]

After the battle, McClernand bragged about his role personally to Lincoln. Grant had no idea what McClernand might be writing to the president and, given the way the Fort Donelson fighting had played out, Grant's fears were reasonable. McClernand was ambitious, at times prickly, and had shown an independent streak in backing Kountz. Grant, for his part, offered only scant praise of McClernand after the battle.[8]

McClernand would try again to gain Grant's trust. After Fort Donelson, Grant was censured by his superior, Maj. Gen. Henry Halleck, in a fabricated controversy that temporarily kept Grant from leading an expedition up the Tennessee River. McClernand wrote Grant a letter of tribute and publicly supported him. Whether this was a genuine attempt at friendship is unknown.

5 Ibid.

6 Ibid., 65-74.

7 Timothy B. Smith, *Grant Invades Tennessee* (Lawrence: University Press of Kansas, 2016), 328-330.

8 Ibid., 390, 402.

It might have been a political calculation, as Grant was the hero of the hour. McClernand might have also surmised that in the feud between Halleck and Grant, the latter was preferable all around. Halleck, after all, despised most political generals that lacked West Point credentials and thought giving them major commands was the equivalent of murder.[9] In any case, whether from McClernand's influence or not, Lincoln intervened in the controversy, and Halleck backed down. McClernand had backed a winner.

Sadly, McClernand's attempt at a renewed friendship failed. Grant ignored McClernand at Shiloh, treating Brig. Gen. William Tecumseh Sherman, whom McClernand out-ranked, as the de facto camp commander and dismissing McClernand's warnings of a possible Rebel attack. Although McClernand was conspicuous in his bravery during the battle, Grant called his report "faulty."[10]

With Halleck and Grant as enemies, McClernand went to Lincoln with a plan to strike at Vicksburg. While Lincoln did not remove Grant after Shiloh, he did consider it several times, and decided to give McClernand command of the Army of the Mississippi. Halleck and Grant succeeded, though, in delaying McClernand and sending Sherman ahead to strike at Vicksburg. The result was the defeat at Chickasaw Bayou. When McClernand did come south, he led an expedition against Arkansas Post. He took the strongpoint and thousands of prisoners. McClernand exclaimed at his victory "Glorious! Glorious! My star is ever in the ascendant. Now, on to Little Rock." Grant's position never looked more fragile, and he uncharitably disparaged McClernand's victory. His former friend was considered a rival for command and would need to be dealt with.[11]

McClernand, now commanding the army's XIII Corps, favored landing troops below Vicksburg and marching on the city. After several failed expeditions in the swamps north of Vicksburg, and a canal scheme, Grant assented, and on April 30, 1863, gave McClernand the honor of crossing first.

9   Larry J. Daniel, *Shiloh: The Battle that Changed the Civil War* (New York: Simon & Schuster, 1997), 32-33.

10   United States War Department, *The War of the Rebellion: A Compilation of the Official Records of the Union and Confederate Armies,* 70 vols. in 128 parts (Washington D.C.: Government Printing Office, 1880-1901), Series I, volume 10, part 1, p. 114 (hereafter cited as *O.R.,* I, 10, pt. 1, 114); Daniel, *Shiloh*, 139.

11   Robert S. Huffstot, "The Battle of Arkansas Post," (National Park Service, 1969). Rose, *Grant Under Fire*, 196-200.

Unfortunately, McClernand turned in an uneven record. He did not do well at Port Gibson, and at Champion Hill he did not press the Rebel right flank. Although he was not ordered to be aggressive, he did not take the initiative.[12]

The last straw for Grant with McClernand came at the gates of Vicksburg. On May 22, Grant launched a grand offensive in order to storm the defenses. McClernand's men did better than most, achieving a small breakthrough at the 2nd Texas Lunette. McClernand requested reinforcements. Grant at first refused until McClernand told him he had captured part of two forts and "The Stars and Stripes are flying over them." After some consternation, Grant ordered another round of attacks. When these failed, Grant lashed out at McClernand, even though Sherman and Maj. Gen. James McPherson had also failed to coordinate their forces. But Sherman and McPherson were friends with Grant and favorites of Halleck, who had long before replaced McClellan as general-in-chief of the army. McClernand, a Democrat despised by Halleck and considered a rival for command, made an easy target.[13] "General McClernand's dispatches misled me as to the real state of facts, and caused much of this loss," Grant wrote to Halleck on May 24. "He is entirely unfit for the position of corps commander, both on the march and on the battle-field. Looking after his corps gives me more labor and infinitely more uneasiness than all the remainder of my department."[14]

On May 30, General McClernand wrote a self-adulatory note to his troops. "As your commander, I am proud to congratulate you upon your constancy, valor, and successes," he began. "History affords no more brilliant example of soldierly qualities." In the recap of the campaign that followed, McClernand implied his men failed in their May 22 assaults because of the shortcomings of others. "The Thirteenth Army Corps, acknowledging the good intentions of all, would scorn indulgence in weak regrets and idle incriminations," he said.[15]

McClernand's report made its way into a Memphis newspaper and

---

12 Rose, *Grant Under Fire*, 233. For a more positive take on McClernand at Champion Hill see Timothy B. Smith's work.

13 Michael B. Ballard, *Vicksburg* (Chapel Hill: University of North Carolina Press, 2004) 340–344.

14 *O.R.*, I, 14, pt. 1, 37.

15 *O.R.*, I, 14, pt. 1, 159-161.

stirred up trouble among the army's other corps commanders. Sherman, in particular, complained bitterly. Secretary of War Edwin Stanton had given Grant permission to remove McClernand as early as January 1863, but he did not move then. The reasons are hard to guess, but it is possible Grant still felt some affection for him; Grant, while not free with praise for McClernand in his memoirs, was kinder than he was to other rivals. McClernand was also then riding high from Arkansas Post, and he was Grant's most experienced corps commander. Removing a popular commander—one who had Lincoln's support—presented a risky proposition. However, with Vicksburg's fate sealed, there was no need to humor McClernand any longer.[16] Grant had in his pocket fresh assurance from Stanton, who had written on May 5 "General Grant has full and absolute authority to . . . remove any person who, by ignorance, inaction, or any cause, interferes with or delays his operation," Stanton affirmed.[17] It is difficult to believe Stanton would have granted such broad discretion without Lincoln's knowledge.

After some debate about the order published in the newspaper, Grant relieved McClernand on June 18 and turned the XIII Corps over to Edward Ord, a Halleck favorite. McClernand remained in the Union army, leading troops in Texas and in the disastrous Red River campaign before leaving in 1864. A loyal Democrat to the end, he campaigned against Lincoln's reelection, but also against the peace faction in his party. When Lincoln was buried, McClernand was present for his old friendly rival. After 1865, he remained active in politics, but was never again a giant of the party.[18]

There is a sadness to the feud between McClernand and Grant. Both men were courageous, devoted, and capable commanders. McClernand showed no great tactical gifts but he was brave, a hard marcher, and good at administration and discipline. After Belmont, Grant and McClernand were compatriots. They had fought their first battle together and came out of it alive. Yet, as Grant was writing his memoirs at death's door, he never even mentioned McClernand's role at Belmont.[19]

---

16 Rose, *Grant Under Fire*, 232-35.

17 *O.R.,* I, 14, pt. 1, 84.

18 Ballard, *Vicksburg*, 358–59; Ibid.

19 Grant, *Personal Memoirs*, 218-229.

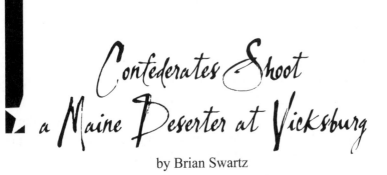

Confederates Shoot a Maine Deserter at Vicksburg

by Brian Swartz

Originally published as a blog post at Maine at War, *an ECW partner, on May 8, 2019, and highlighted on Emerging Civil War on June 6, 2019*

Not every Maine boy donning a Civil War uniform wore Union blue.

More than a few wore Confederate gray or butternut, and the Johnny Rebs shot a particular Maine lad after he bolted for Union lines somewhere in the Mississippi River Valley in early summer 1863.

The story came north with Reverend W. C. Van Meter, who had opened the Home for Little Wanderers and the Howard Mission in May 1861 in New York City. Accompanied by an A. M. Shipman (also "A.H. Shipman") who was eight months a Confederate prisoner at Vicksburg, Van Meter reached Springfield, Illinois, soon after Ulysses S. Grant captured Vicksburg in early July 1863.

With Shipman came a letter written by John B. Marsh, late of the Southern army and of life altogether. Van Meter and Shipman shared the letter with the *Springfield Journal*, which ran Marsh's tale under the subheading "A Boy True to the Last."

Many Union papers then picked up the article; the *Daily Whig & Courier* in Bangor, Maine ran it under the subhead, "A Maine Boy True to the Last."

"Living in the South," Marsh "was conscripted and forced into the rebel army," the *Journal* reported. "Being a Union man, he deserted at the first opportunity, but was caught by the rebels and was shot at Vicksburg a few days ago."

The exact date was not cited, but a bit of digging indicates that Marsh died no later than June 22, 1863.

While in prison, young Marsh slipped a letter to Shipman, whose identity underwent no additional clarification in the *Journal*. Only through Van Meter and the *Official Records* do we learn more about him.

"On my way back home from Vicksburg . . . I met Mr. A.M. Shipman, an Ohio volunteer who was imprisoned for eight months as a hostage in the Vicksburg jail. He was released after the Confederates surrendered on July 4, 1863," Van Meter recalled.

In his letter, young Marsh wrote, "Kind Friend—If you ever reach our happy lines, please have this put in the northern papers that my father, Rev. Leonard Marsh, who lives in Maine, may know what has become of me, and what I was shot for. It was for defending my noble country. I love her and am willing to die for her. Tell my parents I am also happy in the Lord. My future is bright. I hope to see you as I pass out to die."

Marsh signed his name to the letter.

We can only wonder what Shipman thought when guards took Marsh away to die. The guards later returned to the prison, and one soldier told Shipman, "When young Marsh was placed by his coffin, he could speak if he desired it."

Removing his hat, Marsh shouted, "Three cheers for the Old Flag and the Union!"

According to the guard (and the *Journal*), Marsh "then swung his hat and shouted at the top of his voice, 'Hurrah, hurrah, hurrah!'"

There came a rat-a-tat-tat, and that was that for young Marsh, who pitched backwards onto his coffin.

Van Meter later wrote that Marsh, his hands bound behind his back, stepped onto his coffin when permitted to speak. "He cried out, '*Three cheers for the Old Flag and the Union*' (italicized in the original)."

"Of course the patriotic sentiment met no response from that audience," Van Meter commented.

"Then . . . with his eyes lifted as if the flag were in view, he [Marsh] shouted forth his own three cheers, '*Hurrah! hurrah! Hurrah!*' (italicized in the original).

"His clear, ringing voice had scarcely died away when the sharp crack of the musketry added another name to the long roll of martyrs for the dear 'Old Flag,'" Van Meter wrote.

After Marsh's tale ran in certain Maine newspapers, his father hopefully learned about his son's death. We can also assume that someone delivered the boy's letter to his dad.

Van Meter was incorrect regarding one point about Shipman, a member of Co. D, 43rd Ohio Infantry Regiment. He and three other Union soldiers (Bernard Collins, James E. Gaddy, and Nicholas Hoit) had "been held as hostages since December, 1862, for the acts of some of your soldiers in Panola County, Miss.," Confederate Maj. Nathan G. Watts wrote "Maj. Gen. U.S, Grant" from Vicksburg on June 23, 1863.

What exactly happened in Panola County was not spelled out. However, Grant had recently ordered "four Confederate prisoners . . . [held] as hostages for the four Federal prisoners," Watts noted. Since Grant's army besieged Vicksburg, why let eight soldiers remain as hostages? Would Grant transfer the four Southerners to Memphis if Shipman and his comrades were released?

"I this day send across the [Mississippi] River to you four men," specifically the four hostages, Watts told Grant.

Since Shipman was released on June 23, John Marsh was shot sometime before that date. How Van Meter met Shipman is not known, but the two men probably took the same steamboat north.

Sources

"A Maine Boy True to the Last." *Daily Whig & Courier*. Friday, July 10, 1863.

"Facing Execution with Faithfulness, Triumph Amidst Bloodshed: Civil War Soldiers' Spiritual Victories." ed. Craig L. Claybrook and John W. Reed (Primedia eLaunch Publishing: 2012). Chapter IV.

United States War Department, *The War of the Rebellion: A Compilation of the Official Records of the Union and Confederate Armies*, 70 vols. in 128 parts (Washington D.C.: Government Printing Office, 1880-1901), Series 2, volume 6, part 1, p. 37.

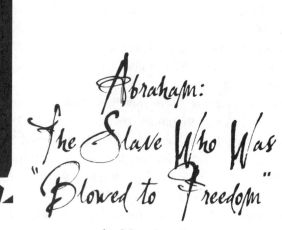

Abraham: The Slave Who Was "Blowed to Freedom"

by Meg Groeling

*Originally appeared on the Emerging Civil War blog
on February 6, 2019, and October 28-31, 2019*

This isn't looking good, said Maj. Samuel Lockett, chief engineer of the Confederate Army of Vicksburg, as he assessed the geological mess at the Third Louisiana Redan. Union Capt. Andrew Hickenlooper's attempt to dislodge the area had made the rocks and soil hold together in a solid mass. *I'd use that 500-pound, black powder thunder keg. It'll loosen that soil until it's like sand*, Lockett said.[1]

The day before, June 25, Hickenlooper's engineers had exploded a massive mine under the redan, creating a crater into which Federal troops had stormed. Hand-to-hand fighting ensued, but the breach of the Rebel line was not permanent. All that remained was a rock-hard field that had been the bottom of the crater.[2]

1   Terry Winschel, "The Engineers at Vicksburg, Part 24: Blasted to Freedom," US Army Corps of Engineers: Engineer Research and Development Center Website, last modified June 22, 2017, https://www.erdc.usace.army.mil/Media/News-Stories/Article/1225290/the-engineers-at-Vicksburg-part-24-blasted-to-freedom/.

2   "The Long, Gruesome Fight to Capture Vicksburg," accessed January 7, 2021, https://www.battlefields.org/learn/articles/long-gruesome-fight-capture-vicksburg.

When Hickenlooper's explosion went off, there was a tremendously loud "bang," but little real damage was done.[3] Not that the Confederate sharpshooters were not doing their jobs; the Union men facing the fort made a game out of placing a kepi on the tip of a ramrod and raising it tentatively above the trenches. Bets were made on the number of times the cap would be hit within a given time.[4]

Now that the Confederates felt they knew the Union plan—to dig beneath the fort and blow up the southern works—Lockett decided to sink a countermine in an attempt to thwart that effort. Rather than risk the lives of white southerners, eight black slaves who accompanied the southern forces were pressed

Andrew Hickenlooper would serve with distinction and go on to a postwar career as a civil engineer. His grandson, John, would go on to a career as a brewer, governor of Colorado, and U.S. Senator. LOC

into service to place the mine. They were under the command of a white corporal, and one of those slaves was known as "Abraham." The slaves, including Abraham, dutifully entered the Confederate tunnels, becoming the unwitting victims of the second Vicksburg Mine.

Or so the tale is told. . . .

*   *   *

In February 2019, as part of Emerging Civil War's commemoration of

3   Andrew Hickenlooper, "The Vicksburg Mine," in *Battles and Leaders of the Civil War*, vol. 3 (New York: The Century Company, 1888), 339-342.

4   Ibid.

Black History Month, I wrote a blog post about Abraham, a formerly enslaved person who was "blowed to freedom" at Vicksburg. This story is verified in several places. It is about a slave who was forced by the Confederate army holding Vicksburg to work underground digging a mine emplacement.

There is, for me, something very compelling about Abraham at that moment. He was young, seemed to be relatively healthy, and had a look on his face—in his *carte de visite*—that is simple and direct. His story struck me as unusual, and it stayed with me for months after I initially read it. I am not sure if anyone knows why someone or something appeals to a person. It seems random to me, but I am no psychologist. Abraham and I just hit it off.

I had many questions concerning Abraham. To whom did he belong initially? Was he really inside the mine? What happened to him immediately after the explosion? What happened later? I wanted to know more. I looked forward

Abraham became a minor celebrity for his "first manned combat flight." *ECW*

to telling as much of Abraham's story as possible. After all this time, he deserves a little justice.

It is difficult to track down information when one is dealing with enslaved people. The destruction of massive amounts of Confederate war records alone is problematic, but slave records are hard to come by, in general, as well. I found some incredible primary source information, including a letter from P. T. Barnum to Union Gen. John Logan. I learned a lot about how slaves were hired by the Confederacy to do jobs that white soldiers did not care to do—like digging a mine. I answered some of my questions, but not all of them. And, of course, I ran into many dead ends.

Before the war, there was an enslaved man called Abraham. His last name is unknown. Here is what is known: The black man known as Abraham was between 18-25 years old at the time of the siege of Vicksburg. He was approximately 5' 6" tall.[5] From all accounts, including Abraham's own, he worked within Confederate-occupied Vicksburg. The Confederate Army often leased groups of slaves from local landowners to do the hard labor of war. Slaves dug ditches, entrenchments, latrines, graves, and apparently mines. It takes strength to do this, but not necessarily a particular skill, so these groups of enslaved men were considered simple laborers.

A look around the Vicksburg area narrowed down the landowners. A check of property lists resulted in no slaves simply named "Abraham" or "Abraham [Landowner's Name]." No Abraham Young, Abraham Harris, or Abraham Marshall. There were few enslaved men with the name of Abraham, which was surprising—unless they changed their names due to Lincoln's election.

Now it was time to look at the land itself. I thought I'd begin my research at the site of the explosion, the Third Louisiana Redan. I looked at maps of the siege area at Vicksburg. I found the site of the redan and quickly saw why the idea of counter-mining the area to create a crater might have seemed like a good idea to the Confederates. So, the mine was dug, the timer set, the explosion occurred and—literally out of nowhere—"Enslaved Abraham" became "Free Abraham" in a matter of seconds. His body arched over the line from the Confederate Third Louisiana Redan to the Union 81st Illinois Volunteer Infantry. As the men in blue helped Abraham to his feet, it began to dawn on the now-former slave that his life would be different than it had been—as Abraham put it, after he had been "blowed to freedom."

Abraham had the pure luck to have landed in the camp of Maj. Gen. John A. "Black Jack" Logan. Although Logan had no military background, was an Illinois Democrat, and was anti-abolition, he was very much against secession. Logan had volunteered with the 2nd Michigan and fought at First Bull Run. He transferred out west where he was severely wounded at Fort Donelson but returned after Shiloh as a brigadier general in command of a division in the XVII Corps of the Army of the Tennessee. John Logan led

5 Annie Wittenmeyer, *Under the Guns: A Woman's Reminiscences of the Civil War* (Boston: E.B. Stillings, 1895), 102-105.

with distinction during the opening phases of the Vicksburg campaign, for which he would gain promotion to major general.

At some point before early 1863, Logan's personal politics underwent a sea change. He saw real slavery for the first time and was deeply affected by it. Just as many Yankees had imagined slavery only in abstract terms, it became real for them as the Northern armies marched further south. These experiences, along with his political support of President Lincoln, changed Logan's mind entirely about the South's "peculiar institution."

When Abraham came down, he was restrained by the soldiers of the 81st Illinois until General Logan could be informed of the situation. Luckily, Logan's headquarters tent was only steps away. The *Chicago Daily Tribune*, published on July 14, 1863, carried the interview.[6] Logan questioned the terrorized Abraham:

> "Why were you fighting us, the friends of the Black man?"
> "I warn't, Massa, swear to Jesus."
> "Where is your gun?"
> "Doan' hab no rifle. . . . I was jus' totin' grub to da men."[7]

This particular response not only satisfied General Logan and the *Tribune*, but it offered another clue as to what Abraham might have been doing for the Confederate army. Abraham was not a laborer—he worked with food in some capacity. On the day of the explosion, he was taking food to a team of men working below ground. These men were laboring inside the seriously damaged Third Louisiana Redan, known as Fort Hill to Federal forces.

The redan had been partially collapsed by the explosion of a mine on June 25, and Confederate leaders, aware of another effort underway to undermine the bastion, had set this party of men to work digging a "countermine." Their goal was to intercept the Federals by running a shaft just above their operation. This would destroy the mine by collapsing the shaft.[8] The number

---

6 *Chicago Daily Tribune*, July 14, 1863, 2. The dialect quoted here and subsequently, which modern ears may find offensive, is that used in the original article.

7 Ibid.

8 Ibid.

Once an ardent anti-abolitionist, John Logan had a powerful conversion after seeing "the peculiar institution" up-close early in the war. His statue in Vicksburg stands near the monument for his home state of Illinois. *Chris Mackowski*

of men involved in the Rebel effort is usually reported as "six or seven negroes, and a white overseer named Private Owen, with all of this group killed"—actually, all killed except Abraham.[9] If all the men inside the mine were killed, and if Abraham was bringing food to the worksite, he might not have been in the mine at all.

Looking at a variety of timelines, this is what probably happened: It was about 1:30 p.m., and Abraham had just arrived at the entrance to the countermine with his delivery when an unearthly "Boom" was followed by a sensation of weightlessness . . . and then, falling . . . rapidly falling. Abraham focused his eyes: the Rebel troops, the Federal troops, the city of Vicksburg were all crystal clear—and a long way down.

The flying man did not know if swinging his arms and kicking his legs

9   Ibid.

A park wayside features a 3-D model of a mine ("Thayer's Approach"). *Chris Mackowski*

caused him to tumble or if that rotation happened of its own accord. But the next thing he knew, his falling ended abruptly. And when he regained his senses, Abraham found himself on his back in a mound of dirt. There were men in blue running towards him, and they all seemed to be shouting.

Apparently, Abraham was interviewed, or at least quoted, after his experience. Perhaps a look at what are claimed to be his own words might shed some light on his origins. One quote is from *Experience in the War of the Great Rebellion*, "By a Soldier of the Eighty-First Regiment Illinois Volunteer Infantry (Edmund Newsome)." On page 71, Abraham is quoted, "I think I went up 'bout tree miles, sah, an' as I was a comin' down I met massa a gwine up."

From another source:

"A DARKEY IN THE AIR"

Abraham, a full-blooded negro, and the only person who escaped with his life at the time the mine under Fort Hill at Vicksburg exploded, was at work with a number of the rebel soldiery "sinking a shaft" for the purpose of discovering any gallery that might have been "run by our miners" beneath their works.

The negro was blown a distance of nearly three hundred yards, and was, when picked up, in a most disturbed state of mind.

"De Lord, massa,"--quoth he—"tink neber should light—yah, yah! Went up 'bout free mile. Ax a white man when I start whar were going, and de next I know'd he was just nowhere but all over."[10]

Silas Trowbridge, Chief Surgeon for the Third Division, was called over to examine the stunned aeronaut. As Abraham sat up, lay down, and rolled over, Surgeon Trowbridge ran his hands along the man's arms and legs, expressing surprise to find nothing broken. However, when Abraham's

10 Lt. Col. Charles S. Greene, *Thrilling Stories of the Great Rebellion* (1864), 286. This book was first published in 1864, then updated to include "Details of the Assassination of President Lincoln," and the "Capture of President Jefferson Davis." "The Story of Abraham" was included, based heavily on *Harper's Weekly* article (August 8, 1863) by Theodore R. Davis. As with the quotes from the *Chicago Daily Tribune* article, the dialect used here is contained in the original book and article. The author and the publisher recognize that many usages considered acceptable in the mid-nineteenth century are no longer such and expressly do not endorse them.

shirt was unbuttoned, his back and either side of his neck were found to be discolored and swollen. Abraham winced when his shoulders were touched. The back of Abraham's head was also found to be badly bruised and swollen. With little knowledge of concussion at the time, all that Trowbridge prescribed was bed rest, sparing quantities of food and water, and time.[11]

Abraham was likely moved to the division hospital, but his dual status as both black and a civilian would have earned him his own tent. It has not been explicitly

Men from Logan's division charge into the crater created by the explosion of the mine (and Eastern Theater fans thought Petersburg's mine/crater were the first . . .). The Volunteer Soldier of America *by John A. Logan*

confirmed, but this is probably where the more enterprising Yankees set up their concession and charged money to other soldiers just to hear Abraham, the "Flying Black Man," tell his story. There are many, many corroborating versions of the quotes above that appear in letters and memoirs.

One thing a political general can do is manipulate the media, and the Abraham incident was no exception. Within a month, Abraham's story had made its way to every major paper (and quite a few minor ones). Written up and illustrated for *Harper's Weekly* by renowned artist Theodore R. Davis, Abraham's story spread nationwide. Versions were also printed in the *Chicago Daily Tribune*, beginning July 14, 1863. From these sources, stories were distributed all over the northern and western United States. The press made Abraham and his aeronautical exploits a thing, and they did not let it go until the turn of the year.

The problem with this type of publicity is that there is often difficulty

---

11   Silas Thompson Trowbridge, M. D., *Autobiography of Silas Thompson Trowbridge* (Carbondale: Southern Illinois University Press, 2004), 145-147.

verifying everything that can be found. According to two Chicago papers, Logan had more interaction with Abraham on July 4, 1863. When the victorious Union army marched into Vicksburg—Maj. Gen. U. S. Grant and his staff officers at the head, followed by Logan—Abraham marched in with Logan's division, right alongside the general and next to the 45th Illinois. It is possible that, while in Vicksburg, Generals Grant, McPherson, and Logan had their carte de visite ("CdV") images taken at the Photographic Studio of Barr and Young. Abraham, likely in company with Logan or lower-level officers, also had his image struck here as well. At least two CdV's of Abraham were made, with lots of copies of those images produced and likely made available as souvenirs for purchase. At least one image exists with "Ole Abe" written across the bottom.

After Vicksburg, Logan departed on leave for a speaking tour mid-July through August. Logan wanted to keep Abraham with the unit, and Abraham reportedly had recovered sufficiently for Surgeon Trowbridge to attempt to make use of him as a "general hand" in the division hospital. After about three weeks, Abraham was relieved of his duties. Personal letters tell researchers that Dr. Trowbridge expressed great dissatisfaction with Abraham's performance. What is not known is how much of this "lack of satisfactory performance" was due to possible brain injury of Abraham, or how much may have been due to Dr. Trowbridge's ideas concerning Abraham's race. Nevertheless, Abraham was an uneducated man being requested to perform unfamiliar hospital duties. As a lifelong slave, Abraham had been taught *not* to anticipate orders but, instead, to wait for those orders and then carry them out promptly. Independent thinking such as might be necessary for a medical setting would have been difficult.[12]

One more mention of Abraham occurs in *Under the Guns: A Woman's Reminiscences of the Civil War*, published in 1895 by Annie Wittenmeyer:

> a slave boy, about 18 years old, was blown into Union lines as a result of the Fort Hill mine explosion. He was often seen by me at General Logan's headquarters . . . and after the war, he went to Washington with them, I think, and remained some years.[13]

---

12 Ibid.

13 Wittenmeyer, *Under the Gun*, 102-105.

From August 1863 until June 1864 there is no military record of Abraham, except the claim in *Vicksburg and the War* that "Abraham last appears in the records at Atlanta on the staff of Major General McPherson, as a cook. After McPherson died on July 22, 1864, Abraham vanished from recorded history."[14]

The remainder of the story is yet to be uncovered. Some letter or diary entry may make mention of Abraham's next assignment. Too many soldiers and officers knew about the "Vicksburg incident," and Abraham would have still possessed minor celebrity status. Abraham might have found another U.S. Army assignment as a cook or joined the "camp followers" that attempted to tag along as Sherman marched through Georgia. My guess is that he stayed with the Logans. Mrs. Logan was in camp with her husband during most of the war and writes in her biography, *Reminiscences of a Soldier's Wife: An Autobiography*, that several former slaves travelled with them back and forth to their home in Illinois.[15]

A particularly exciting discovery—for so many reasons—was finding a letter in the Library of Congress. The General John A. Logan Museum, in Murphysboro, Illinois, notified me that there was a letter to General Logan, dated December 31, 1863, from none other than the Great Showman himself, P. T. Barnum. The museum explained that the letter requests "something... regarding the 'former slave Abraham, blown to Freedom.'"[16]

Barnum's American Museum
New York, Dec. 31, 1863

My dear Genl Logan

I claim to be a great "blower", but you took the wind out of me when you blew up Abraham. I have felt inclined to reach under

---

14 Gordon A. Cotton and Jeff T. Giambrone, *Vicksburg and the War* (LA: Pelican Publishing, 2004), 76-77; Miriam Szubin, "Behind the Scenes of 'Bound for Freedom's Light'," National Portrait Gallery, accessed January 7, 2021, https://npg.si.edu/blog/behind-scenes-"bound-freedom's-light".

15 Mrs. John A. Logan, *Reminiscences Of A Soldier's Wife: An Autobiography* (New York: Charles Scribner's Sons, 1913), 122-168.

16 Meg Groeling, email message to Mike Maxwell, December 2020.

(out?) to you, for that "blow" shriveled the biggest hurricane down to the mildest zephyr. Still a sort of feeling of jealousy prompts me to the desire to have a puff at colored Abraham. When you think you can share your Abraham (and I hope it will seem consistent to you to let him off, long before you are called to the ORIGIN? Of his name for he is considerably higher up than the big wind. I should feel flattered to get the latter "culture" from you for a while with such a letter of notification & identification as you would permit me to publish. I hear from one mutual friend T H Davis Esq. that Abraham can tell his story and do a thing or two, and if you should feel like it ship him along by Express <u>C. O. D.</u> I will be most happy to take charge of him & use him well & make him satisfied. I shall also be most happy to reciprocate your kind help if ever opportunity offers—if not I'll do it for some other clever fellow.

I have a niche in the Museum for Jeff Davis if you will only catch him. For <u>that</u> attraction I will pay high—in fact if I could exhibit Jeff in the Museum six months, I would give more than this whole Confederacy will be worth until he leaves it.

Wishing you a happy New Year & health & happiness as well as a glorious success in <u>squelching</u> this worse than damnable rebellion. I am with sentiments of the highest regard

Very Truly Yours, P. T. Barnum[17]

A close reading of this discovery uncovers jokes, puns, and smart, delightful wordplay. Barnum continued to entertain even in his letter, written on New Year's Eve. Like most successful entrepreneurs, he saw Abraham as a viable business asset and promised General Logan that "colored Abraham" would be well taken care of. The real surprise comes in the middle paragraph. Barnum went into Republican politics the last third of his life, and these comments on Jefferson Davis are priceless.

---

17   P.T. Barnum to General John Logan, December 31, 1863, Letter, Library of Congress.

The other obvious topic is: what happened to Abraham? So far, there is concrete evidence concerning the formerly enslaved man known as Abraham up to the fall of 1863. It is at that point that information begins to conflict or does not exist at all. There is official information about army cooks and undercooks. The 45th Illinois Volunteer Infantry was the first regiment to make use of black men to do the cooking, doing so after the siege of Vicksburg. The 45th Illinois used the services of seven or eight men. These men were assigned to Companies A, G and K. Two men were recorded as having been promoted from Undercook to Cook. None of them are Abraham.

Did Vicksburg Abraham transfer to one of the Mississippi U.S.C.T. regiments? A check of the roster of the 66th Regiment U. S. C. T. finds five men with the first name of Abraham and last names of Handman (or Hendman), Jacob, Nelson, Wilson, and Vaughn (or Voghn or Vohn.) There is no record

Any story where P. T. Barnum shows up, even in a cameo, becomes five times more colorful. *LOC*

of the 1st, 2nd, 3rd, 4th, 5th, or 6th Regiments of Mississippi Infantry, which were organized at Vicksburg in December 1863. However, upon investigation, the 6th Mississippi Infantry (African Descent) was renamed 58th Regiment U.S.C.T., and the other units were renamed, as well. After exhaustive searching to little avail, I currently think Abraham probably stayed with his newly found Union friends.

Oddly enough—because it is usually Confederate records that are incomplete—the staff members, officers, and enlisted—including black cooks and undercooks—of Confederate generals are recorded at the National Park Service's Soldiers and Sailors Database. A search for similar lists for Union Generals Logan, McPherson, and Grant turned up nothing.

In June 1864, mention is made in *Vicksburg and the War,* as well as a Smithsonian Institution blog supporting the National Portrait Gallery exhibition "Bound for Freedom's Light," that Abraham joined the Union war effort.[18] "Abraham last appears in the records at Atlanta on the staff of Major General McPherson, as a cook," it says. "After McPherson died (July 22, 1864) Abraham vanished from recorded history. . . ."[19]

This next theory is a little different. Perhaps, after General McPherson died, Abraham went "home" to General Logan. The Logans were the first married couple Abraham met after the mine explosion, and Mary Logan, who spent much of the war with her husband in camp and on campaign, was well known for hiring newly freed men to work on their farm in Cairo, Illinois. Her biography speaks of this often.[20] General Logan succeeded Sherman in command of the XV Corps, then temporarily took over the Army of the Tennessee after McPherson was killed during the battle of Atlanta. Logan returned to the XV Corps when O. O. Howard was given permanent command of the army. This puts Logan and Abraham in very close proximity. After the Carolinas campaign and a brief, abortive foray to assist George Thomas, Logan accompanied Sherman to Washington where he led the Grand Review's second day in May 1865. And I like to think Abraham marched with him.

I have continued to research Abraham's story and have not been able to find out any more than what I have indicated above. I wish I could have written that Union soldiers were sensitive caregivers to this formerly enslaved person, but they were not. I hope that, after his time as a cook for McPherson, he went further North and found a better life for himself than what he had in Vicksburg, but I have no indication at all of his future. My only reason for the inclusion of this story is that the war was made up of a great many stories, and whenever possible we should not forget them. When I first read about Abraham, I found him memorable. I share this with our readers in hopes that they will do so as well.

---

18   Cotton, *Vicksburg and the War,* 76-77. Szubin, "Behind the Scenes of 'Bound for Freedom's Light.'"

19   Ibid.

20   Logan, *Reminiscences,* 122-168.

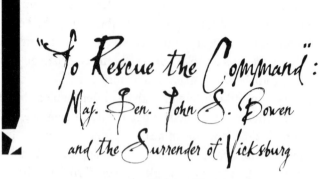

"To Rescue the Command: Maj. Gen. John S. Bowen and the Surrender of Vicksburg

by Kristen Trout

Originally published as a blog post at Emerging Civil War on July 9, 2018

On July 3, 1863, after a dangerous crossing through no-man's land, Maj. Gen. John S. Bowen and Lt. Col. Louis Montgomery entered the Union siege lines surrounding Vicksburg to deliver a message from the Army of Vicksburg's commander, Lt. Gen. John Pemberton, inviting a discussion on surrender. Stricken with dysentery himself, Bowen commanded a division of Missourians and Arkansans who were slowly dying of starvation and disease within the blockaded river city. Bowen hoped that through his personal connections with Army of the Tennessee commander Maj. Gen. Ulysses Grant (Grant "knew him well and favorably before the war"), he could somehow negotiate reasonable terms of surrender to save the army—and his own men.[1]

Though Grant initially refused to meet with his former St. Louis, Missouri, neighbor and friend, Bowen at least loosened the tension between the two warring armies positioned in and around the "Gibraltar of the

---

1 Ulysses Grant, *Personal Memoirs of U.S. Grant,* vol. 1 (New York: The Century Company, 1895), 466.

Confederacy." A veteran of the Camp Jackson affair, Shiloh, Iuka, Corinth, Champion Hill, and the entirety of the campaign to defend Vicksburg, Bowen was considered one of the best division commanders in the Confederacy. His reputation and performance on the battlefield were commended by many of his fellow officers, including Gen. P. G. T. Beauregard, who called him a "meritorious officer."[2] Additionally, Bowen cared deeply for his men, aiming to save lives and prevent further bloodshed. In a letter to Pemberton the day before, he revealed his desire "to rescue the command by making terms with the enemy. . . . If accepted, we get everything we have any right to hope for."[3]

After returning to the Confederate lines, Bowen delivered Grant's message to Pemberton. "The useless effusion of blood you propose stopping by this course can be ended at any time you may choose," Grant wrote, "by an unconditional surrender of the city and garrison."[4] Though disappointed with Grant's stubborn insistence on an unconditional surrender, Bowen told Pemberton that Grant would be willing to meet the defeated Southern general to discuss the terms of surrender later that afternoon.[5] The ball was once again in the Rebels' court to end the bloodshed.

Around 3:00 p.m. along the Confederate defense works, flags of truce rose and the firing was silenced. Pemberton, Bowen, and Montgomery rode out on horseback toward a swale along the Jackson Road between the siege lines, where Grant, James McPherson, A. J. Smith, John Logan, Edward Ord, and other Union officers were waiting. After dismounting, the enemies shook hands before discussing the heavy matter at hand. A mediator and natural diplomat, Bowen served largely as a voice of reason for Pemberton.

---

2 Report of P.G.T. Beauregard, April 11, 1862, in *War of the Rebellion: The Official Records of the Union and Confederate Armies*, ser. 1, vol. 10, pt. 1, (Washington, DC: Government Printing Office, 1880), 390.

3 Reply from John S. Bowen to John C. Pemberton, July 2, 1863, in *War of the Rebellion: The Official Records of the Union and Confederate Armies*, ser. 1, vol. 24, pt. 1 (Washington, DC: Government Printing Officer, 1880), 282-283.

4 Letter from Ulysses Grant to John Pemberton, July 3, 1863, in *Personal Memoirs of U.S. Grant*, vol. 1 (New York: The Century Company, 1895), 466.

5 Michael Ballard, *Vicksburg: The Campaign That Opened the Mississippi* (Chapel Hill: The University of North Carolina Press, 2010), 397.

Recalling what Bowen told him, Pemberton said to Grant that it was his understanding that the Federal commander wished to meet with him regarding Vicksburg's surrender. Grant, with a puzzled expression, denied that he ever said that to Bowen and had no intention of further negotiations. Slightly embarrassed, Bowen admitted to making it up in hopes of initiating negotiations and settling the surrender. Just as before, Grant refused anything but unconditional surrender. Pemberton thought it was hopeless. "I can assure you, you will bury more of your men before you enter Vicksburg," he threatened.[6]

Confident but casual, John Bowen would find himself on July 3, 1863, caught between a rock and a hard head. *LOC*

To prevent further destruction and death between the two armies, Bowen suggested that Grant and Pemberton leave their four subordinates to negotiate the terms of surrender. As Grant and Pemberton withdrew, falling into reminisces and fond memories of their Mexican War days, Bowen, Montgomery, McPherson, and Ord were left to determine the fate of the Confederate garrison at Vicksburg. Their meeting resulted in a cease-fire and further negotiations of the details of surrender. With the meeting late in the day, the formal surrender itself had to occur the following day. Terms were finalized through an exchange of notes that culminated at dawn on July 4—Independence Day.

At 10:00 a.m., Grant's victorious troops marched into Vicksburg. All of Pemberton's Confederate troops were to be paroled and to march east to locations designated for exchange. Just under 30,000 Rebel troops surrendered The siege of Vicksburg was finally over.

---

6 John C. Pemberton, "The Terms of Surrender," in *Battles and Leaders of the Civil War,* vol. 3 (New York: The Century Company, 1887), 545.

Though many Confederate soldiers were exchanged and able to continue their fight in the war, Bowen's service was about to come to an end, just like the thousands of his fellow Rebels who perished at the hands of disease during the Vicksburg Campaign. The day of the surrender, Bowen's health took a dark turn. He was cared for in Vicksburg until he could recover. On July 11, 1863, his physician and chaplain decided that he needed better medical care in Raymond and departed that day by ambulance. Bowen's wife, Mary, and newborn baby spent the siege in nearby Edwards, Mississippi, and they joined the entourage there.

Just six miles outside of Raymond, on July 12, the caravan was forced to stop at the small wooden home of John Walton. The heat and humidity took a tremendous toll on Bowen, and he could not survive the rest of the journey to Raymond. In the morning of July 13, Bowen passed away. Using a coffin built by a local carpenter, the fallen Rebel general was buried in the backyard of the Walton home. Later, Bowen's body was re-interred with a military headstone at Cedar Hill Cemetery in Vicksburg, where many of his men are buried today.

Though hardly known beyond historians and students of the campaign, Bowen's role at Vicksburg and in its surrender to the Federals was tragic, but quite important. Through his negotiations with the Union high command, he sought peace to end the bloodshed and inglorious deaths suffered on both sides. Bowen's legacy can be seen at Vicksburg National Military Park, where a bust of him stands today. In his book, *Vicksburg: A Guided Tour Through History,* historian Mike Sigalas wrote that Bowen "saved the surrender negotiations between Grant and Pemberton."[7] Bowen biographer Phillip Thomas Tucker considered him "the forgotten Stonewall of the West," noting the commander's tragic early demise and his remarkable ability as a leader of men.[8] He is undoubtedly one of the most understudied Confederate generals, yet had major roles in many of the Western Theater's most important battles and campaigns, from Shiloh to Vicksburg.

---

7   Mike Sigalas, *Vicksburg: A Guided Tour* (Guilford, CT: GPP Travel, 2010), 14.

8   Phillip Thomas Tucker, *The Forgotten "Stonewall of the West": Major General John Stevens Bowen* (Macon, GA: Mercer University Press, 1997).

"Independence Forever!"

by Chris Mackowski

*Originally published as a blog post at Emerging Civil War
on July 4, 2019, with additions adapted from a blog post,
"The Secession of Mississippi," published on January 9, 2021*

To commemorate 1826's July Fourth celebrations in Quincy, Massachusetts—which marked the 50th anniversary of the Declaration of Independence—the organizing committee approached the town's elder statesman, John Adams, to furnish a few "appropriate comments." Adams, the single most important voice of the independence movement in the Second Continental Congress, was by that time one of only three surviving signers of the Declaration (another being the document's primary author, Thomas Jefferson, nominated for the job by Adams).

Adams, 90 years old, was nearly blind, nearly deaf, and in feeble condition, but his boisterous spirit remained as vibrant as ever. For his remarks, he said, "I will give you 'Independence forever!'" When asked if he didn't want to elaborate, he replied, "Not a word."[1]

I wonder how many people in Vicksburg, Mississippi, might have recalled Adams's proclamation 37 years later: July 4, 1863.

On that Fourth of July, Ulysses S. Grant's Union forces, led by Gen. John Logan, marched into the beleaguered city along the river after a siege

---

1 This iconic tale is told many places, but for the Pulitzer Prize-winning version, see David McCullough, *John Adams* (New York: Simon & Schuster, 2001), 645.

that had lasted since mid-May. The commander of the city's garrison, Gen. John Pemberton, had acquiesced the day before to a surrender, choosing July 4th because he felt he would get better terms on the patriotic holiday. "I know their peculiar weaknesses and their national vanity," he had told a gathering of his officers called to help him decide the matter; "I know we can get better terms from them on the Fourth of July than on any other day of the year."[2]

Grant, not feeling especially magnanimous on that day, offered terms little better than the "unconditional surrender" that had made him famous at Fort Donelson in the winter of 1862.

And so John Logan, at the head of his division, "with 'stars and stripes,' with streamers from

John Logan rides at the head of the column as Federals enter Vicksburg. "Sleek horses, polished arms, bright plumes—this was the pride and panoply of war," wrote Vicksburg resident Dorra Miller. "Civilization, discipline, and order seemed to enter with the measured tramp of those marching columns." The Volunteer Soldier of America *by John A. Logan*

the fleet, with martial music, with booming cannon, with a huzza," marched into the city, wrote one Wisconsinite, whose "regiment joined its cheer in that grand jubilee which a nation at home celebrated with Te Deums of thanksgiving."

"It was a glorious Fourth of July for us to get Vicks on that great day," wrote Pvt. Charles Beal of the 11th Illinois Infantry. "We marched in town on the Fourth and when we come to the court house we seen the glorious Stars and Strips floating, on the court house and we give it three cheers."[3]

---

2 Grant quotes Pemberton's official report in his memoirs. *Ulysses S. Grant, Grant: Memoirs and Selected Letters*, Mary Drake and William S. McFeely, editors (New York: Library of America, 1990), 380.

3 As quoted in *In Their Letters, In Their Words: Illinois Civil War Soldiers Write Home*, Mark Flotow, editor (Carbondale, IL: Southern Illinois University Press, 2019), 76.

Meanwhile, glum residents, looking on, wept or stood silently by, shell-shocked. "[A]nd the heart turned with throbs of added pity to the worn men in gray, who were being blindly dashed against this embodiment of modern power," added one diarist.[4]

Whether anyone in Vicksburg's populace recounted Adams's words or not, the day's sardonic twist was not lost on them. Their Confederacy had sought independence, yet the surrender of Vicksburg was a crushing blow against that aim. Independence might be forever, but it was not for the Confederacy at all.

Just what did independence mean? For Adams's generation, it meant independence from tyranny from the King of England. For those pushing for Southern independence, it meant independence from what they saw as the tyranny of the central government in Washington.

But, similar to words like "freedom" and "liberty," "inde-

Independence Day, said John Adams, "ought to be solemnized with pomp and parade, with shews, games, sports, guns, bells, bonfires and illuminations from one end of this continent to the other from this time forward forever more." His statue in his home town of Quincy, Massachusetts, stands at street level, inviting visitors to engage with him and his ideas. *Chris Mackowski*

pendence" is a slippery term that means different things to different people. The Founding Fathers discovered this almost as soon as the Articles of Confederation were ratified, and again when they tried to hammer out, and then ratify, the Constitution. Everyone thought they knew what those words meant but, as Adams and Jefferson themselves exemplified, there were very different and often mutually exclusive visions of what those ideas meant.

---

4   Dorra Miller, "A Woman's Diary of the Siege of Vicksburg", The Century, Illustrated Monthly Magazine, (New York: The Century Co, & London: Warne & Co, Vol. XXX, May 1885), accessed December 16, http://www.natchezbelle.org/oldtime/diary.htm.

Even during the Founding, Northerners began to call out Southerners who cried out for liberty yet kept black men and women in bondage. James Madison, after ratification of the Constitution, observed that "It seems now to be pretty well understood that the real difference of interests lies not between the large and small but between the northern and southern states. The institution of slavery and its consequences form the line of discrimination." It took the notorious three-fifths compromise, counting slaves as three-fifths of a person for purposes of representation, and omission of the word "slave" from the Constitution for delegates to reach a final deal.

In the end, it's worth noting, the Founders thought it was more important to bring the new nation together than it was to abolish slavery, which would have sundered the country before the nation ever got off the ground. I wasn't there, so I won't second-guess their decision or pass judgment from my comfortable seat in the present; rather, I recognize that they wrestled with the issue and came to a decision that says something important about their priorities and reasoning.

Adams, not present for the Constitutional Convention, considered slavery "an evil of colossal magnitude."[5] Others, like Jefferson, considered it an unsolvable dilemma. "We have the wolf by the ear, and we can neither hold him, nor safely let him go," he wrote in 1820. "Justice is in one scale, and self-preservation in the other."[6] Jefferson, himself a slave owner and bound to the security it provided his otherwise shaky finances, proved Exhibit A. He felt the question of slavery would fall to a younger, more vigorous generation to solve.

And so issues of race, freedom, liberty, and independence competed for decades, wrapped in increasingly sectional and bitter politics. By 1860, when the South sought its independence by declaring secession, what did these words really mean? States claimed to seek independence from tyranny, but did that speak for—and apply to—all its residents, or really only just for its white citizens?

Mississippi chose to explicitly lay out its argument in a document

---

5   John Adams to William Tudor, Jr., 20 November 1819, *Founders Online,* National Archives, https://founders.archives.gov/documents/Adams/99-02-02-7261.

6 Thomas Jefferson to John Holmes, 22 April 1820, *The Works of Thomas Jefferson, Volume 12,* Paul Leicester Ford, ed. (New York: G.P. Putnam's Sons, 1905), 159.

The Mississippi state house in Jackson as it appeared in a *Scribner*'s sketch in 1874, much as it appeared in 1861; the building is now the Old Capitol Museum, operated by the state Department of Archives and History. *LOC*

with the labyrinthine title "A Declaration of the Immediate Causes which Induce and Justify the Secession of the State of Mississippi from the Federal Union," which the state's Secession Convention issued in conjunction with its January 9, 1861, Ordinance of Secession.[7] "Our position is thoroughly identified with the institution of slavery—the greatest material interest of the world," the document began.

> Its labor supplies the product which constitutes by far the largest and most important portions of commerce of the earth. These products are peculiar to the climate verging on the tropical regions, and by an imperious law of nature, none but the black race can bear exposure to the tropical sun. These products have become necessities of the world, and a blow at slavery is a blow at commerce and civilization. That blow has been long aimed at the institution, and was at the point of reaching its consummation.

7 For the full document, see https://avalon.law.yale.edu/19th_century/csa_missec.asp.

> There was no choice left us but submission to the mandates of
> abolition, or a dissolution of the Union, whose principles had
> been subverted to work out our ruin.

Worried that people would think the conventioneers "overstate[d] the dangers to our institution," they went on to reference "a few facts" in their document. What followed was essentially a bulleted list that outlined the ways the Federal government denied "the right of property in slaves."

"The hostility to this institution commenced before the adoption of the Constitution," the document said. Among the other grievances it outlined, the document said the Federal government "refuses the admission of new slave States into the Union, and seeks to extinguish it by confining it within its present limits, denying the power of expansion."

The delegates felt they had no alternative but to secede. "Utter subjugation awaits us in the Union, if we should consent longer to remain in it," they concluded. "We must either submit to degradation, and to the loss of property worth four billions of money, or we must secede from the Union."

The Mississippi Secession Convention was held in the state capital of Jackson, a town named for former President Andrew Jackson, who once famously declared "Our Union—It Must be Preserved." Jackson's dinner toast served as a salvo against an idea called Nullification, pushed by southern states, that held the individual states could nullify the laws of the Federal government.

Jackson's own vice president, South Carolinian John C. Calhoun, was one of Nullification's chief proponents. His rebuttal to Jackson, while clever, had none of the force of the president's pithy toast: "The Union: next to our Liberty the most dear: may we all remember that it can only be preserved by respecting the rights of the States, and distributing equally the benefit and burden of the Union!"

As a Civil War-era storyteller, Frazer Kirland, would later explain it, "In that toast was presented the issue—liberty *before* Union—supreme State sovereignty—false complaints of inequality of benefits and burdens—*our rights* as we choose to define them, or *disunion*."[8]

And so read the "Declaration of Immediate Causes" drafted in Jackson

---

8 Frazer Kirland, *The Pictorial Book of Anecdotes and Incidents of the War of the Rebellion...* (Hartford, CT: Hartford Publishing Co., 1867), 23-24.

and approved on December 9: "our rights" as Mississippi chose to define them, secured only through "disunion."

The hero of New Orleans might have rolled over in his grave at the outcome of Mississippi's secession vote, but that same vote and its "Declaration of the Immediate Causes" clearly defined the Magnolia State's notions of freedom, liberty, and independence on the eve of civil war.

The war changed much in the two-and-a-half years between the convention in Jackson and the fall of Vicksburg, some forty-five miles to the west. To the city's besieged citizenry and bedraggled Confederate army, with their bellies lean and their rations and pets gone after 47 days of siege, hunger more than politics dominated their thinking. High-minded ideals of independence had shriveled like stomachs into hard, stubborn pride, made all the harder to swallow as Logan's men raised the flag of the United States of America above the courthouse.

Isaac Jackson of the 83rd Ohio Infantry, among those troops occupying the fallen city on July 4, declared it "the most Glorious Fourth I ever spent." Sgt. Charles Wilcox of the 33rd Illinois elaborated: "This day in American history is only second to the one of which today is the 87th anniversary."

In fact, in 1776, John Adams predicted the adoption of the Declaration of Independence would be "celebrated by succeeding generations as the great anniversary festival . . . with pomp and parade, with shows, games, sports, games, bells, bonfires, and illuminations from one end of this continent to the other from this time forward forever more."

But in Vicksburg, Mississippi, the memory of that Independence Day would stay bitter in the mouths of residents. As the story goes, townsfolk refused to celebrate the Fourth of July for another one hundred years, disproving, at least in one locale, Adams's prediction.[9]

I can only wonder what the feisty old Founder would have thought.

---

9   And that's what it is, says historian Terry Winschel—a story.

Atop one of Vicksburg's tallest hills, in one of its most historic buildings, Federals raised the Stars and Stripes over the courthouse when they entered the city. Today, the national flag and the Mississippi state flag fly out front. The building now houses the Old Courthouse Museum, which contains a mind-bogglingly impressive collection of Civil War stuff—mostly (but not all) Confederate memorabilia—well worth a visit. *Chris Mackowski*

The Civilian Experience at Vicksburg: In Their Own Words

by Paige Gibbons Backus

The Siege of Vicksburg was the culminating point of nearly a year's worth of campaigning by the Federal Army to gain complete control over the Mississippi River. Lasting for 47 days, from May 18 to July 4, 1863, the important city of Vicksburg, Mississippi, and its garrison under Lt. Gen. John C. Pemberton were surrounded on land by Maj. Gen. Ulysses S. Grant's army and on water by US Navy gunboats.

Before the city was completely besieged, many civilians, including men, women, children, and the enslaved, tried to escape but were forced to return after encountering Pemberton's troops. As a result, the thousands of civilians left in the city were forced to endure days of terror and uncertainty as they were bombarded. Unable to flee, civilians along with nearly 30,000 Confederate soldiers, faced shortages of food, water, medicine, and comforts. It is hard to fully understand what those people went through during one of the most famous sieges in American history. Fortunately, a large number of participants wrote descriptive accounts of their experiences, either during the siege or shortly after. Below are some of those contemporary experiences from three prominent diarists who survived the siege.

In the days leading up to the siege, as Confederate forces retreated into Vicksburg, many civilians closely followed the events as they unfolded, including Emma Balfour, a diarist who lived next to Pemberton's

This photo of the caves dug into the hillside near the Shirley House has become one of the most iconic images of Vicksburg. Today, traces of only a few of the caves remain around the city, although at the time of the seige, Vicksburg was "so honeycombed with caves that the streets look[ed] like avenues in a cemetery." *LOC*

Headquarters. An observant recorder, Balfour wrote often of what she witnessed in Vicksburg. In one of her earliest entries, written on May 17, 1863, Mrs. Balfour wrote:

> I hope never to witness again such a scene as the return of our routed army! From twelve o'clock until late in the night, the streets and roads were jammed with wagons, cannons, horses, men, mules, stock, sheep—everything you can imagine that appertains to an army being brought hurriedly within the entrenchment. . . .

> What is to become of all the living things in this place when the boats commence shelling, God only knows. Shut up as in a trap, no ingress or egress, are thousands of women and children, who have all fled here for safety. Then all the mules and horses belonging to this department—and all the stock of all kinds for fifteen or twenty miles around! The Dr. [her husband] thinks human life will be endangered by the stampede amongst

these creatures when terror seizes them—for I fear we have not provender to feed them for long.[1]

Emma Balfour was right. Soon the shelling of the city began and finding food and water, as well as safe shelter, became a primary concern for those trapped inside. In order to gain protection from the constant shelling of the city and its surrounding forts, soldiers and refugees who could burrowed themselves into the ground, excavating caves to live in.

One of the most comprehensive accounts of what it was like living in a cave during the siege comes from 26-year-old Mary Webster Loughborough, who had only planned on visiting Vicksburg but got trapped in the city. Loughborourgh wrote of her experiences in *My Cave Life in Vicksburg*. In her "letters of trial and travel" she described not only building the cave, but what it was like to live inside:

> Our policy in building had been to face directly away from the river. All caves were prepared, as near as possible, in this manner. As the fragments of shells continued with the same impetus after the explosion, in but one direction, onward, they were not likely to reach us, fronting in this manner with their course. . . .

Mary Loughborough's *My Cave Life in Vicksburg* goes behind the scenes—and under the hills—of the beseiged town. *LOC*

I went regularly to work, keeping house under ground. Our new habitation was an excavation made in the earth, and branching six feet from the entrance, forming a cave in the shape of a T. In one of the wings, my bed fitted; the other I used as a kind of a dressing room; in this the earth had been cut down a foot or two

---

1 Emma Harrison Balfour, *Mrs. Balfour's Civil War Diary: A Personal Account of the Siege of Vicksburg* (Vicksburg: Third Printing, 2011), 12-13.

below the floor of the main cave; I could stand erect here; and when tired of sitting in other portions of my residence, I bowed myself into it, and stood impassively resting at full height—one of the variations in the still shell expectant life.[2]

However, not everyone was able to get into a cave, and those had to find other shelter. One such person was diarist Dorra Miller:

> June 9th. - The churches are a great resort for those who have no caves. People fancy that are not shelled so much, and they are substantial and the pews good to sleep in. We had to leave this house last night, they were shelling our quarter so heavily. The night before, Martha forsook the cellar for a church. We went to H_'s office, which was comparatively quiet last night. H_ carried the bank box; I the case of matches; Martha the blankets and pillows, keeping an eye on the shells. We slept on piles of old newspapers. In the streets the roar seems so much more confusing, I feel sure I shall run right in the way of a shell. They seem to have five different sounds from the second of throwing them to the hollow echo wandering among the hills, and that sounds the most blood-curdling of all.[3]

No one was safe over the course of the siege. Homes were damaged and, in Mrs. Balfour's words, even if "most people live entirely in [the caves], for there is no safety anywhere else—indeed there is no safety there. Several accidents have occurred. In one cave, nearly a whole family was killed or crippled."[4]

> One afternoon, amid the rush and explosion of the shells, cries and screams arose—the screams of women amid the shrieks of

---

2   Mary Webster Loughborough, *My Cave Life in Vicksburg*, (Vicksburg: Vicksburg and Warren County Historical Society, 1990), 61-62.

3   Dorra Miller, "A Woman's Diary of the Siege of Vicksburg", *The Century, Illustrated Monthly Magazine*, (New York: The Century Co, & London: Warne & Co, Vol. XXX, May 1885), accessed December 16, http://www.natchezbelle.org/oldtime/diary.htm.

4   Balfour, *Civil War Diary*, 29.

Many caves, said one inhabitant, were "altogether quite . . . large and habitable . . . were it not for the dampness and the constant contact with the soft earthy walls." *LOC*

falling shells. The servant boy, George, after starting and coming back once or twice, his timidity overcoming his curiosity, at last gathered courage to go to the ravine near us, from whence the cries proceeded, and found that a negro man had been buried alive within a cave, he being alone at the time. Workmen were instantly set to deliver him if possible; but when found the unfortunate man had evidently been dead some little time. His wife and relations were distressed beyond measure, and filled the air with their cries and groans. . . .[5]

Food was a critical concern for the thousands of civilians within the city while it was besieged. Competing against tens of thousands of soldiers also confined there, food and water quickly became scarce:

Some families had light bread made in large quantities and

---

5 Loughborough, *My Cave Life,* 63.

subsisted on it with milk (provided their cows were not killed from one milking time to another), without any more cooking, until called on to replenish. Those most of us lived on corn bread and bacon, served three times a day, the only luxury of the meal consisting in its warmth, I had some flour, and frequently some hard, tough biscuit made from it, there being no soda or yeast to be procured. At this time, we could, also, procure beef.[6]

Dorra Miller had a similar experience as early as May 28, as recounted in her diary:

I am so tired of corn-bread, which I never liked, which I eat it with tears in my eyes. We are lucky to get a quart of milk daily from a family near who have a cow they hourly expect to be killed. I send five dollars to market each morning, and it buys a small piece of mule-meat. Rice and milk is my main food; I can't eat the mule-meat. We boil the rice and eat it cold with milk for supper. Martha runs the gauntlet to buy the meat and milk once a day in a perfect terror.[7]

These are only a few excerpts from well-known primary accounts describing just several aspects of the civilian experience during the siege of Vicksburg. There are additional reports available that provide a more comprehensive story of the civilian, enslaved, and soldier experience. For many today, this is an incomprehensible situation to be put into and the resilience of these people in the face of seemingly unending danger is amazing to read about.

---

6   Ibid., 60-61.

7   Miller, "A Woman's Diary."

A Sacred Service:
Sister Ignatius Sumner and the Sisters of Mercy during the Vicksburg Campaign, 1862-63

by Andrew Miller

The campaign and siege to capture Vicksburg, Mississippi in 1862-63 has left historians with a wealth of letters and diaries of not only the combatants fighting over the landscape, but also of the civilians who endured the violence. Of the latter, one of the most unique is the "Register of the Events from the Foundation of Convent of the Sisters of Mercy, Vicksburg, Miss.," compiled by Sister Ignatius Sumner.

Born in 1826 in Baltimore, Maryland, Frances S. "Fannie" Sumner grew up in that city, but the Sumner family was originally from Massachusetts. Her father, Henry Sumner, was the youngest brother of the renowned Abolitionist senator Charles Sumner. Henry died early in young Fannie's life and her mother, Frances Steele Sumner, in her grief, searched out relief in the Catholic Church. Fannie would follow her mother's example. While her famous uncle was advocating for the immediate abolition of slavery, Frances S. Sumner was confirmed into her new life with the Sisters of Mercy, choosing the name Mary Ignatius.[1]

---

1   Mary Paulinus *Oakes and Ignatius Sumner, Angels of Mercy: an Eyewitness Account of Civil War and Yellow Fever by a Sister of Mercy: a Primary Source* (Baltimore, MD: Cathedral Foundation Press, 1998); Mary Eulalia Herron, "WORK OF THE SISTERS OF MERCY IN THE UNITED STATES: ARCHDIOCESE OF BALTIMORE 1852 to 1921." Records of the American Catholic Historical Society of Philadelphia 34, no. 1 (1923): 50-78. Accessed January 1, 2021. http://www.jstor.org/stable/44208593; Mary Ignatius Sumner, "Register of the Events from the Foundation of the Convent of the Sisters of Mercy, Vicksburg, Mississippi," Register of the Events from the Foundation of the Convent of the Sisters of Mercy, Vicksburg, Mississippi, (1860).

In October 1859, a request for the Sisters of Mercy to establish themselves in Vicksburg, Mississippi, was approved, and a small group of nuns left Baltimore on October 9 for the hill city. Arriving in Vicksburg, the sisters were both surprised and relieved "that they were coming to some half-Indian place . . . and had been mentally resolving to suffer all the imaginary deprivations patiently."[2] Vicksburg was a city of roughly 5,000 individuals and was anything but the "half-Indian" town of the sisters' imagination.

From its humble, hardscrabble beginnings in 1825, Vicksburg had grown into a cosmopolitan city by 1860. As noted by Christopher Morris in his wonderful work "Becoming Southern: the Evolution of a Way of Life, Warren County and Vicksburg, Mississippi, 1770-1860," "Owning on average fewer slaves, living in a city of several thousand people, making their living off the cotton trade to be sure, but as investors, merchants, and lawyers and not by overseeing its production directly . . . thus, a step removed from the plantation elite, and a step closer to a national elite joined by an expanding urban and economic system, they began to reflect new sensibilities . . . very much in line with elites of New York or London."[3]

This was the Vicksburg in which the Sisters of Mercy set up their convent at the Cobb House on Crawford Street on October 15, 1860. Five days later, the Convent opened its doors and welcomed the first group of students. This happy occasion was marred by the escalating events of a national crisis and civil war that was rapidly approaching. South Carolina seceded in December and Mississippi called a secession convention, ultimately voting for secession on January 9, 1861.

The war finally came to Vicksburg when Flag Officer David G. Farragut's fleet of Union naval vessels steamed up the Mississippi River and arrived south of the city on May 18, 1862. Demanding the surrender of Vicksburg, the civil and military authorities of the city declined the Federal's request, and time was given for local inhabitants to leave before the ships opened a bombardment.[4]

---

2 Ibid, 2.

3 Christopher Morris, "A Place Apart From The Countryside: The City of Vicksburg." Essay. In *Becoming Southern: the Evolution of a Way of Life, Warren County and Vicksburg, Mississippi, 1770-1860*, (New York: Oxford University Press, 1999), 131.

4 Edwin C. Bearss, *Rebel Victory at Vicksburg* (Wilmington, NC: Broadfoot Publishing, 1989).

"The northerners came with their Gun boats to attack Vicksburg," noted Sister Ignatius, and

> by the second week in . . . [the] same month, all the inhabitants having fled into the surrounding country; those who could not get houses camping out in the woods, and living in caves which they dug in the sides of the hills. On Ascension Day (May 29), Father [Francis Xavier] Leray, being anxious about our safety, six of the Sisters accepted the invitation of Major Cook and his wife, went to their plantation and four of them remained a month, three of them having returned to the Convent to nurse the sick soldiers, with which the house was filled after their departure. Sickness, terror, death, reigned everywhere, soldiers without shelter, or else lying on the bare floor, were scattered through the town.[5]

Confederate authorities established a military hospital in Mississippi Springs, southwest of Jackson, where Sister Ignatius and her group moved to better provide for the sick and wounded. Within a couple of days, 700 sick soldiers and civilians were overflowing the hospital. "The sick had been hurried out of Vicksburg, fearing it would be taken by the enemy," she wrote, "and the house was dirty and neglected, entirely unfurnished, the mattresses burned on the cars coming out, and [we] were without the necessary means of cooking, or supplying the soldiers with necessities, so that the Sisters suffered much in seeing the sick suffer."[6]

In July, as the Federal navy severely bombarded Vicksburg, the military hospital at Mississippi Springs was dissolved, the Sisters of Mercy being requested to staff the Institute for the Deaf and Dumb, which was converted into a hospital. In the fall, the sisters moved north to Oxford to work at the Confederate hospital at the university. "The hospital at Oxford was composed of twelve large buildings forming an immense circle," she wrote. "It had been used as a College, and contained about one thousand sick. Many were extremely ill and neglected and the whole place in a disorderly

---

5 Mary Ignatius Sumner, "Register of the Events from the Foundation of the Convent of the Sisters of Mercy, Vicksburg, Mississippi.," *Register of the Events from the Foundation of the Convent of the Sisters of Mercy, Vicksburg, Mississippi,* (1860), 5.

6 Ibid.

condition." The assignment at the University of Mississippi would be a trying time for the Sisters of Mercy, who worked diligently to improve the living conditions of the sick and wounded. "It was a wide field of labor and the place, and the condition of the sick were gradually improving and even the invariable collegiate tobacco juice, was disappearing from the walls, when, at the end of the month (November), we were warned to prepare in haste for flight, as the Federals were momentarily expected."[7]

A hasty couple of days were spent in loading the train with the sick and hospital supplies. A sense of relief came over everyone as the train moved out of Oxford heading south. Within a few hours, Maj. Gen. Ulysses S. Grant's Army of the Tennessee had taken possession of the college town. The following evening, the train cars pulled into Canton, and the ragged sisters got out. "The guard at the depot, catching a glimpse of our coifs, hastened towards us, thinking we were wounded Yankees and was some what abashed to find only peaceful Sisters." The sisters arrived in Jackson the next day.[8]

The Sisters of Mercy would spend their spring in Jackson, working with Confederate Surgeon Daniel Warren Brickell in a small hospital when Grant's army crossed the Mississippi River on April 30, 1863. The Federals arrived at Jackson on May 14 and cut off the Sisters of Mercy from their convent and home. Sister Ignatius and her sisters would not see Vicksburg for over a year until May 28, 1864. Vicksburg by then was a very different city, now under martial law, and Union soldiers had even taken possession of their buildings.[9]

The following August the sisters were finally able to move back to their house and convent. The sisters cleaned the buildings and grounds which were scarred from Federal occupation. School was reopened in November and as the war came to a close, the Sisters of Mercy were once again providing their Catholic services to the community of Vicksburg.[10]

---

7   Ibid, 5-6.

8   Ibid, 7.

9   Mary Ignatius Sumner, "Register of the Events from the Foundation of the Convent of the Sisters of Mercy, Vicksburg, Mississippi," *Register of the Events from the Foundation of the Convent of the Sisters of Mercy, Vicksburg, Mississippi* (1860).

10   Mary Paulinus Oakes and Ignatius Sumner, *Angels of Mercy: an Eyewitness Account of Civil War and Yellow Fever by a Sister of Mercy: a Primary Source* (Baltimore, MD: Cathedral Foundation Press, 1998).

In the Wake of Vicksburg, U.S. Grant as Commander of the Army of the Potomac!

by Chris Mackowski

Originally published as a blog post at Emerging Civil War on August 15, 2017

By early August, 1863, Ulysses S. Grant had settled into administrative routine following the fall of Vicksburg, Mississippi—but Grant wasn't one to sit idle long. He had set his eye on Mobile, Alabama, which he was "very anxious to take" and which he thought he could do "with comparative ease."[1]

But even as Grant eyed Mobile, forces in Washington, D.C., were eyeing him. Word had begun to circulate in the upper reaches of the War Department, among influential politicians in the capitol, and even at the White House itself that perhaps Grant might best be used not in Alabama but in Virginia.

In the Eastern Theater, George Gordon Meade's victory at Gettysburg

---

1   For the full exchange between Grant and Dana, including the text of the August 5 letter from Grant to Dana and the August 18 reply from Dana to Grant, see *The Papers of Ulysses S. Grant*, vol. 9: July 7, December 31, 1863, John Y. Simon, ed. (Carbondale, IL: Southern Illinois University Press, 1982), 145-148. Available online at https://msstate.contentdm.oclc.org/digital/collection/USG_volume/id/2725/rec/1.

had earned the Army of the Potomac commander great praise—which was almost immediately stripped by his inability to deliver a killing blow to the Army of Northern Virginia in the days following the battle. Robert E. Lee slipped across a swollen Potomac River on July 14, and for Meade, things went downhill for the rest of the month.

Lincoln wrote but did not send a scolding letter. "I do not believe you appreciate the magnitude of the misfortune involved in Lee's escape," he lamented. "[T]o have closed upon him would, in connection with our other late successes, have ended the war—As it is, the war will be prolonged indefinitely."[2] Although Lincoln tucked the letter away, his frustration over the missed opportunity was no secret.

Although Grant (right) did not replace Meade (left) in the summer of '63, he would supercede him in March 1864, replacing him in practice if not in actuality. Ironically, Grant came to respect Meade a great deal and equated him with Sherman as "the fittest officers for large commands I have come in contact with." *LOC/LOC*

One of those "other late successes" he mentioned was, of course, Grant's major victory at Vicksburg. Already, events had positioned Meade and Grant in such a way that Lincoln began looking at them in parallel—and the comparison already favored Grant.

2 The full text of Lincoln's unsent letter to Meade can be found in many places, including on the American Battlefield Trust's website: https://www.battlefields.org/learn/primary-sources/lincolns-unsent-letter-george-meade.

Meanwhile, Dan Sickles, the former commander of the Army of the Potomac's III Corps, wounded at Gettysburg after disobeying orders and sent to Washington to convalesce, had immediately set to work telling his own version of events—a tall tale that set him at the center of the victory and minimalized Meade. Politically well connected, Sickles only flamed the doubts people had about Meade's leadership.

It was in this context that military and political leadership began considering Grant as a possible candidate for command in the east.

Word of such talk had circulated back to Grant, who heard of it at least in a July 22 letter from Assistant Secretary of War Charles Dana.[3] In his August 5 reply, Grant addressed the rumors head on. "[I]t would cause me more sadness than satisfaction to be ordered to the command of the Army of the Potomac," he admitted. He went on to outline the reasons for his reluctance:

> Here I know the officers and men and what each Gen. is capable of as a separate commander. There I would have all to learn. Here I know the geography of the country, and its resources. There it would be a new study. Besides more or less dissatisfaction would necessarily be produced by importing a General to command an Army already well supplied with those who have grown up, and been promoted, with it.

Although the Army of the Potomac had gone through a parade of commanders—McClellan, Burnside, Hooker—Meade had found his improbable place in that parade through the very process Grant had described. Meade had, to use Grant's phrase, "grown up, and been promoted" from brigade command to division to corps to army through stalwart service on the battlefield and with absolutely zero political grandstanding. As the victor at Gettysburg, he was the first of that string of army commanders to score a clear-cut victory over Lee—and that *did*, it turned out, merit him some consideration.

---

3 The letter from Dana to Grant seems to have been lost to time, although Grant's reply to the letter exists among the Grant Papers at the Ulysses S. Grant Presidential Library. According to archivist Ryan Semmes at the library, "There is no reference to it in the Published files either except a note from the Editors in 1977 stating that 'we don't have it.' I think it's just a letter lost to time." John Marszalek to author, 7 January 2021.

"There is no probability of any change in the Army of the Potomac. . ." Dana admitted to Grant in an August 18 letter. But then he added a cautionary note: "There is however, much dissatisfaction with the present state of things, but it takes a long time to make any movement at Hd. Qtrs."

Dana's words would prove prophetic. As he predicted, it would take "a long time to make any movement," but Grant would finally be called east in March 1864—some eight months after the fall of Vicksburg—to take command of all Union armies, not just the eastern Army of the Potomac. In the intervening time, Grant would lift the siege of Chattanooga, and his time in command of the Western district would give him valuable large-scale operational experience he would need as general in chief, so perhaps it's just as well that he did not get pulled eastward sooner than he did.

Meanwhile, almost simultaneous with Grant's success at Chattanooga, Meade found himself stymied before imposing Confederate works along Mine Run. "I expect your wishes will now soon be gratified, and that I shall be relieved from the Army of the Potomac," Meade wrote to his wife shortly thereafter.[4] He would, however, keep his command—solely at Grant's discretion, as it would eventually turn out. Upon first meeting Meade, Grant recognized his mettle and professionalism. "This incident gave me even a more favorable opinion of Meade than did his great victory at Gettysburg the July before," Grant admitted in his memoirs years later.[5]

One reason for the delay in Grant's promotion after Vicksburg could be attributed to his longtime jealous nemesis and former commander, General in Chief of the Army Henry Halleck—although Halleck took great pains to keep Grant from knowing about his machinations against him. For instance, as early as February 1862, Grant referred to Halleck as "one of the great men of the age" even as Halleck was trying to convince then-General in Chief George McClellan to sack or at least censure Grant.[6] "[T]here are not

---

4   George Gordon Meade to wife, 2 December 1863, George Gordon Meade, *The Life and Letters of George Gordon Meade, Major-General United States Army*. Vol. 2 (New York: Charles Scribner's Son, 1913), 156-9.

5   Ulysses S. Grant, *Memoirs and Selected Letters*, Mary Drake and William S. McFeely, eds. (New York: Library of America, 1990), 470. Hereafter cited as *Memoirs*.

6   Ulysses S. Grant to Julia Dent Grant, 1 March 1862, *Papers*, vol. 4. 306. Grant repeated the assertion in an April 30 letter to Julia, as well: Reprinted in *Memoirs*, 1006.

two men in the United States who I would prefer serving under than Halleck and McClellan," the oblivious Grant naively proclaimed.[7]

Halleck would finally overplay his hand in August 1863, however. Afraid of giving Grant the chance to earn yet one more possible accolade, Halleck would deny Grant's petition to move on Mobile. Instead, Halleck began to strip Grant's men from him and farm them out as reinforcements elsewhere. "The General-in-chief having decided against me," Grant later wrote, "the depletion of an army, which had won a succession of great victories, commenced. . . ."[8] Grant effectively became a commander without a command.

But his victory at Vicksburg had put the wheels in motion, and although he did not yet get the call eastward, Grant would soon see himself lifted out from under Halleck's thumb by Lincoln himself.

But on August 5, when Grant wrote to Dana, he still credited Halleck's patronage, as well as Dana's, for keeping him in the west. "I feel very grateful to you for your timely intercession in saving me from going to the Army of the Potomac," Grant wrote. "Whilst I would disobey no order I should beg very hard to be excused before accepting that command."

---

7 Ulysses S. Grant to Julia Dent Grant, 1 March 1862, *Papers,* vol. 4, 306. Grant repeated the assertion in a March 23 letter to Julia, as well: Reprinted in *Memoirs,* 992.

8 Grant, *Memoirs,* 259.

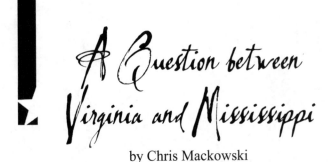

A Question between Virginia and Mississippi

by Chris Mackowski

*Originally published in the July 2021 issue
of* America's Civil War *magazine
in conjunction with the release of this book*

What if Robert E. Lee sent troops to Vicksburg in the spring of 1863?

That question was certainly on the mind of Confederate Secretary of War James Seddon that season. By default, then, it was also on Lee's.

Vicksburg, a bluff-top city high above the Mississippi River, lay hundreds of miles away from Lee's own position along the banks of Virginia's Rappahannock River. The city's topographical dominance gave Confederates the ability to control traffic on the river and also keep open a vital connection to the Confederacy's Trans-Mississippi region.

Because of its strategic importance, Union Maj. Gen. Ulysses S. Grant had made stabs at the city for months, although to no avail. That the tenacious Grant kept trying worried once-confident Mississippians. The overall Confederate commander in the western theater, Gen. Joseph E. Johnston, had a highly regarded reputation, but he made his headquarters in far-off Tullahoma, Tennessee. The local commander, Lt. Gen. John Pemberton, was a Pennsylvanian who had thrown his loyalty in with the Confederacy— and thus, to some, he could not be trusted. Worse, he had never held such an important field command before.

Jefferson Davis (left, as he appears in a painting that hangs in Vicksburg's Old Courthouse Museum) was a native Mississippian but his prewar service in government had given him a national view as president of the Confederacy. General Robert E. Lee (right), as a native Virginian, held a Virginia-centric view of the war. Secretary of War James Seddon (center) was caught between them as he tried to find reinforcements he could send to the west. *Old Courthouse Museum/LOC/LOC*

As the situation along the Mississippi looked more and more questionable, Seddon looked for possible solutions. One option would be to send reinforcements directly to Pemberton. Another would be to send them to Johnston, who could then lead them to Pemberton's relief.

But where to get those reinforcements from?

Lee had reason to be concerned about the question. Confederate President Jefferson Davis was a Mississippi resident who saw Vicksburg as "the nail head that holds the South's two halves together."[1] On a more personal note, Davis and his brother both owned plantations right outside Vicksburg. The urge to protect the riverside bastion and deny Federals free, full access to river navigation was strong.

Lee had another reason to be concerned. From a logistical point of view, he already had two divisions on detached duty from his army as winter thawed toward spring in 1863: John Bell Hood's and George Pickett's men, under the overall command of James Longstreet. In mid-February, Lee had sent them to southeast Virginia on a foraging mission to shuffle much-needed

---

1   Quoted ubiquitously, but here taken from Terrence Winschel, *Vicksburg: Fall of the Confederate Gibraltar* (Abilene, TX: McWhitney Foundation Press, 1999), 14.

supplies back to the rest of the Army of Northern Virginia. Their absence from the Confederate line along the Rappahannock presented a double benefit, too, by alleviating the need for those supplies on the front. "At this time but few supplies can be procured from the country we now occupy," Lee told Seddon on March 27 as part of a series of urgent correspondence about the dire state of the army.[2]

Longstreet acknowledged Lee was "averse to having a part of his army so far beyond his reach."[3] Detached as they were from Lee's immediate control, the two divisions looked like tempting chess pieces that Seddon could move across the Confederate board to Vicksburg. Complicating matters further, Ambrose Burnside's Federal IX Corps shifted to the western theater, increasing the need for Confederate counter-forces out west.

Could reinforcements "safely be sent from the forces in this department," Seddon inquired of Lee on April 6, going so far as to muse aloud whether "two or three brigades, say of Pickett's division" could be spared. "[T]hey would be an encouraging re-enforcement to the Army of the West," he added.[4]

No one seemed eager to get on Lee's bad side, though; his fiery temper, usually kept hidden under a courtly exterior, was an open secret. Besides, Lee had strung together impressive victories since assuming command in June 1862, so he had earned a certain amount of deference. "I know . . . that your army is largely outnumbered by the enemy in your front, and that it is not unlikely that a movement against you may be made at any day," Seddon admitted. "I am, therefore, unwilling to send beyond your command any portion even of the forces here without your counsel and approval."[5]

Lee responded on April 9 with a letter that demonstrated he, too, had his eye on the chessboard. "I do not know that I can add anything to what I have already said on the subject of reinforcing the Army of the West,"

---

2   United States War Department, *The War of the Rebellion: A Compilation of the Official Records of the Union and Confederate Armies*, 70 vols. in 128 parts (Washington D.C.: Government Printing Office, 1880-1901), Series I, volume 25, part 2, p. 687 (hereafter cited as *O.R.*, I, 25, pt. 2, 687).

3   James Longstreet, *From Manassas to Appomattox: Memoirs of the Civil War in America* (Philadelphia: J.B. Lippincott Co., 1896), 328.

4   *O.R.*, I, 25, pt. 2, 709.

5   Ibid.

he opened before launching into a string of suggestions. Just as Seddon had suggested a Pickett-for-Burnside shift west, Lee countered with a corresponding shift of troops from southwest Tennessee. "If a division has been taken from Memphis to re-enforce Rosecrans, it diminishes the force opposed to our troops in that quarter," Lee pointed out, urging offensive action there that might reverse the Federal departure and instead tie them down. He pointed, too, to rumors of a Federal troop shift along the Tallahatchie River that would free up Confederate troops there. He also suggested "judicious operations" in the west that could occupy Burnside on his arrival in Kentucky, which would do more to relieve pressure on Johnston than sending more troops would.[6]

Seddon, as secretary of war, certainly had his pulse on these developments more so than Lee, who got them second- and third-hand in his camp in Fredericksburg. But Lee's attention to them demonstrates the larger strategic view he had beyond his own army, which served as a protection *for* his army. His big-picture view served his operational interests.

And Lee's army did have immediate concerns to think about. Rumors circulated everywhere that Fighting Joe Hooker, on the far side of the Rappahannock, was preparing to shake the Army of the Potomac from its winter slumber. Lee set a May 1 deadline, determining to take the offensive himself if Hooker didn't do something by then. That, too, could help address Seddon's concerns out west. "Should Genl Hooker's army assume the defensive," Lee suggested, "the readiest method of relieving the pressure upon Genl. Johnston . . . would be for this army to cross into Maryland. This cannot be done, however, in the present condition of the roads. . . . But this is what I would recommend if practicable." Already Lee was looking north of the Mason-Dixon Line, foreshadowing future events.[7]

Lee admitted that Pickett's men seemed to offer an easy fix for Seddon, but he warned the secretary not to be deceived. "The most natural way to reinforce Genl Johnston would seem to be to transfer a portion of the troops from this department to oppose those sent west," he admitted, "but it is not as easy for us to change troops from one department to another

---

6 Ibid., 713-714.

7 Ibid, 713.

as it is for the enemy, and if we rely on that method we may be always too late."[8]

As events would tell, this proved a self-fulfilling prophecy. By not shifting troops, Lee's "better never than late" logic assured there'd be no reinforcements at all. For a man once described as "audacity itself," this abundance of overcautiousness seems curious.

Lee's intentional pessimism is easily explained by the fact that he had a vested interest in keeping Pickett's troops attached to his army. Longstreet already felt he didn't have enough troops to robustly carry out his foraging mission, Lee informed Seddon. "If any of his troops are taken from him," he explained, "I fear it will arrest his operations and deprive us of the benefit anticipated from increasing the supplies of this army."[9]

The flurry of correspondence between the two over the previous weeks had clearly laid out the case for Lee's supply concerns, so this comment was no lame excuse suddenly pulled from thin air. Furthermore, Seddon himself had attributed the supply urgency to "impediments to their ready transportation and distribution." In particular, Seddon had admitted, "our railroads are daily growing less efficient and serviceable."[10] To depend on those same railroads to quickly shift troops to the west might be asking for trouble.

Lee knew this well enough, too, but instead of closing his letter by saying "check mate," he deployed his usual rhetorical deference. If Seddon thought it "advantageous" to send troops to the west, "General Longstreet will designate such as ought to go." Couched in such terms, Lee knew Seddon would *not* find it advantageous and, better, would think it his own idea.

* * *

Like his parries with the Army of the Potomac, though, Lee's victory on the Vicksburg question was but a temporary one.

As rumor foretold, Hooker's army did rumble to life, and the two forces clashed at Chancellorsville, Fredericksburg, and Salem Church May 1-4.

8 Ibid.

9 Ibid, 714.

10 Ibid., 693.

Hooker slipped away on the night of May 5, giving Lee little time to assess his army's condition before he received another message from Richmond about events in Mississippi.

Even as Lee had beaten back Hooker at Chancellorsville, Grant had begun his spring campaign against Vicksburg in earnest. On April 29, he landed two of his three corps on the east bank of the Mississippi River at Bruinsburg, south of Vicksburg, then fought his first action of the campaign two days later just a few miles inland at Port Gibson.

On May 6, with Grant moving around the Mississippi interior, Pemberton pleaded with Richmond for reinforcements. "The stake is a great one," he told Seddon. "I can see nothing so important."[11] Davis himself responded the next day: "You may expect whatever is in my power to do."[12] By that time, he and Seddon had directed Gen. P. G. T. Beauregard, in command of the military district that included Charleston and Savannah, to send reinforcements. Those five thousand men boarded trains on May 6, and lead elements began arriving in the Mississippi capital by May 13, eight days later, where they would rendezvous under Joe Johnston's leadership for Vicksburg's relief.

Davis had explicitly ordered Johnston to Mississippi as an answer to a call from several prominent citizens, including editors of the *Mississippian* newspaper in Jackson. The people did not have "confidence in the capacity and loyalty of Genl. Pemberton, which is so important at this junction, whether justly or not . . ." the editors wrote in a private letter to Davis on May 8. "Send us a man we can trust," they pleaded, "Beauregard, [D. H.] Hill or Longstreet & confidence will be restored & all will fight to the death for Miss."[13]

Lee himself was not an option. On the angst-filled evening of April 20, 1861, when he decided to decline Lincoln's offer to command U.S. forces in

---

11   *O.R.*, I, 24, pt. 3, 838.

12   Ibid., 842.

13   Quote from *The Mississippian* by Cooper and Kimball to Jefferson Davis, 8 May 1863, Jefferson Davis Papers, Louisiana Historical Collection, Howard-Tilton Memorial Library, Tulane University, New Orleans, quoted by Michael B. Ballard, *Pemberton: A Biography* (Jackson, MS: University Press of Mississippi, 1991), 153. For newspaper editors, Cooper and Kimball used atrocious punctuation, so I've added commas to the quote to improve readability.

"Send us a man we can trust," pleaded Mississippi newspaper editors in May 1863, "Beauregard, [D. H.] Hill or Longstreet & confidence will be restored. . . ." However, Davis despised Beauregard; Hill was even then (once again) proving himself prickly; and Lee didn't want to give Longstreet up. By fall, after Vicksburg fell, Davis seemed to learn a lesson and transferred both Hill and Longstreet to Bragg's embattled Army of Tennessee where they would perform well on the field but make a bad command situation even worse.
National Archives/LOC/LOC

the war, Lee had resolved, "Save in the defense of my native State, I never desire again to draw my sword." Sincere as that vow was, he ended up stretching "defense of Virginia" enough to include an invasion of the north in the fall of 1862, and even now he contemplated stretching it again for another. Most importantly, Lee's vow reflected his Virginia-centric view of the conflict and his role in it. As a professional soldier, he no doubt would have obeyed any direct order to go west, but as a wily negotiator who knew better than anyone how to manage his own president, he surely would have found a way to make Davis see things *his* way.

But if Lee wasn't going anywhere, Seddon at least wanted to shift Pickett's division westward, and said so in a May 9 dispatch. Lee was simultaneously deferential and oppositional in his reply the next day. "The distance and the uncertainty of the employment of the troops are unfavorable," he wrote. "But, if necessary, order Pickett at once."[14]

At the heart of the brief note, Lee laid out the situation in terms as stark as possible: "it becomes a question between Virginia and the Mississippi." Davis, seeing the note, told Seddon, "The answer of General Lee was such

14 Ibid.

as I should have anticipated, and in which I concur."[15] Davis's answer is often taken to suggest his agreement with Lee's priorities, but in fact, Davis was agreeing that the shortage of resources in the face of twin crises created an unfortunate binary choice.

Lee followed his short dispatch to Seddon with a longer one later in the day. He blamed the delay on the garbled transmission of Seddon's telegram, which couldn't be "rendered intelligibly" until almost noon. It may have been, though, that Lee actually needed a little time to think through his response. He did, after all, have much vying for his attention, including the aftermath of battle and the deteriorating condition of trusted subordinate Thomas "Stonewall" Jackson, who would die that very day.

Lee's reply laid out careful arguments against any move to Mississippi. Sincerely meant at the time, the note now teems with unfortunate irony when read with hindsight.

"If you determine to send Pickett's division to Genl Pemberton," Lee wrote, "I presume it would not reach him until the last of this month. If anything is done in that quarter, it will be over by that time, as the climate in June will force the enemy to retire. The uncertainty of its arrival and the uncertainty of its application cause me to doubt the policy of sending it. Its removal from this army will be sensibly felt. . . . I think troops ordered from Virginia to the Mississippi at this season would be greatly endangered by the climate."

Lee predicted any action in Mississippi would be over by month's end, but we now know that did not turn out to be the case. Instead, by month's end Grant was just settling into a siege. Even factoring in the questionable condition of the railroads and the distance to travel, it's reasonable to think Pickett's men could have arrived in the Magnolia State in time to be of use. The timely movement of Beauregard's men from South Carolina and Georgia demonstrated as much. Certainly the vulnerabilities of the railroad, called into stark relief by the supply issue, offered cause for realistic caution, but a little more audacity would not have hurt.

Pickett's arrival would have added 7,500 troops to Johnston's assembled force of 15,000 men in Jackson—a significant threat to Grant's isolated army. In fact, one reason Grant rushed into assaults on May 19 and 22 was

15   *O.R.*, I, 25, pt. 2, 790.

that he had one eye on Johnston operating in his rear and feared an attack from behind. Johnston never made a move, but perhaps an additional 7,500 men would have inspired action. (Doubtful—but one can wonder. . . .)

Lee's May 10 letter also became ironic because he predicted "the climate in June will force the enemy to retire." Of course, Grant ended up doing no such thing, opting to "outcamp" the besieged force in Vicksburg for forty-seven days. One of Lee's underlying assumptions proved wildly off the mark, something Seddon suspected from the beginning. The secretary of war said, "Grant was such an obstinate fellow that he could only be induced to quit Vicksburg by terribly hard knocks"—and even that prediction proved wrong as the two failed assaults demonstrated.[16]

Lee expressed an extra concern about the Mississippi climate in his letter, as well. He worried that "troops ordered from Virginia to the Mississippi at this season would be greatly endangered" by it. Of the divisions detached from his army, though, Hood's at least contained a brigade of Alabamians and two brigades of Georgians, so they, if no one else, would have been accustomed to the Deep South climate. If acclimatization was truly a concern, Lee could have also offered up William Barksdale's brigade of Mississippians from another of Longstreet's divisions commanded by Lafayette McLaws. Carnot Posey's brigade also consisted of Mississippians.

Again, though, Lee had a vested interest in keeping his army intact, so he was not taking any ownership of Seddon's larger strategic problem or offering solutions that negatively impacted his own immediate situation. "Unless we can obtain some reinforcements," he said, turning the tables on Seddon, "we may be obliged to withdraw into the defenses around Richmond. We are greatly outnumbered now. . . . The strength of this army has been reduced by the casualties of the late battles."[17]

Indeed, Chancellorsville had cost Lee 13,460 men. Compounding those losses, intelligence suggested Hooker's army was already replenishing its own casualties. "Virginia is to be the theater of action, and this army, if possible, ought to be strengthened . . ." Lee wrote to Davis on May 11, underscoring the point he made to Seddon the day before. "I think you will

16 Longstreet, 328.

17 *O.R.*, I, 25, pt. 2, 790.

agree with me that every effort should be made to re-enforce this army in order to oppose the large force which the enemy seems to be concentrating against it."[18]

In that same letter, noting that troops from the Department of South Carolina, Georgia, and Florida had been sent to Vicksburg—the 5,000 men Beauregard had shipped out—Lee let slip an idea that had weighed increasingly on his mind since Chancellorsville. "A vigorous movement here would certainly draw the enemy from there . . ." he said.

Lee didn't just want reinforcements for defense. He was thinking about taking the fight to the Federals.

*   *   *

With Stonewall Jackson struggling to recover from his wounding and with James Longstreet not yet back from Suffolk, Lee felt the loneliness of command even as he tried to figure out what to do next. How should he follow up Chancellorsville? What should he do about the army in light of Jackson's absence? What could he do to replace the tremendous battle losses his army had sustained? Yes, even perhaps, how might Vicksburg tie into his own plans?

"There are many things about which I would like to consult Your Excellency," Lee wrote to Davis on May 7, "and I should be delighted, if your health and convenience suited, you could visit the army." Lee depended here on Davis not as president but as a former United States Secretary of War—one of the country's most organized and successful. Davis was a notorious micromanager as a politician, but he and Lee had come to a hard-earned trust on military matters. If Davis visited, Lee promised him a comfortable room near his headquarters, "and I know you would be content with our camp fare."[19]

Alas, Davis was, at the time, too sick to travel. Lee would have to plan a trip to Richmond instead—which he volunteered to do—but with a wounded Army of the Potomac lurking on the far side of the Rappahannock, and with his own army and officer corps still reeling from its recent bloodletting, Lee

18   Ibid., 791-792.

19   *O.R.*, I, 25, pt. 2, 783.

did not yet feel comfortable slipping away. He would have to brood over his plans in solitude.

As it happened, James Longstreet would have been happy to talk things over. The battle at Chancellorsville had triggered a hurried recall of the First Corps commander and his two divisions, but the fighting ended before they could make it back. Lee subsequently ordered his Old Warhorse not to stress his divisions with a forced march.

On the trip north, Longstreet had plenty of time to chew over the Confederacy's overall strategic situation. Since at least late January, he had contemplated moves where one corps of the Army of Northern Virginia would hold the line at the Rappahannock while the other corps would operate elsewhere, and his operations around Suffolk had confirmed the idea's viability.[20] He longed to "break up [the enemy] in the East and then re-enforce in the West in time to crush him there."[21] By May, Longstreet had a particular eye on Vicksburg. "I thought that honor, interest, duty, and humanity called us to that service," he later said.[22]

Traveling ahead of his divisions, Longstreet arrived in Richmond on the evening of May 5 and spent the next day conferring with Seddon. What if, the Secretary of War offered, we sent Pickett's and Hood's divisions not northward to the Rappahannock but, rather, westward toward the Mississippi?

Longstreet did Seddon one better. Rather than send troops to Vicksburg where they would move against Grant directly, he suggested reinforcements concentrate instead in middle Tennessee under Johnston—reinforcements that would include Hood and Pickett, with Longstreet himself along for good measure. Johnston could then combine with Braxton Bragg's Army of Tennessee in a move against Maj. Gen. William Starke Rosecrans's Army of the Cumberland encamped in Murfreesboro. "The combination once made should strike immediately in overwhelming force upon Rosecrans, and march for the Ohio River and Cincinnati," Longstreet argued.[23] That sudden

20 *O.R.*, I, 27, 959.

21 Ibid., 960.

22 Longstreet, 331.

23 Ibid.

dire threat would force a Federal response. "Grant's was the only army that could be drawn to meet this move, and that the move must, therefore, relieve Vicksburg," he concluded.[24]

Longstreet's plan reflected the same principle Lee had articulated in April when he contemplated a move on Maryland but for the muddy spring roads. A serious movement into the northern interior would panic state governments and the Lincoln administration into a response that would sap Union operations of any initiative and momentum while they dealt with a Confederate invasion.

Lee's Old Warhorse was not being disingenuous with his commander in proposing this plan. As soon as he finally reported to Lee on May 9, he presented his idea for Vicksburg's tangential relief to Lee and "asked the aid of his counsels with the War Department, and reinforcements from his army for the West, to that end."[25]

As Longstreet later recalled, Lee "reflected over the matter for one or two days."[26] This was either a generous or a forgetful retelling. The same day Longstreet pitched the idea to him, Seddon's garbled telegram arrived asking to transfer Pickett's division west—a telegram no doubt inspired by Seddon's conversation with Longstreet. Lee didn't respond until May 10, and during that time he sent for Longstreet for further discussion.

"I thought we could spare the troops unless there was a chance of a forward movement," Longstreet explained to a confident, Texas Sen. Louis T. Wigfall. "If we could move of course we should want everything, that we had and all that we could get."[27]

Indeed, Lee had begun thinking of moving, not defending, and his early afternoon reply to Seddon suggests a mind firmly made up. Lee's thinking shifted away from the Mississippi, and away from Longstreet's suggestion of the Ohio River and Cincinnati, toward his own northern frontier instead. "To that end he bent his energies," Longstreet wrote. "His plan or wishes

24   Ibid 327.

25   Ibid, 331.

26   Ibid.

27   Longstreet to Wigfall, quoted in Jeffrey D. Wert, *General James Longstreet: The Confederacy's Most Controversial Soldier—A Biography* (New York: Simon & Schuster, 1993), 245.

announced, it became useless and improper to offer suggestions leading to a different course."

But even as Lee settled on his plans—and set his mind to reclaiming Longstreet's two divisions—John Pemberton was penning frantic letters to Richmond about Grant's movements through the Mississippi interior. Davis, because of his illness, was largely silent in reply, but he confided "intense anxiety over Pemberton's situation" despite public confidence.[28]

In fact, the timing of Grant's river crossing could not have worked out better for him in relation to events in the east, which presented more urgency to Richmond because of their proximity. Chancellorsville, virtually on Richmond's doorstep compared with the Magnolia State, sucked up all the oxygen. Davis's illness kept him uncharacteristically passive, and even before he recovered, Stonewall Jackson's death provided additional, mournful distraction.[29] Davis and Seddon did agree to send reinforcements west from Beauregard, but at a time when additional troops might have also come from the Army of Northern Virginia, Robert E. Lee was feeling his oats after his Chancellorsville victory.

Lee finally had his much-hoped-for conference with Davis on May 15 when the army commander traveled to Richmond to hash it all out. He arrived on a day of "calamity," as described by Confederate clerk John B. Jones. A fire had torn through the Tredegar Iron Works and Crenshou's woolen mill, mostly destroying them, and news had just arrived of Grant's capture of Jackson, Mississippi. "[Vicksburg] may be doomed to fall at last," Jones wrote.[30] If so, it would be "the worst blow we have yet received."[31]

Lee looked thin and a little pale, Jones noted, and Davis himself, just back to work after days of illness, was "not fully himself yet." The president's frailty so alarmed Lee that, upon his return to Fredericksburg days later, he wrote, "I cannot express the concern I felt at leaving you in

---

28 Quoted in William C. Davis, *Jefferson Davis: The Man and His Hour* (New York: Harper Collins, 1991), 501.

29 For more on this, see William C. Davis, 500-501.

30 John Beauchamp Jones, *A Rebel War Clerk's Diary at the Confederate States Capital*, vol. 1 (Philadelphia: J. B. Lippincott & Co., 1866), 325.

31 Jones, *Rebel War Clerk's Diary,* 324.

such feeble health, with so many anxious thoughts for the welfare of the whole Confederacy weighing upon your mind."[32]

No record exists of the discussion that day—ironic for an event, says historian Stephen Sears, that "easily qualifies as a pivotal moment in Confederate history."[33] But from that confab came the Gettysburg campaign, or at least the general outlines of it. (On May 31, Davis would write to Lee claiming, "I had never fairly comprehended your views and purposes until the receipt of your letter yesterday [May 30]."[34])

The results were obvious on May 16, at any rate. "It appears, after the consultation of the generals and the President yesterday, it was resolved not to send Pickett's division to Mississippi," Jones observed. Pickett's column marched northward through the city, "Pickett himself, with his long, black ringlets," accompanying them, "his troops looking like fighting veterans, as they are."[35]

In the weeks that followed, Davis might have felt buyer's remorse for his troop allocations. Grant assaulted Vicksburg twice and failed to capture it, so besieged the city instead. "The position, naturally strong, may soon be intrenched," Davis said. He also noted Grant had the additional advantage of connecting his army with gunboats and transportation on the Yazoo River to the north of Vicksburg, allowing Federals to bring in more troops, supplies, and big guns—none of which were now available to the cut-off city.

"It is useless to look back," Davis wrote to Lee, "and it would be unkind to annoy you in the midst of your many cares with the reflections which I have not been able to avoid."[36] Davis had put the needs of the Confederacy ahead of his home state but now could not stop wondering whether he had prioritized the crisis properly. What if Lee had sent troops to Vicksburg? Would it have made a difference? Was the gambit worth it?

Lee's foray north of the Mason-Dixon line was about to begin. The answers to Davis's questions awaited.

---

32 *O.R.*, I, 25, pt. 2, 810.

33 Stephen W. Sears, *Gettysburg* (Mariner's, 2004), 1.

34 *O.R.*, I, 25, pt. 2, 842.

35 Jones, *Rebel War Clerk's Diary*, 326.

36 *O.R.*, I, 25, pt. 2, 843.

From Civil War to World War: The Missouri State Memorial at Vicksburg National Military Park

by Kristen Trout

Originally appeared as a blog post on Emerging Civil War blog on November 4, 2017

Along Confederate Avenue in Vicksburg National Military Park, near the Stockade Redan, sits the Missouri State Memorial. It is one of the only memorials at Vicksburg that is dedicated to both Federal and Confederate troops who served in this consequential campaign in the Western Theater.[1] Made of Missouri red granite, the memorial is 42 feet tall (representing 42 Missouri units—27 Union and 15 Confederate—engaged in the campaign) with two flanking wings depicting each side's role there. On the center pylon, the Spirit of the Republic stands upon a pedestal underneath a granite relief of the Missouri State Seal. Two bronze reliefs are on the wings of the memorial; the right wing depicts the Confederate defenders, while the left illustrates the attacking Federals. The Missouri State Memorial is not only significant as a piece of art but, most importantly, also as a symbol of brotherhood, reconciliation, and unity in postwar America.

On October 17, 1917, more than fifty-four years after Vicksburg,

---

1 As does Kentucky's (see pp. 26-27).

Missouri was especially—and sometimes brutally—divided during the war, so reconciliation and unity were especially important themes for many Missouri veterans. *National Park Service*

hundreds of veterans and civilians alike gathered around the new memorial to, as inscribed in bronze, "commemorate and perpetuate the heroic services, the unselfish devotion to duty, and exalted patriotism of the Missouri soldiers, both Union and Confederate." The ceremony of the monument was quite reconciliatory in spirit, with a particular focus on the theme of "brother against brother." The memorial was strategically placed where Union and Confederate Missourians literally fought one another. The symbolism of brotherhood became, like many memorial dedications in the postwar era, "the possibility of patriotic reflection, when orators declared that America's greatness was revealed in this uniting of former enemies."[2] These same messages used to showcase reconciliation amongst Missouri veterans once divided by civil war were also used to push unity and patriotic themes as the United States had, just months prior, declared war on Germany.

---

2   Nina Silber, *The Romance of Reunion: Northerners and the South, 1865-1900* (Chapel Hill: The University of North Carolina Press, 1993), 1-2.

By the time the Missouri State Memorial was dedicated and erected at Vicksburg National Military Park, the United States had been at war for over six months, preparing for the deployment of four million military personnel to the Western Front and the Atlantic Ocean. As the nation's "boys in blue and gray" erected monuments to their fallen comrades and to their courageous actions on the battlefield, they and others who partook in the commemorations looked to the ongoing conflict overseas to help in the war effort and to connect the past with the present.

"The sons and the grandsons of those soldiers . . . are now at cantonments and in training as soldiers of the United States," William T. Rigby of the Vicksburg Park Commission told the crowd. He went on to say, "After their training is ended and when, somewhere in France, these young Missourians go over the top of the parapet and charge the Germans, let them start the Rebel Yell, the fiercest battle cry that ever leaped from the lips of fighting men."[3]

Today, when visitors stroll through Vicksburg National Military Park and come across the Missouri State Memorial, they may not know the deeper history and context of both the monument and its dedication. It is not just a monument to a state—instead, it is a monument that represents brotherhood, reconciliation, suffering, courage, and national unity amongst Missourians, who, from 1861-1865, were bitterly divided. It is also a testament to postwar reunion; though engaged in civil war over fifty years before, the symbols of reunification and "shaking hands over the bloody chasm" united the next generation of American soldiers to fight a greater enemy abroad.

---

3 "New York and Missouri Memorials Dedicated," *The Vicksburg Herald* (Vicksburg, MS), October 18, 1917.

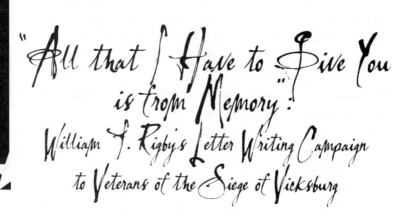

"All that I Have to Give You is from Memory": William T. Rigby's Letter Writing Campaign to Veterans of the Siege of Vicksburg

by Andrew Miller

Vicksburg National Military Park's first resident commissioner was William Titus Rigby. The former captain of the 24th Iowa Infantry and veteran of the campaign and siege of Vicksburg had been selected as the initial secretary of the Vicksburg National Military Park Association, as well as a member of the board of directors of the association for preparing a bill for establishing the military park to be presented to Congress. Rigby was instrumental in obtaining the lands comprising the siege lines, fortifications, and historically important points of interest to ensure that the preservation of the battlefield would live on in perpetuity.

But maybe Captain Rigby's most important contribution to the development of Vicksburg National Military Park was the rapport, relationships, friendships, and information he obtained through constant letter writing to the veterans of the great campaign. One only needs to provide a few examples of the wealth of information these letters contain.

Rigby looked to the veterans themselves to confirm the locations where their regiments assaulted, defended, camped, and languished for forty-seven days in the summer of 1863. The veterans of the respective regiments, both

North and South, wrote to each other to reconnect and revitalize those old memories of time spent in the armies. One or two veterans from each regiment would make it their personal mission to get Rigby the most accurate information by contacting their comrades across the United States. A general consensus would be established, and iron marker tablets would be cast and placed along the siege lines that gave the park its first real interpretation.

Forty years had passed since the war ended and many of these veterans were well into their "golden years" as they attempted to remember where exactly their units had fought. Humor was often the guise of a "defective" memory. However, the veterans wanted to ensure those historical moments and details were told. Marcus D. Elliott, living in Holly, Michigan in 1903, lamented in his response to Rigby that "all the data I had of the Vicksburg campaign was destroyed by fire the 1st day of Nov. 1891, and all that I have to give you is from memory. . . ."[1]

During the siege of Vicksburg, Elliott had been in command of a section of the 8th Battery, Michigan Light Artillery. He mentions watching Grant and Pemberton meet under the oak tree for the initial conference to discuss surrender terms. Elliott and his squad of artillerists, along with Lieut. Henry Foster's company from the 23d Indiana, were the ones that grabbed Abraham, "the old colored man that was blown over the works" during the second mine explosion on July 1, 1863.[2]

Elliott's best memory of the siege was during the June 25 mine explosion, "when the rush was made in the crater, some smarty suggested that an artillery officer be ordered to take charge of the throwing the hand grenades, and as I was the first one there, I was the one ordered and I made the remark that it was a piece of dam foolishness. The idea was started to put me under arrest, but no one wanted my place, so it was not done." Perhaps Elliott's memories were embellished but they make for great stories.[3]

Rigby's devotion to the most accurate information also led veterans to

---

1   Marcus D. Elliott Letter to Capt. E.E. Lewis, "Dear Sir," Vicksburg, Mississippi: War Department Park Commission, 1890-1933, file 481, Vicksburg National Military Park, December 12, 1903.

2   Ibid.

3   Ibid.

squabble with who was right while trying to remain polite. Responding to a letter from Rigby, the Louisiana Monument Commissioner Louis Guion, formerly of the 26th Louisiana Infantry, felt the need to express a point of error on another Confederate officer's location of the brigade headquarters during the siege. Time and nature had changed the viewshed of the ravines behind the Confederate lines around the Stockade Redan Complex, but Guion was adamant his memory was correct. Guion was upset that, having pointed out Gen. Francis Shoup's brigade headquarters location on his previous visit to the park, his memory was now questioned by park commissioners.

"I do not pretend to say that after the lapse of forty years, and with the changes of time in the natural features of the country, that I may not have been wrong, and Mr. McCutchen right . . ." Guion noted. "We desire to have it placed of record, that it (Shoup's headquarters) was in the rear of the 26th La." Doubling down on his previous statement to Rigby, Guion adamantly stated, "I AM willing to swear in the rear of the 26th La., and in the rear of Capt. Bisland's Co (H) and . . . that it was anywhere in the rear of the 27th or the 28th [La. Regiments]." Guion's final snipe at his former Confederate comrade-in-arms put the issue to bed in the Louisianan's mind for good. "While Mr. McCutchen came each morning to deliver his reports [to the brigade headquarters] . . . I was as likely to be correct as he was, because being on the staff of Gen. Shoup, wherever his headquarters were, I remained."[4]

Remembering and identifying the correct information regarding the African Brigade, which had fought so determinedly at Milliken's Bend on June 7, 1863, also became a part of Captain Rigby's rigorous letter writing campaign. Charles R. C. Koch was the assistant secretary and treasurer of the "Commission to Ascertain and Mark Positions of Illinois Troops at the Siege of Vicksburg." Having concluded a letter about the Illinois-Vicksburg Commission, Koch wanted "to take up another matter" with Rigby. "I am deeply interested that the colored troops at Millicen's Bend [*sic*] who fought so bravely and heroically, shall be properly recognized by the National

---

4 Louis Guion Letter to William Titus Rigby, "My Dear Captain," Vicksburg, Mississippi: War Department Park Commission, file 104, Vicksburg National Military Park, April 29, 1903. Guion later served as the Confederate representative on the park commission following the death of S. D. Lee.

Commission at or near Grant's monument." Koch had been commissioned a captain in the 49th United States Colored Troops (formerly the 11th Louisiana Infantry, African Descent) and understood the importance of their service.[5]

Koch wrote a long letter noting the different resources, stating the disproportionate casualty figures of the 9th and 11th Louisiana Infantry, African Descent, suffered during that hot June morning. "The accounts of the individual bravery performed by this Command at the bloody fight of Milliken's Bend, have never been fully recorded in history and probably never will be." Koch had been in communication with his former commander of the 49th USCT, Lieut. Col. Cyrus Sears, who kept a memorandum book at the time of the battle. The book listed 369 men who went into action that day with an aggregate of 132 killed or wounded and another 114 missing. Confederate after action reports stated they only took 50 prisoners which, if the numbers are correct, shows at least that the 11th Louisiana Infantry, African Descent, had 64 others unaccounted for.[6]

Koch had a record of his personal company's casualties from that day "which shows 13 killed on June 7th in my Company alone and gives their names, and considering that this Company had been in the service at that time only 17 days, and that four other Companies of the Regiment had only been in the service four days, the heavy mortality is easily accounted for because they were not trained to take care of themselves or protect themselves. That they did not run and throw away their arms is what is most surprising. . . ." Koch wanted to set the record straight. "I submit it to show to you that the colored troops at Milliken's Bend were not the cowards that [Rear Admiral David Dixon] Porter painted them."[7]

The War Department Park Commission correspondence runs from 1890 through 1933, when the National Park Service took over the administration and preservation of Vicksburg National Military Park. Within the files is a fascinating leap into the hearts and minds of the veterans who were reliving

---

5   Charles R.C. Koch Letter to William T. Rigby, "Dear Captain," Vicksburg, Mississippi: Vicksburg National Military Park, War Department Park Commission 1890-1933 papers, file 245, April 1, 1902.

6   Ibid.

7   Ibid.

the glory days of their youths. It is no surprise that every single veteran's letter leaves off with hope for another response from Captain Rigby and for his continued health in preserving the hallowed ground they all fought so heroically on. Rigby's efforts brought hundreds of letters documenting the locations of the men who fought at Vicksburg and his continued health would do this important work until his passing in 1929.

William Rigby of the 24th Iowa later served as one of the three original commissioners who established Vicksburg National Military Park. He and his wife are now buried in the national cemetery. *Chris Mackowski*

COVID and the USS Cairo: A Summer at Vicksburg

by Caroline Davis

The year 2020 was not what any of us had anticipated, and it was no different for me. January and February brought trepidation and anxiety. March brought fear and isolation.

In February, I found out I would be working a seasonal position at Vicksburg National Military Park. I was ecstatic, but I knew things would be different this time around. Just as the battle at Vicksburg was unique in its time, my experience at the park would be quite different from the summers I had spent at other battlefields.

For me, being a historian has always been a dream. As far back as I can remember, I have been fascinated with the stories told about our nation. At the age of eight, I cried when I got to hold a gun owned by David Crockett—the magnitude not lost on such a young mind. By eleven, I was asking the front desk clerk why the hotel we were staying in was called The Blockade Runner, enthralled with the story I was told about the naval blockade of the Southern \orts during the American Civil War.

Even now, into my 30's, I find myself entranced by the stories of men who fought against each other more than 150 years ago—men whose bravery and patriotism changed the course of American history.

I often joke that I am with "my people" when working at a battlefield.

Few understand the drive and passion I feel for our country's story. My friends will laugh and say, "Well, there she goes again," when I launch into a tale about one of my favorite battles in the middle of a conversation. I got that same feeling with Vicksburg as soon as I arrived. I was with "my people." I was surrounded by my passion. I was home.

Historians, specifically those in the field of public history, thrive on the interactions between faculty and guests and on the presentation of history to eager minds. That personal interaction was impossible with the park closed to prevent the spread of COVID-19.

The closure produced much frustration for the staff at Vicksburg, but it gave us the unique opportunity to reset, refresh, and connect with history on a more personal level. As a historical interpreter, it is my job to help others form connections with the past. But it is easy to focus on someone else and lose track of the connection we ourselves feel.

Still, working at Vicksburg had always been a dream of mine. So, regardless of the coronavirus pandemic, I was eager to take in all the park had to offer. I spent my first day exploring the park with my fellow seasonals and had lunch near the USS *Cairo*. It was my first time seeing the massive vessel in person.

The USS *Cairo* was one of seven "city-class" ironclad warships built at the beginning of the Civil War. The *Cairo*, named after the city in Illinois, was built specifically to help the Union secure control of major waterways, thus facilitating the movement of troops and supplies while preventing the Rebels from doing the same.

The USS *Cairo* first saw action in May 1862 at Plum Point, but is famous for what happened during the following month: the capture of the Confederate garrison of Fort Pillow on the Mississippi River, which allowed Union troops to occupy Memphis.

Unfortunately she met her demise just six months later on the Yazoo River. The date was December 12, and the *Cario* was part of a small flotilla making its way upriver north of Vicksburg. The primary objective was to destroy the Confederate batteries and clear the river of mines, known at the time as torpedoes.

Cairo's mission was part of the larger operation to capture Vicksburg. In November, Union Maj. Gen. Ulysses S. Grant began a southward advance from Grand Junction, Tennessee, into northern Mississippi. As suggested

The USS *Cairo* is a must-see attraction for any Civil War buff. Visitors can walk around the ship for an immsersive experience. *Chris Mackowski*

by Maj. Gen. William T. Sherman to Navy Admiral David Porter, a thrust up the Yazoo and Yalobusha rivers toward Grenada would greatly assist Grant's endeavor while at the same time putting Confederate Gen. John Pemberton in a tricky situation.

So it was that on December 12 the flotilla was making its way up the Yazoo River when Capt. Thomas O. Selfridge, Jr. directed *Cairo* to assist the USS *Marmora,* which had paused to look for mines. Shots were fired from the Confederate battery atop Drumgould's Bluff and the USS *Cairo* returned fire, unaware of the real threat ahead.

Cairo sank to the bottom of the Yazoo in just twelve minutes after she collided with two mines in the river, making her the first warship in US history to be sunk by an electronically-detonated torpedo. Aid was provided to all souls onboard, but the boat itself would lie alone at the bottom of the river for the next 102 years.

In 1956, three historians set out to locate the USS *Cairo*: Edwin

Bearss, Don Jacks, and Warren Grabau. Though it would take nine years from the date of their discovery for the vessel to be lifted out of the river, it is due to the preservation efforts of these three men that *Cairo* sits where she does today.[1]

Cairo was returned to Vicksburg in June 1977 after Congress approved legislation allowing the National Park Service to restore the ironclad and put her on display at the park. *It had been a long time coming, but the USS Cairo was finally home.*

At this point the reader may assume that I have launched into one of my stories and lost track of my original subject, COVID-19. The connection between this story and the pandemic is the *Cairo* itself, which brought me peace this summer as I struggled to understand my role at Vicksburg without guests.

Each morning at Vicksburg I would stand on my front porch and gaze at the magnificent vessel. The year 2020 was anything but normal. And 1862 wasn't normal, either. During both years, Americans were faced with fear, anxiety and unprecedented hardship. When I look at the USS *Cairo*, I can't help but hope that the people living in 1862 had a similar space that brought them peace.

As I mentioned earlier, there are times when historians lose sight of their personal connections with history. My summer at Vicksburg—though not what I had anticipated—gave me the opportunity to reconnect with the past. Every time I laid eyes on that gunboat, it was as if I were holding Crockett's gun and waiting for the next part of the story.

---

1   E.C. Bearss, *Hardluck Ironclad* (Baton Rouge: Louisiana State University Press, 1966), 89-104.

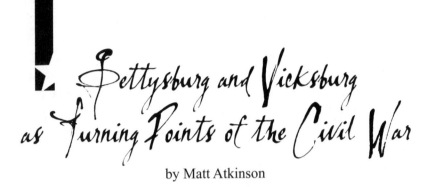

Gettysburg and Vicksburg as Turning Points of the Civil War

by Matt Atkinson

This is an edited transcript based on a presentation
from the 2018 Emerging Civil War Symposium at Stevenson Ridge,
delivered August 8. It subsequently aired on C-SPAN 3's
American History TV. You can watch the full program at
https://www.c-span.org/video/?449402-6/gettysburg-vicksburg-turning-points.

From Matt's introduction:

Matt Atkinson has an undergrad degree from the University of Mississippi and a master's degree from the University of Louisiana Monroe (to which Matt says, "We beat Alabama one time.") Matt has been a park ranger at Petersburg National Battlefield and has worked in Manassas, Vicksburg, and Gettysburg. He will tackle the elephant in the room about Gettysburg versus Vicksburg. Being a native Mississippian and having worked at both parks, which one of these two battles does he consider to be the biggest turning point, Gettysburg or Vicksburg? I will let Matt get up here and explain.

(applause)

Matt Atkinson:

I understand you all had a row last night about something. You had a list of the most important turning points—a "Top 10" turning points of the American Civil War—and Gettysburg was left off. Can you believe that?[1] I'm sure the speaker did not leave Gettysburg off unintentionally.

The real question, to me, is what is the most important battle to *Matt?* I think *that* would be the relevant question. The most important battle in the Civil War to Matt Atkinson is wherever Matt Atkinson happens to be working. (laughter) Thank you. Thank you very much. (applause)

I would also like to acknowledge the other elephant in the room. I tell people this at Gettysburg a lot. I caution them, if you go to other Civil War sites, don't go into a visitors' center and tell them that you have been to Gettysburg. Don't tell a park ranger that, because they don't want to hear that. They have heard that. I have worked at other sites, and I have heard it multiple times, sometimes multiple times in the *same day*. Multiple times.

Obviously this is an Emerging Civil War conference and so forth. We have a plethora—not bad for Mississippi public education right there, "a plethora"—of subjects back there [referring to the book sales tables in the back of the room] from which you can choose. Books, etc. What is the most important turning point? The list could go on and on. We can put Chickamauga up there. We can put Chancellorsville up there. We can put Spotsylvania up there.

You could really argue: what is the turning point? *Is* there a big turning point?

I am supposed to write a book about Vicksburg for the Emerging Civil War Series—and I sincerely thank the editor of ECW, Chris, for his patience with me on this book on Vicksburg, which is almost at 500 words if I remember correctly (laughter) maybe about 2,000. I don't know. If and when that book is ever published, which will obviously be the master work on Vicksburg, gee, right there, the problem is—let's stare this in the face—it is not going to sell.

---

1   To kick off the 2018 Emerging Civil War Symposium at Stevenson Ridge, themed "Turning Points of the Civil War," historian Bert Dunkerly offered his Top 10 Turning Points of the Civil War as a point of departure for conversation. He omitted Gettysburg from the list, which of course prompted lots of discussion and good-natured exasperation for the rest of the weekend. Bert's talk is available on C-SPAN 3: https://www.c-span.org/video/?449337-5/civil-war-turning-points-overview.

Why is it not going to sell? People do not buy the same number of books about subjects on the Western Theater like they do on the Eastern Theater. If I can slap something on there like "Vicksburg: The Gettysburg of the West," I would sell 10,000 more copies about it. (laughter)

I hate to let the elephant out of the room, but I don't think the question is which is more important, "Gettysburg or Vicksburg?" I think the relevant question is, *why* is Gettysburg bigger than Vicksburg? Why is that? Is anybody really going to debate that with me? In the American psyche, I don't think there's any question that Gettysburg is bigger than Vicksburg. Why is that? That is something I don't know if I will be able to answer today, but we will try.

First things first: a quick overview of both campaigns.

The Gettysburg campaign really does not need any introduction. It is the culmination of all of Robert E. Lee's battles. According to Lee, if you're going to win the war through military means, you probably have to win a decisive battle on Virginia soil or have a victory on Northern soil. Robert E. Lee knows he can keep whipping the Yankees—and I use that word still here in Virginia—time and time again, but what does it solve? None of those battles are decisive, so what does it accomplish?

After the battle of Chancellorsville in May of 1863, Robert E. Lee is going to get an opportunity. He has the initiative, and he is going to use that opportunity to invade the North. Basically he swings to the west and uses the mountain ranges as cover, and it is a perfect conduit into the North. Once he gets into Pennsylvania, he splits his forces up. The Union army starts to dovetail kind of behind him, but they are not exactly flush with him as he comes up.

On the night of June 28, everything changes for him in Chambersburg. A scout—or spy, if you will—comes in and drops a bomb on Robert E. Lee: "Hey, the Union Army is not in Virginia. It is actually in Maryland. As the crow flies, it is not that far away from you."

What most people miss is that the scout tells Lee that the Union army is not moving north, it's moving west. So everything is based off that false intelligence. Right there, Robert E. Lee believes the Union army is moving behind him, not towards him. So Lee calls a junction of his forces at Gettysburg to keep the Union army on the eastern side, or the Washington side, of the mountains.

Then we have the first day of the battle of Gettysburg, ladies and gentlemen, and that first day ends up as a Confederate victory. But I think it is the worst thing that could have possibly happened to Robert E. Lee. Why is that? Because Robert E. Lee wins the first day, and it sets up the next two. If he lost the first day, he might have gotten away from it. But he wins, and when you are winning—I don't know if you've ever pulled a slot machine—when you are winning, it is fun. (laughter) When it is not, it is not.

Anyway, Confederates chased the Union forces back through town, and Robert E. Lee renews the offensive the next day—the second day. He ends up attacking the south end of the Union line at places like Little Round Top, Devil's Den, Peach Orchard—places that you all have heard about, written into American history. He comes *this* close, really. A couple breaks here or there, like a football game, he might have had a little bit more success. But the Union army is fighting hard—harder than the Confederates estimated they would. Basically, the Union army holds on.

On the third day—it is fourth down and one, with two seconds left on the clock—and Robert E. Lee decides to punch it up the gut. We all know how that worked out. That's Pickett's Charge.

But Pickett's Charge has captured the American imagination. When I talk about the overall subject of Gettysburg versus Vicksburg, obviously Vicksburg does not have a Pickett's Charge. If you like, if this is the proper word for it, Pickett's Charge embodies the "romance of war." After all, how much grander does it get than Pickett's Charge? I can't tell you how many times, as a boy in Mississippi, in my parents' pasture, how many times I walked across the terrain with my little toy musket and Rebel flag that the Ole Miss cheerleaders gave me and I was reenacting Pickett's Charge. That's what captured my imagination. It was the seminal moment. I had not even read William Faulkner's *Intruder in the Dust* yet. (laughter)

An excerpt from Faulker's novel captures that moment:

> For every Southern boy fourteen years old, not once but whenever he wants it, there is the instant when it's still not yet two o'clock on that July afternoon in 1863, the brigades are in position behind the rail fence, the guns are laid and ready in the woods and the furled flags are already loosened to break out and Pickett himself with his long oiled ringlets and his hat in one hand probably and

his sword in the other looking up the hill waiting for Longstreet
to give the word and it's all in the balance, it hasn't happened
yet, it hasn't even begun yet, it not only hasn't begun yet but
there is still time for it not to begin against that position and those
circumstances which made more men than Garnett and Kemper
and Armistead and Wilcox look grave yet it's going to begin,
we all know that, we have come too far with too much at stake
and that moment doesn't need even a fourteen-year-old boy to
think This time. Maybe this time with all this much to lose and
all this much to gain: Pennsylvania, Maryland, the world, the
golden dome of Washington itself to crown with desperate and
unbelievable victory the desperate gamble, the cast made two
years ago. . . .

But Pickett's Charge ends in defeat. It is a huge debacle, a bad mistake,
and it really can't be justified. I can offer you a whole hour's worth of
excuses on why he did it, but I can't really justify it in the end. Robert E.
Lee, if he ran out of options, would hit you head on. Think of the Seven
Days campaign. Think of the Wilderness. Look at the pattern with Robert E.
Lee. He will hit you head on if he runs out of options. That is Robert E. Lee.

After that defeat, the Union army pursues the Confederate army. Here
is one of the great What Ifs of the war; I wish I had more time to spend
on it: the Union army has a chance to bottle up Lee's army next to the
Potomac River at a place called Williamsport, Maryland. Think about that.
George Meade has just won the battle of Gettysburg. The man was placed
in command on June 28, three days before the battle—three!—then he goes
up against Lee. And he wins.

George Meade, I think he is exhausted, and he is trying to shoo those
old Rebs across the river. He is happy to see Lee go if he will go. Meade has
an opportunity to win the war right here should he attack, but for now, he is
happy just to see Lee go.

Lincoln was furious. Why? Because he had been telling Meade, "Destroy
them. Destroy them. End the war right here." When Lincoln finds out that
Meade has allowed Lee to escape, he writes him a letter and he is furious.
When Lincoln is assassinated a couple years later, that letter is found in his
desk. Lincoln wrote on the outside of it something like "letter not sent." I

have remembered that. One thing Lincoln has taught me right here is that I cannot tell you how many times I have written an email and waited—try it yourself—and waited 24 hours before I sent it. Most of the time, I do not send it. That is what Abraham Lincoln taught me.

Now, what about General Meade? General Meade is very happy with the campaign. He thinks it is a brilliant success. He would write in his official report about the defeat of the enemy at Gettysburg and Lee's compulsory evacuation of Pennsylvania, Maryland, and withdrawal from the upper valley of Shenandoah after losing three guns, 41 standards, and more than 13,000 prisoners. Federals collected 24,978 small arms on the battlefield. Meade finds it all to be a rounding, rounding success. Lincoln doesn't feel that way.

There is a whole lot of color in between here and Grant coming to the east and so forth. Suffice to say, I do believe Meade's failure to attack at Williamsport is the start of his demise. You can add in Bristoe Station.

Now we are flipping away 850 miles. I can tell you the mileage because I drove it last week, all the way down to Houston, Mississippi. I got within five miles of my parents' house, with two girls screaming in the back and one boy that is tired, and I am doing 79 miles an hour down the highway, and at the top of the hill, there greeting me was the Mississippi Highway Patrol. (laughter) I got pulled over and I said to him, "You know, I made a detour to Montgomery. I went to see Hank Williams's Cadillac. I have been telling my girls, my little three-year-olds, about Hank Williams and how they know the story of how he drank too much beer and died in the back of that Cadillac. So we went by the grave and everything." I am trying to get out of this ticket, so I reach inside my pocket and I pull out this Hank Williams Museum ticket, and I hand it to him. He goes, "What is this for?" He has the flat hat on and everything, and he is leaning over the window. I'm like, "I'm just saying, I have been to Hank Williams Museum." He goes, "I will be right back." I go, "That is the best excuse you've heard all day." (laughter). It did not work. If you would like to see the ticket from the museum, it is in my car. (laughter)

In a nutshell, Vicksburg, Mississippi, becomes the last Confederate stronghold—with a small shout-out to Port Hudson, Louisiana, which is *really* the last Confederate stronghold on the Mississippi River. Both commanders-in-chief, Jefferson Davis and Abraham Lincoln, put a high priority on Vicksburg. You've got to remember that Vicksburg is Davis's backyard. This is the hometown, folks. He is very familiar with it. He referred to it as the nail head that held the South together. Abraham Lincoln said, "See what a lot of land these fellows hold, of which Vicksburg is the key. The war can never be brought to a close until that key is in our pocket."

There are a lot of failed attempts to take Vicksburg. In fact, my master's thesis was on the battle of Chickasaw Bayou, which was one of the failed attempts. If I ever get around to it, I will publish that one time. My mother has a copy. (laughter) She thinks I ought to name the book "Dead Yankees in a Swamp." (laughter)

Here is the campaign of Vicksburg. General Grant actually starts on the Louisiana side. His ultimate objective is to get to high and dry ground behind Vicksburg. How do you do that? The Mississippi River is to the west of Vicksburg, and the Big Black River is to the south and east. And then you have the Yazoo River to the north. That is a huge problem for Grant to overcome.

What he ends up doing is he has the Union gunboats run past the city from the north, and his army marches down the Louisiana side and rendezvous with the fleet. They cross over the Mississippi River in what is the largest amphibious landing of U. S. forces until North Africa in World War II. He ends up fighting five battles, the first one at Port Gibson. A couple weeks later, he fights at Raymond, then the battle of Jackson. Raymond, by the way, is the only battlefield in the country that has a cannon for every gun that was historically on the battlefield.

What is Grant's ultimate objective? It is to cut the railroad between Jackson and Vicksburg. It does not really matter where he breaks it, so he breaks it at Clinton on May 13 and Jackson on May 14, and then marches towards the west. He ends up meeting the Confederate garrison at a place called Champion Hill. It is a battle that is roughly around 60,000 men. It goes back and forth all day, with General Grant's career tottering with it, and it ends up being a decisive Union victory. They drive the Confederates back. It is nothing but a matter of time from there.

The Confederates fight a rearguard action, and then Confederate commander John Pemberton, in all of his infinite wisdom, gets himself bottled up inside the city. After that, it boils down to a siege, which I think is very interesting within its own right. You are talking about a Union field army having to convert themselves into engineers. When the siege starts, within his army of 42,000 men, Grant has three engineers. These farm boys from Illinois and Indiana and all of the rest out there have to learn how to be engineers.

They do a darn good job. They start thirteen approaches toward the Confederate works and, as Grant would say in his memoirs, they would out-camp the enemy for 47 days. That would end up resulting in the surrender of the city. With that comes 29,500 Confederate soldiers who will be stacking arms out there. An entire Confederate army is taken off the board. In addition, the Federals find themselves in possession of 172 pieces of artillery, 38,000 artillery projectiles, 58,000 pounds of black powder, and 4,800 artillery cartridges. In addition, I might add that they got 50,000 small arms along with 600,000 rounds of ammunition and 350,000 percussion caps. Quite a haul, to say the least. Compare that to the numbers Meade bragged about.

So, that's the quick overview. Now, "Gettysburg/Vicksburg," which is more important? How are you going to wrestle with this question? How do you wrap your arms around a subject that is basically subjective?

A couple of quotes for you. New York City diarist George Templeton Strong would write on July 5 and 6—it was a memorable day in his diary: "Glorious news proved to be half true. Tidings from Gettysburg have been arriving in fragmentary installments with a steady crescendo towards complete, overwhelming victory. July 6. The results of this victory are priceless. The charm of Robert Lee's invincibility is broken. The Army of the Potomac has at last found a general that can handle it and has stood up nobly to the terrible work in spite of its list of hard-fought failures."

On the Confederate side, John B. Jones—and, I might add, in the fifth grade, I actually slogged my way through his entire diary. Yes. And I look back on that, and I wonder why I haven't read that again. From Jones: "July 8. we have sad tidings from the west. General Johnston telegraphs from Jackson, Mississippi, that Vicksburg capitulated on the fourth instant. This is a terrible blow. And it produced much despondency. If Lee falls back again, it will be darkest day for the Confederacy that we have seen yet." Jones, in Richmond, is learning about Vicksburg before Richmonders learn about Gettysburg. Interesting, isn't it, how information travels?

Henry Adams would write to his father, who is the minister to Great

Britain: "July 23, 1863. The disasters of the rebels are unredeemed by even any hope of success. It is now conceded that all idea of intervention is at an end." Meaning foreign intervention.

Colonel Josiah Gorgas—most of you have never heard of him, but he was the chief of ordnance for the Confederacy. He made cannonballs down in Richmond. "July 28, 1863. Events succeeded one another with disastrous rapidity. One brief month ago, we were apparently at the point of success. Lee was in Pennsylvania threatening Harrisburg and even Philadelphia. Vicksburg seemed to laugh all of Grant's efforts to scorn. Port Hudson had beaten off Banks' forces. All looks bright. Now the picture is as somber as it was bright then. Lee fell at Gettysburg, and as we crossed the Potomac and resumed the position of two months ago, covering Richmond, Vicksburg and Port Hudson capitulated. It seems incredible that human power could affect such a change in so brief a space. Yesterday, we rode on the pinnacle of success. Today, absolute ruin seems to be our portion. The Confederacy totters to its destruction."

So when we get into this, when you get into "Gettysburg versus Vicksburg," how do you differentiate? It's impossible. Impossible.

I'm sure to the people of Illinois and Iowa, those farmers who could not get their produce down to New Orleans and out to the rest of the world—and who, by the way, were having the railroad jacking up the prices on them when they tried to ship it east—to them, I'm sure Vicksburg was a big deal. And I might add, the people from the west—from the western northern states—especially families, probably had a lot more vested in Vicksburg because that is where their boys were fighting at the time.

Gettysburg, on the other hand, is arguably going to save Washington, D.C. If Washington, D.C., falls, what is going to be the consequence of that? Or if Washington does not fall, what are the consequences of Confederate victory on northern soil?

So Vicksburg splits the Confederacy in two and opens up "the Father of Waters unvexed to the sea." It also brings to the forefront William T. Sherman, right? Grant's right-hand man. Grant is going to get promoted to the east. Sherman is going to get command in the west. And that is all basically related to Vicksburg, with a subsequent success in the Chattanooga area. That rolls it all up right there.

The question begs itself, talking about Sherman and Grant, could the war have been won without them? Can the North win the war without Sherman and Grant? That is an open-ended question for you to ponder. You note takers ought to be writing right now. (laughter)

Of the commanders—Sherman, Grant, and Meade—which ones are indispensable? It's a debatable question, but Grant obviously has to be up there.

Think about the battlefield parks and the veterans—what does it mean to them? There is a reason that the veterans choose the five original Civil War parks—Chickamauga-Chattanooga, Gettysburg, Shiloh, Vicksburg, and Antietam. When the veterans congregate after the war, they are going to get together at these original battlefields when they do that.

I would urge you to go through, ladies and gentlemen, and look at some of the more modern interpretation. It is all over the place. Name a book that covers both Gettysburg and Vicksburg at the same time. The author's viewpoint really depends on what subject he is writing about. Obviously, if he is writing about Gettysburg, he will feel that is more important. If he is writing about Vicksburg, he will feel *that* is more important.

Historian Edwin Coddington says, "In conclusion, these accomplishments were substantial, but in return, Lee paid an excessively high price in lives lost and the destruction of the myth of invincibility. Nor did he succeed in forcing the withdrawal of a single soldier from the siege of Vicksburg, which had been one of the major main reasons of the campaign. Although the real meaning of the victory of Gettysburg emerged only with the passage of time, its immediate effect was to give the Army of the Potomac a sense of triumph which grew into an imperishable faith in itself. The Confederates put forth their best efforts and best army, but they were not strong enough. The Army of the Potomac, weak as it was, finally lived up to its promise."

Historian Maj. Gen. J. F. C. Fuller, writing about Vicksburg, is going to say "the drums of Champion Hill sounded the doom of Richmond." Bruce Catton, who I have recently rediscovered—I have fallen in love again with Catton. He does not get the credit he is due. He is a fantastic writer—he said at the end of *Grant Moves South*, after Vicksburg: "Grant was ready at last, the time of testing was over and he had reached his full stature. Better than any other northern soldier, better than any other man save Lincoln himself, he understood the necessity for bringing the infinite power of the growing nation to bear on the desperate weakness of the grave and tragically archaic little nation that opposed it. He understood, too, that although rebellion must be crushed with the utmost rigor, the Rebels themselves were men who would again be friends and fellow citizens. Now, it was time to go on. Sherman had said it. Sling the knapsacks for new fields."

I did a little research—we like to use the word "research" in the business—I did a little research on Google. I wanted to see how many hits I would get when I put in the word "Gettysburg," and I wanted to see how many hits I would get when I put in the word "Vicksburg." I filtered it by books. What I came up with, approximately: I got 7,000 hits on "Gettysburg." I got 1,000 hits on "Vicksburg." Yeah. That's what I'm saying.

Why is that *that* much bigger? Why is Gettysburg overshadowing Vicksburg?

I would like to leave you with one last rhetorical question, as far as the Gettysburg and Vicksburg debate. What if we looked at this in a completely different way? Why don't we quit looking at it from the lens of victories for the Union and why don't we look at it through a different lens. This gets hypothetical but nevertheless: what would have happened if those Union forces would have been defeated? What would be the repercussions from that? If you look at that question of Gettysburg versus Vicksburg in a reverse form, you might possibly come up with a better idea of why it was important that both Union armies won in the first place.

I know everybody's waiting with bated breath on me to pronounce which one is more important. I have to say that, in the immediate aftermath—and this is my opinion—if Gettysburg had been a defeat, that would have been highly more problematic for the North than Vicksburg would have been. I don't think I am going too far out on a limb on that.

However, I would also like to say, for Vicksburg, if General Grant is defeated outside of Vicksburg—of course I can't say this with one hundred percent accuracy—we may not see Lee versus Grant in 1864. General Grant may very well have been sacked. Going back to one of my earlier questions, could the war have been won without Grant, William T. Sherman and the rest of the Union high command that ends up winning it? That question is for you to ponder.

In the end, ladies and gentlemen, maybe the reason Gettysburg is so big in the American psyche has to do with someone else entirely. What if Abraham Lincoln had gone to Vicksburg instead?

Thank you all very much. I appreciate it. (applause) Thank you. Thank you very much.

Questions from the audience:

Q: We talk about Gettysburg and Vicksburg. Didn't John Bachelder have a lot to do with Gettysburg's popularity and his dedication to bringing that to bear?

A: John Bachelder is the first historian of the battle of Gettysburg. Out of the five original parks, I can't name the original five historians, but every park had someone who came up and took an interest in it. Bachelder was the first. He got to Gettysburg in 1863 before there was any thought of a park. He started researching. We have the Bachelder papers. Vicksburg had a guy named William Rigby. He corresponded with the veterans. Antietam had a gentleman of its own. So on and so forth. These people paved the path.

The question was, did John Bachelder pave the way for Gettysburg to becoming so important? In a way he did, he definitely facilitated to a greater extent our understanding of the battle because he is already corresponding during the war with these Union generals. I hate to say I believe some of that correspondence was lost in a fire. I would love to have that if I had a time machine.

But nevertheless, I think what really helps Gettysburg besides the geographical location—and you can say this over Vicksburg, you can say this over the battlefields around Fredericksburg, etc.—Gettysburg is fought in an area that is left unmolested immediately after the battle. In other words, these families, these historians, these people that want to see the battlefield, they can come to Gettysburg, Pennsylvania, and not have to worry about Confederate cavalry jumping into the town. It is not an active combat area. I think that helps get Gettysburg rolling—and, of course, that Bachelder guy.

Q: Elisha Hunt Rhodes of the 2nd Rhode Island mentions in his diary "glorious day" right after the battle. He talks about Gettysburg and Vicksburg together. He's at Gettysburg, but he's referring to events that happened in the west. How did he hear so soon?

A: As far as information traveling fast, it's a hard thing to say. It kind of pieces out in the news, depending on where you are. People in New York will hear about Gettysburg before they do Vicksburg. But you might argue that people in Chicago might hear about Vicksburg before they do Gettysburg. Especially in the rural areas when you get out there, it is really weird how it disseminates. I have some letters from my ancestor who was going to Ole Miss in 1861. It is like two or three weeks after the firing at Fort Sumter. They still had not heard the news. They heard they were firing over there, but two weeks later, there was no news to reach Oxford, Mississippi. It is weird, but it is caught in the moment: he is writing his parents saying, "I wonder what is happening over there."

Q: Matt, is there any way that Grant could have realistically helped in Pennsylvania with his troops once it was known that Lee was in Pennsylvania? It seems like that is a long distance to pull a whole bunch of men.

A: Well, the debate was whether to pull them out. I agree with you, it is not realistic to get the Union army all the way from Mississippi, all the way up to the north. It is not what you asked, but let me give you one example. When the Confederates surrendered at Vicksburg, I said they surrendered close to 30,000 men. Admiral David Porter came to Grant and said, "I could get them up north, but it is going to take a long time." If you think about it, that is a lot of men. By the time the Vicksburg campaign is over, Grant probably has, with reinforcements, close to 75,000 men. You think about moving the components of it. Any realistic Union reinforcements probably would come from the middle of Tennessee or Kentucky or something like that.

FOLLOWING SPREAD: The Tullahoma Campaign of 1863 began on the banks of Stones River at Murfreesboro, Tennessee. To start the year, the Federal Army of the Cumberland dealt a battlefield defeat to the Confederate Army of Tennessee, which withdrew to the south, allowing the Federals to enacamp outside of the town for the winter and turn it into the launchpad for their summer advance toward Chattanooga. *Chris Heisey*

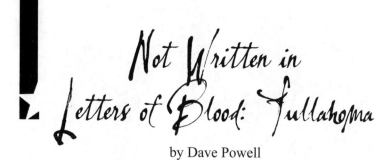

Not Written in Letters of Blood: Tullahoma

by Dave Powell

Adapted from blog posts originally published at Emerging Civil War on July 8, 2016, and September 25, 2020

Edwin M. Stanton to Major General William S. Rosecrans, July 7, 1863:

> We have just received official information that Vicksburg surrendered to General Grant on the 4th of July. Lee's army overthrown; Grant victorious. You and your noble army now have the chance to give the finishing blow to the rebellion. Will you neglect the chance?[1]

Upon reading this dispatch in his newly established headquarters at Tullahoma, Tennessee, Rosecrans must have been stunned. Certainly he was angered.

The Army of the Cumberland had just concluded its own arduous operation; an extended turning movement aimed at outflanking Gen. Braxton Bragg's Confederate Army of Tennessee from a line of hills south

---

1 United States War Department, *The War of the Rebellion: A Compilation of the Official Records of the Union and Confederate Armies,* 70 vols. in 128 parts (Washington D.C.: Government Printing Office, 1880-1901), Series I, volume 23, part 2, p. 518 (hereafter cited as *O.R.,* I, 23, pt. 2, 518).

of Nashville, where Bragg's men had been since the retreat from Stones River, 6 months before. This movement did not result in a climactic battle, like the one in Pennsylvania; nor did it result in the capture of an entire Rebel army, like Vicksburg.

Stanton's subtext was clear: "What have you done for me lately?"

On the heels of Rosecrans's victory at Stones River, the administration's gratitude flowed down the telegraph wires in virtual torrents. Over the spring and summer, that tone changed. Carping and complaint ruled the day. Lincoln and Stanton needed action; Rosecrans preferred meticulous preparation.

Unquestionably, Rosecrans erred on the side of caution that spring. In early June, when Bragg's army was being depleted in order to reinforce the Rebels confronting Grant in Mississippi, Rosecrans first denied those troop movements were occurring, and then suggested that it would be better for his army to wait and see the outcome of Grant's campaign; if his army should be defeated, then only Rosecrans's Army of the Cumberland would be left to redress the balance.

This was a flawed strategy—a poorly thought-out argument coming from a man who usually had a firm grasp of military affairs.

Which is why Rosecrans commenced his long-awaited—and long prepared-for—advance barely three weeks later, on June 24.

Bragg's army was stretched across a front of about 30 miles, with cavalry on each flank; his infantry deployed at Shelbyville, Wartrace, and the hamlet of Beech Grove. Bragg's supply depot lay at Tullahoma. Guy's Gap, Liberty Gap, and Hoover's Gap lay between Rosecrans and his opponent; narrow defiles which, if stoutly defended, offered Rosecrans only the prospect of bloody frontal assaults.

So Rosecrans opted for a different approach. By feinting against the gaps while flanking Bragg to the east, Rosecrans intended to march a corps unopposed first into Manchester and then on to Tullahoma. Capturing that place would not only cripple Bragg's logistics, but it would also potentially cut Bragg's best retreat route.

The strategy worked. By June 27, the Union XXI Corps entered Manchester. But strategy, no matter how carefully planned, could not overcome the vagaries of weather. Drenching rains slowed both armies' movements, but with Bragg moving on the chord while Rosecrans maneuvered on the rim of the circle, Bragg escaped the trap. Bragg retreated to Tullahoma before Rosecrans could seize the place. Subsequently, Bragg retreated out of middle Tennessee entirely, falling back to Chattanooga rather than risk battle.

Rosecrans was elated. Yes, Bragg had escaped, but some of the most difficult terrain ahead was now in Union hands with barely a shot fired, and Rosecrans could embark on the planning for his next objective, Chattanooga. Losses were light. Rosecrans suffered a total of 570 casualties. Confederate losses were never fully articulated, but the Yankees reported the capture of 1600 prisoners, with at least 300 known combat losses.

Not that Tullahoma was without its moments. There were sharp fights at Hoover's and Liberty Gaps, a sizeable cavalry engagement at Shelbyville, and a number of smaller actions usually waged for control of various river crossings. One such scrap occurred on July 2, 1863, on the banks of the Elk River—which produced at least seven awards of the Medal of Honor, all to men of the 104th Illinois Infantry. This is an impressive number, given the size of the fight. On the same day at Gettysburg, amid the largest battle of the war, only 22 such medals were awarded.

It is not surprising, all things considered, that Rosecrans felt slighted when he read Stanton's telegram and the implied rebuke. Rosecrans's reply speaks volumes:

> You do not appear to observe the fact that this noble army has driven the rebels from Middle Tennessee, of which my dispatches advised you. I beg on behalf of this army that the War Department may not overlook so great an event because it is not written in letters of blood.[2]

---

2   Ibid.

The 1863 Tullahoma Campaign

by Chris Kolakowski

*This is an edited transcript based on a presentation
from the 2019 Emerging Civil War Symposium at Stevenson Ridge,
delivered August 3. It subsequently aired on C-SPAN 3's*
American History TV. *You can watch the full program here:
https://www.c-span.org/video/?463239-2/1863-tullahoma-campaign.*

From Chris's Introduction:

Chris Kolakowski, Emerging Civil War's chief historian, is the author of two books published by the History Press, *The Civil War at Perryville: Battling for the Bluegrass* and *The Stones River and the Tullahoma Campaigns: This Army Does not Retreat.*

Chris Kolakowski:

I see you all have drunk your coffee this morning, judging by the energy by which you respond to me. That's good news. It's great to be here.

How many people have ever been to Tullahoma, Tennessee? (a number of hands go up) That's actually a lot more than I thought. How many of the rest of you knew, before you saw it in the program, that there was a place called Tullahoma, Tennessee? (more hands go up) Well, that's also really, really good. There must be a bunch of Air Force people in here.[1]

I want you to see if you can name this operation. It occurred in late June

---

1 Arnold Air Force Base is located in Tullahoma. They do a lot of scientific testing. It was the old Camp Forrest from the 1943 MA maneuvers.

and early July of 1863. It drove a major Confederate army back in defeat and secured a major geographic area for the United States. Are there any guesses in the room—and that's a rhetorical question because I know, in this audience, I will get many. I am, of course, referring to the Tullahoma campaign of 1863, June 24 to July 4. It is part of what turns out to be a very eventful series of weeks for both sides in the Civil War. In many ways, it gets overshadowed, and I will touch on that a little bit later in the conversation.

The Tullahoma campaign was fought between the Army of the Cumberland under Maj. Gen. William Starke Rosecrans's 70,000 men and 45,000 men of the Army of Tennessee under the command of Gen. Braxton Bragg. Rosecrans will take the cavalry into the operation under Gordon Granger, along with George Thomas's XIV Corps, Alexander McCook's XX Corps, and Thomas Crittenden's XXI Corps. Bragg, for his part, has two infantry corps under Leonidas Polk and William J. Hardee, plus cavalry under Joe Wheeler and some other detachments. Some very prominent people here. A lot of them are familiar with each other. In many ways, this is the second round in the series of battles between Rosecrans and Bragg in middle Tennessee, southeastern Tennessee and northern Georgia from the late fall of 1862 and all the way through the fall of 1863. I think everybody views the battles between Bragg and Rosecrans through the prism of Chickamauga and focuses on that, and it tends to overshadow everything that they go through. But in reality, the two rounds before that, Stones River and Tullahoma, deserve far more attention.

To understand the story of Tullahoma, we have to understand the context in which it's fought and the continuum in which it's fought. A lot of times when you look at campaign histories, oh, it starts this day and ends this day, but you often forget that what has gone before sometimes overshadows and influences what is coming. So having said that, let me now explain the context of Tullahoma because in many ways to understand, particularly Bragg's army, you've got to understand that context. So let me rewind from July of 1863 back to January 5, 1863, when Bragg leaves Stones River and the area of Murfreesboro, Tennessee.

After the three-day battle there on December 31 through January 2, the Yankees have more reinforcements coming in, and Bragg has to withdraw southeast about 15 miles or so to the area of the Highland Rim, which is high ground between Murfreesboro and Tullahoma. They will camp there

William Rosecrans (left) is one of the most over-looked—and perhaps under-appreciated—Union army commanders. Braxton Bragg (right), meanwhile, is perhaps the most vilified Confederate army commander, in the same "easy-to-take-potshots-at" league as Union general George McClellan. *LOC LOC*

and spend time in middle Tennessee until the whole operation begins in June of 1863. Almost immediately, the Confederate press goes after General Bragg. On New Year's Eve, Bragg had confidently predicted victory and said "We have driven the Federals everywhere except on the extreme left" and implied that Rosecrans was finished. We had this great victory and Bragg is retreating. Why is that, especially when the armies in Mississippi and Virginia won great victories and are holding their ground if not advancing?[2] And so newspaper reports and editorials began to come out about General Bragg and impugning the performance of the Army of Tennessee. And that causes Bragg to plant ill seeds that will bear ill fruit.

On January 11, against the advice of his staff, he sent a message to his corps commanders: if you advise me to retreat, please publicly say so. Put it in writing. We had a conference about it, you told me about it, so put it

2 Chickasaw Bayou in Mississippi (Dec. 26-29) and Fredericksburg in Virginia (Dec. 11-13).

in writing and let us stand together against opprobrium coming from the press. That's a close paraphrase. He also said something else: if I have lost the confidence of my generals, I will retire without a murmur. Talk to your brigade commanders, as well, and get their opinions before responding.

I don't care who you are and what organization you're with, if you are a CEO and you put yourself in front of your subordinates, even if you win that vote of confidence, you can't command that same respect. This is a capital error on the part of Braxton Bragg.

The replies are very quick in coming. Polk is on leave. He has a couple of lawyers in his corps. They take a look at this and say, "Is Bragg really asking us two questions or asking one?" They wait until late January to get back. Other commanders get back and say, "Yes, we advise retreat. We're happy to say that. By the way, we think a change in the command of this army is necessary." Polk gets back at the end of January and writes

Known as "the fighting bishop" because he was a West Point-trained man of the cloth, Lt. Gen. Leonidas Polk lived up to his nickname mostly by fighting with his superior. *LOC*

back to Bragg, "Is there one request or two?" Bragg: "I only meant one question in there." He tries to shut it down.

Polk decides it's a good idea to write to President Davis. He packages all of this correspondence, which he provides copies of, and sends a message to Davis, saying, "We didn't give our response about the fitness of the command of the army, but our opinions coincide with those of the other corps." And when Davis gets this, he is angry. It's like, "What is this?" And he wonders, "Why Bragg would submit himself to that tribunal is beyond me."

He decides to send Joe Johnston, Confederate commander of the

Western Theater: "Go to Tullahoma and figure out what the heck is going on." In early February, Johnston goes to Tullahoma, and he talks to the commanders. Bragg wanted to be relieved at this point, but he doesn't force the issue by resigning. What Johnston finds is that the morale among rank and file is pretty good. They feel good about going against the dastardly Yankees. But he also figures out some people are just putting on a pretty good face. Even though Bragg may be a cantankerous codger, they have to show a good face to Johnston.

So Johnston writes a report and disappears. You think it's smoothed over, right? Now is the time for the paperwork and battle reports for the battle just concluded. Now it's time to refight the Stone River Campaign. How many of you have looked at the official records of the Stones River campaign? (only a few hands go up) They're interesting for two reasons. Several of the officers allow their feelings about the Emancipation Proclamation to show up in their description of the enemy. They start talking about the emancipationist fiends and a whole bunch of other horrible language that shows up about the enemy, which makes sense since these reports are written in February of 1863.[3]

For our purposes, the big thing to understand is Bragg, who gets all of these reports and then writes his own. He cannot resist the opportunity in his own report to start striking back at those people who were most against him in that referendum of sorts in January. He paints those people in the worst possible light, to the point—and I have seen this nowhere else in the official records—to the point where John Breckinridge of Kentucky writes his divisional report and Bragg writes an addendum and proceeds to use the polite equivalent of lying as much as he can to point out where Breckinridge was wrong and at fault, and he pins the whole failure of the battle on John Breckinridge. During the Kentucky campaign the year before, Bragg advised Jeff Davis in the fall of 1862, "We must leave the garden spot of Kentucky to its cupidity." That's how Bragg feels about the Bluegrass State and the officers from there. Breckinridge is from Lexington, which doesn't help matters.

Once again, this fissure in the high command has opened publicly. Jeff

---

3 Lincoln issued the final Emancipation Proclamation on January 1, 1863, while Bragg's and Rosecrans's armies were still in the middle of the battle of Stones River.

Davis at this point decides to act. He tells Johnston, "Go to Tullahoma, take command, and send Bragg to Richmond for consultation." But Johnston doesn't like to create the impression he is pulling down a brother officer so he can take the field command he really wants. When he shows up, he has a convenient excuse to not actually execute the order. Why? Mrs. Bragg is with the army, and she has drunk some bad water and is down with typhoid. She can't travel for a few weeks. So Johnston tells Davis that Mrs. Bragg can't travel, so Bragg himself can't travel to Richmond, and he is going to suspend the orders for the time being.

For the next six weeks, until April 1863, here is the situation in the Army of Tennessee headquarters in Tullahoma: You have Joe Johnston, supreme commander in the West, nominally in command because he is the senior officer, and Braxton Bragg, who is not relieved from the command—everyone knows he should be, but he is still there. Who is in charge? I don't think they ever figured it out.

Now, who is the one person who could referee all of this and cut that knot and solve the whole problem? Jefferson Davis. The fact that Jefferson Davis does not is a severe indictment of him as a commander-in-chief of the Confederacy. I call it in my book—and I do not withdraw the comment now—*dereliction of duty*.

Finally, when Mrs. Bragg is ready to travel, it's early April of 1863, getting on toward mid-April of 1863. The problem is now Joe Johnston. His Virginia wounds have flared up. He is unfit for field duty. When he *is* fit for field duty in late April, is anything else going on in the West that might demand his attention at this point? That's when Porter runs the batteries at Vicksburg, and it becomes clear that the Mississippi front is about to get really, really active, which, of course, it does with the Vicksburg campaign. And so Johnston is ordered away with elements of Bragg's army to go and counter that. That is, in part, the detachment that will be defeated at the battle of Jackson in May of 1863.

So where are we in the Army of Tennessee at this point? Is this a happy organization, ready to take the field, a good team of leaders? No—emphatically no. The wounds begin to heal over again once Johnston leaves and everyone realizes Bragg will be here and they have to work together and continue to work together. The wounds begin to heal, but a few weeks later, the scabs are ripped off again. I invite you at some point to go look at the

Kentucky campaign official records. You'll notice half of the reports were done in the fall of 1862. The other half were done in the spring of 1863, including Bragg's official report on the Kentucky campaign. It rips all those scabs back off again.

And at this point, Bragg—even though in 1862 he had no problem with Polk's decision to act on his own initiative and abandon the city of Bardstown—he's going to court-martial Polk.[4] He gathers all of the evidence, gets everything together, and at the last minute decides he's not going to court-martial General Polk. You have to laugh—it's all you can do—because it's a tragedy that so many men's lives will depend on the ability of this army's high command to function well, and you can see what's happening to it.

Do you know when the last actual correspondence relating to the Kentucky campaign was dated? June 20, 1863. So this is going on literally up to 96 hours before Rosecrans moves for the Tullahoma campaign. There is a report between Polk and Hardee dated May 1863, and Hardee tells Polk, "If you want to rip up the Kentucky campaign, now is the time to do it." In other words, the impending court-martial.

Polk writes back and says, "It's not the time to do that, but you're absolutely right that we need to watch Tullahoma as much as we watch Murfreesboro." Why is that important? Who is there? The Federal army, the enemy. The Army of the Cumberland. You have to watch them because they're going to advance at some point, and you're going to fight another battle with them. And who is in Tullahoma? Where is the Army of Tennessee headquarters? It's Tullahoma. So what Hardee and Polk are saying is that we have two enemies. We have an enemy in the front, but we have an enemy in the rear as well, our ostensible boss, Braxton Bragg. We will talk more about that as we get closer.

Over in Murfreesboro, all is not well with the forces there, either. Rosecrans doesn't move out in force. He will send cavalry and skirmishing parties here and there. Sometimes they get the better of the Confederates, other times they don't. They are in the area and won't move until June 1863.

---

4   Polk abandoned Bardstown on October 2 during the lead-up to the battle of Perryville, Kentucky, on October 8, 1862.

Rosecrans, striking his best Napoleon pose, addresses members of the 32nd Indiana in camp outside Murfreesboro. *LOC*

How does that look in Washington, by the way: the second-largest army in the Federal service doesn't move for practically six months? It does not look good, does it? Rosecrans gets in trouble with Washington.

A good manager can manage the people below them and above them. You have to manage your relationship with superiors. Rosecrans finds time to lecture the commanding general and the secretary of war about warfare. How does that go down, especially in the wake of what George McClellan did the year before?[5] Rosecrans did not have the animosity against Lincoln and Stanton that McClellan did, but there he was in 1863, still planning a campaign instead of moving.

I will say this: he does have a couple of points. The first point is that most of his cavalry needs remounts. They're not in very good shape. Most have just come back from prison, having been captured the previous year. And he has another problem, and this is something, when people consider the Army of the Cumberland, they neglect to point out: How far is the Army of the Potomac's line of communication at any point in its career? Fifty miles to Washington or to one of the river ports in eastern Virginia. How

---

5 McClellan had a notoriously prickly relationship with his superiors, whom he did not respect—and often let that contempt show.

about the army out in Mississippi? They can rely on the United States Navy going up and down the Mississippi River, right? Good, relatively short, secure lines of supply. What about the Army of the Cumberland?

The forward base is Nashville, which is 30 miles northwest of Murfreesboro. You can supply in through the Cumberland River, but it can be very fickle, shall we say. There are times, because of the shoals just downstream from the city of Nashville, you can't get steamers up. You have the option of the Louisville-Nashville Railroad, which parallels modern Interstate 65 and, at Nashville, picks up the Nashville and Chattanooga Railroad and is paralleled by modern Interstate 24. Basically, everything you are going to need is going to have to ride the rails on a single-track railroad.

Now, once you leave Louisville, between Louisville and Nashville, when you're in that 183-mile stretch, at best you are going through neutral territory. Even though Kentucky has voted to remain loyal to the United States, it is at best neutral territory. Morgan has made a career at this point of cutting that railroad. You know how much that railroad was fully operational? Seven months and twelve days. So for almost five full months of that twelve-month period, that railroad was not fully operational. And it's not just bridges; it's not just taking up rails. There is a 2,000-foot-long tunnel just north of the town of Gallatin, Tennessee, 30 miles north of Nashville that Morgan had blown up and burned and blocked and knocked out of commission for two months in the fall of 1862.

Whenever you think of the Army of the Cumberland, you must remember, why does Rosecrans operate in fits and starts? Why does he spend so much time building up supplies? It's the tenuous nature of his lifeline back to Nashville and back to Louisville. That's why his army always stops to fix the railroad and bring up supplies. It's not just rhetoric or an excuse. He needs it.

The other thing about that railroad is, what do you think that does to the army's supplies? During the winter of 1862, the army was down to three days of reserve supplies in their warehouses. This is an army not far away from starvation because of the railroad insecurity. Rosecrans is not going to move before he has good cavalry or sufficient supplies on hand, especially because he has Nathan Bedford Forrest to his south, to the west of Shelbyville, to the west of the Army of Tennessee. And who does Rosecrans have on the eastern flank? Who does he have over in the hills aiming back to his home state? John Hunt Morgan—two of the great raiders in the history of the Confederate cavalry. Joe Wheeler is not bad, either. I would be worried about my railroad, too. Wouldn't you?

One of the things that Rosecrans builds up is a huge base of supplies. You can visit part of it today, Fortress Rosecrans, part of Stones River National Battlefield. More importantly, when his troops leave Murfreesboro, they'll take eleven days of supplies with them. He is going forward, banking on a big reserve. He is going to ride on a very big cushion of supplies. I think this is very prudent on his part because he knows there is a pretty good chance he is going to lose railroad communications at some point.

Of course, what does this look like in Washington, particularly because of what happens in Mississippi in May of 1863—the Vicksburg campaign? And what happened in Virginia in May of 1863? The battle of Chancellorsville—the largest single engagement in North American recorded history up to that point, to be precise. Meanwhile, Rosecrans sits in Nashville and, by June of 1863, the War Department threatens him with relief: "Are you going to move anytime soon?" He writes back and says, "If 'now' means 'tomorrow,' no. But if it means in five days, yes." And that's good enough. That's good enough.

And so Rosecrans, looking for the right opportunity, looking for the right amount of supplies, looking for the right way to go, begins to cast his plans to go after General Bragg.

To understand the story I'm about to tell you, let's take a moment to review the geography of middle Tennessee, because to understand this, you have to understand the geography.

From Murfreesboro, it's about 25 miles straight south to Shelbyville. From Shelbyville to Tullahoma, it's another 18 miles southeast. From Tullahoma, you go down the rail line about eight miles to the key rail bridge at Estill Springs. Once you cross there, you go through Decherd, the major rail tunnel at Cowan, and climb up into the Cumberland Plateau. Then you reach the University Place, Sewanee, the home of the University of the South. The cornerstone had been laid and the war intervened. As a matter of fact, the cornerstone was laid in 1860 by General Polk, whom we have spent time with already in this presentation.

There are two big things you need to know about this ground. The first thing, the area between Shelbyville-Murfreesboro and the gaps, that is known as the Highland Rim. Those mountains extend anywhere from 500 to 900 feet up, and they're very steep. They can only be crossed by three gaps: Guy's Gap, Liberty Gap, and Hoover's Gap. There is one all-weather road that runs out of Murfreesboro, today's Route 41; it runs south through a gap down to Manchester and continues southeast toward Chattanooga. That's the ground that we're going to focus on. Bragg has deployed his army to cover the gaps with his infantry and extend his cavalry in several directions. Forrest and Wheeler will be west toward the Duck River and, in the northeast between Woodbury and McMinnville, will be Morgan—at least until June 20, 1863, when he embarks on a raid into Kentucky and disobeys orders and goes into Indiana and Ohio and will be captured. So, he'll disappear just before the campaign starts, and Rosecrans has been waiting for that.

Polk will be in and around Shelbyville, protecting Guy's Gap. Pat Cleburne's division of 8,000 men will hold Liberty Gap. Alexander P. Stewart's division of 6,000 men will hold Hoover's Gap. There is cavalry, being an alarm force in case the Federals decide to move out from Murfreesboro. The idea is to warn the infantry so they'll have time to move up into the gaps and stop the Federals. That's the basic plan Bragg's army has come up with.

This is Rosecrans's plan for the operation:

> Positive information from various sources concurred to show the enemy intended to fight us in his entrenchments at Shelbyville should we advance by that route and he would be in good position to retreat if beaten and retard our pursuit through winding roads which lead up into the Barrens and inflict severe loss towards the mountains of their base. I was determined to render useless their entrenchments and if possible secure their line of retreat by turning their right and moving on the railroad bridge across Elk River.[6]

Where's the railroad bridge across the Elk River? Allisona and Estill Springs. That is the key ground, the key point to the entire campaign—

---

6 United States War Department, *The War of the Rebellion: A Compilation of the Official Records of the Union and Confederate Armies,* 70 vols. in 128 parts (Washington D.C.: Government Printing Office, 1880-1901), Series I, volume 23, part 1, p. 404 (hereafter cited as *O.R.,* I, 23, pt. 1, 404).

Rosecrans's objective. And if he takes that and Bragg is still around Tullahoma or Shelbyville, Bragg's army will be in very, very deep trouble, because they will be cut off from Chattanooga. Rosecrans said that would compel a battle on the Federal's own ground or drive Confederates in a disadvantageous line of retreat.

"To accomplish this," Rosecrans continued, "it was necessary to make Bragg believe we would advance on him by the Shelbyville route and keep up the impression if possible until we reached Manchester with the main body of the army."

Let me translate that plan for you. Granger's Reserve Corps and David Stanley's Cavalry Corps—a grand total of 25,000 men all told—along with Alex McCook's XX Corps moving south of Murfreesboro, will operate in the area southwest of Murfreesboro and keep Polk thinking they'll try to force Guy's Gap and Liberty Gap. Meanwhile, the bulk of the army, George Thomas's XIV Corps, 25,000 men, and 20,000 men with Thomas L. Crittenden's XXI Corps, will march east of Murfreesboro and aim for Manchester, at which point they'll be in a good position to operate directly against Tullahoma or down toward the rail bridge across the Elk River.

What do you think of the plan? Good plan, isn't it? It's a good plan. One problem, though. Speed is the vital factor. It's been a really nice dry summer, but when these troops start marching out on the morning of June 24, 1863, it starts raining. Of the next seventeen days, it will rain at least once—and I'm not talking about a sprinkle, but a gully-washing thunderstorm—at least once on fourteen of those seventeen days. So what do you think these roads turn into? And by the way, when it's not raining, it's overcast, 90-something degrees with 100% humidity. This is miserable. For those of you familiar with the retreat from Gettysburg, the horrible rain they had to go through starting July 4. Well, some of that weather comes from middle Tennessee, washes over Rosecrans's men, and meets the other armies up in Pennsylvania later. This is atrocious weather and should always be remembered when you consider the Tullahoma Campaign.

In the early morning hours of June 24, the Army of Cumberland gets in motion. The decoy forces begin to move into their area and do their job.

OPPOSITE: TULLAHOMA CAMPAIGN—By feinting toward Shelbyville, the Federal forces tricked Confederates into shifting their attention in that direction while the Army of the Cumberland actually marched toward Manchester, outflanking the Confederate position, forcing the Army of Tennessee to fall back.

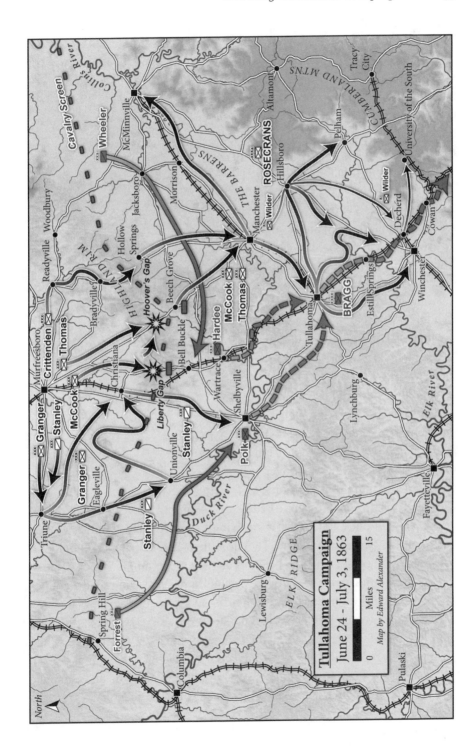

Tullahoma Campaign
June 24 - July 3, 1863

Miles
0   15

Map by Edward Alexander

They skirmish with Cleburne at Liberty Gap on 24th and 25th of June. The main elements of Thomas's corps begin to move southeast toward Hoover's Gap. In the front is a very special unit of mounted infantry— they don't want to be called cavalry—under the command of an intrepid 33-year-old Indiana colonel named John Wilder. Wilder had tried to chase Confederate cavalry with marching infantry and realized it wasn't going to work. He thought, "I want as many horses and mules as I can," and he fronted the money to give his men seven-shot Spencer rifles. And they have gone out and done very good work. Now they are in front. Of course, some of the real cavalry is like, "Oh, you're tadpole cavalry." That's the word they use: "tadpole cavalry." But they know what they're doing.

On this day Wilder wants to prove himself, and his men are out front as the rains start to come in. About seven miles out from Murfreesboro toward Hoover's Gap, they run into the 1st Kentucky

Col. John Wilder's mounted infantry, with their seven-shot repeating rifles, moved and fired as fast as lighting, earning themselves a flashy nickname: The Lightning Brigade. *LOC*

Cavalry. How do you think these Federals do charging forward with Spencers against spread-out Confederates with single-shot rifles? It's quickly over, and the Kentucky lines collapse. They lose their battle flag and begin to fall back under the pressure of the Federals as they move into Hoover's Gap.

As the Confederates try to make a stand right there, they send a courier riding as fast as he can back toward Fairfield to wake up Stewart's division and get them moving. Wilder realizes the situation, and he sends his vanguard unit, his 17th Indiana, into the attack. They scatter the Confederates and push into the gap itself. His orders only are to stop to take the foot of the gap and wait for the main body of the Federal infantry to come up and complete the assault. But Wilder realizes those trenches aren't occupied. "And if I

A memorial to the Confederate dead of Hoover's Gap stands in the Beech Grove Cemetery, located near the gap. *Brian Swartz*

wait," he thinks, "they might be occupied by people very unfriendly to me," so he orders his men into the gap and through the gap and actually takes position on a ridge on the other side, near a place called Jacob's Store. If you go there today, that's where the Confederate cemetery is and the battlefield pavilion they have right off I-24.

They take a position right there, and they will stay there all afternoon because they can hear the long roll in the distance, thanks to acoustics, of the Confederate infantry coming up. They will withstand several attacks by Confederate infantry that afternoon, and as one of the Illinoisans said in that brigade, they "went after it shooting." They inflict over 200 Confederate casualties and send most of the Confederates back. They would hold their own at three-to-one odds.

Thomas, when he gets up to the battlefield with the main body of the infantry, surveys what Wilder has done. For those of you who know George Thomas, he's not a demonstrative man, but comes over to Wilder, shakes his hand, pumps it, gushes, "You've saved me 20,000 men!" Thomas will consolidate there. And the next day, he publishes an order that says, because of their fast move and hard strike, this brigade, Wilder's brigade, shall ever after be known as the Lightning Brigade. This is where they get their famous name, which they will carry on to greater glory through the Georgia campaign of 1864.

Both sides expect Bragg to make a counter offensive. But Bragg doesn't, and Rosecrans decides to move towards Manchester on the morning of the 26th. The largest battle of the campaign is in and around Beech Grove, the Jacob's Store area, where Thomas's men will basically shove aside the Confederates, much like opening a hole in the line in football. Federals will push them south and begin to progress southeast and reach Manchester on the morning of June 27, where they finally find Crittenden's corps. Crittenden's boys have had to march up around Bradyville, up a slope. No joke. Forty-five degrees. There have been orders put out, decrease your wagon train, decrease your baggage as much as you possibly can. Tommy Wood, one of the division commanders, obeyed that order to the letter, but the guy in front, John Palmer, said, "No, I know better. We're taking everything. I don't know what's on the other side of the hills."

They are marching through roads that, no joke, are knee high with mud. One of the brigade commanders, William Hazen, would say, "Between marching through the fields and on the road, I didn't know where the road was because of the mud." What do you think happens to those wagons and artillery? Even on flat land, they start sinking. And so it takes them two days to get up that height. And how do they do it? You line up infantrymen on both sides of the wagon and then, with the teamsters using their animals as hard as they can, they run up to the hill and, as they falter, the infantry men come in, grab the wheels and push and begin to turn and crank them up. Literally crank them up the hill. It takes them two days to do that. One of the officers who had seen many fights on many battlefields would say that was the worst march of the war.

This distance, in dry weather—thirty miles—should only be covered in two days, three days of march, right? It takes them four full days. What do you think their condition is when they reach Manchester? They're exhausted. They are blown.

This is also the day, by the way, where Bragg finally decides he's going to do something. He sends a message to General Polk on the 26th, and comes to see Polk and says, "Look, I have a plan. I want you to take the 15,000 men of your corps and advance up through Guy's Gap, and then I want you to turn right and I want you to fight your way up towards Murfreesboro." Polk asks, "Do we know what's on the other side of those hills?" Bragg says, "You can take care of it, you'll be fine."

Polk used the phrase "man trap" to describe what Bragg was proposing. He said, "This is nothing short of sending us into a man trap." And he's right. He's absolutely right.

Bragg gets back to his headquarters, and what does he find waiting for him there? He finds waiting for him news of the defeat at Beech Grove, that Hardee's men have been shunted aside towards Fairfield. Bragg sends a message to Polk, and the wording is significant and indicative of Bragg's quality of leadership. He said, "Movement proposed for tomorrow is postponed." First of all, he'd ordered the movement. Why did he say he was proposing it? Now he's postponing it, which means it's not canceled, and sends a series of questions to Polk. Should we stand at Shelbyville, retreat to Tullahoma, or try to fight it out somewhere?

I leave you to unpack that as you see fit.

Here's where the bitter fruit of January, February, March, April, and May really comes to ripeness. Somewhere else on the map, there's another Confederate army that twice in the war sets up a defense behind a major geographic obstacle, expecting the Federals to try to cross that obstacle, and will have two or three contingency plans ready to engage when the Yankees get active. That, of course, is the Army of Northern Virginia setting up on the south bank of the Rappahannock River in the winter of '62–'63, and on the south bank of the Rapidan River in the winter of '63–'64. Lee is ready. He's talked about it with his team and knows what he needs to do, but it's a matter of activating the contingency plan. That's called good communication, coordination, and collaboration—what a successful organization needs to achieve its objective and get done what it needs to get done.

Do you think any of that is present in the Army of Tennessee? Absolutely not. You see it in the flat-footed reaction by General Bragg. Here we are almost 72 hours into an active campaign, and Bragg is only now thinking of what he needs to do. He tries to cobble together a counter offensive under a general he just tried to court martial a couple of weeks earlier. This is one of the saddest stories in Confederate military history. In American military history, I would submit to you, as well. They spent so much time in the spring and summer fighting paper battles over what had gone before that they forgot the enemy in front of them wearing blue uniforms, and they were caught flat-footed.

One option I would submit to you is actually the best option Bragg has because, once they get out of the Highland Rim, the advantage is all Rosecrans's. What Bragg should have done is order Polk to move from Shelbyville up to Fairfield and make a dawn attack on the morning of June 27, north to Beech Grove and try to retake Hoover Gap. Why would you do that? Because if you manage to threaten that area, you force Rosecrans at Manchester to turn around and reopen his line of communications back to Murfreesboro, and if you manage to take Hoover's Gap, you've now cut the Army of the Cumberland in two. Two corps at Manchester and the rest of the army leaderless because Rosecrans is with Thomas at Manchester on the other side of the Highland Rim.

That's a pretty decent plan, isn't it? Isn't that a reasonable contingency they might have thought about before the campaign started? There's no evidence they ever even considered that in the course of events, though, so on the night of the 26th Bragg orders everybody to concentrate on Tullahoma.

The rest of the campaign, after they leave the Highland Rim, is somewhat anticlimactic because with Rosecrans at Manchester and Bragg at Tullahoma, Bragg is ready to fight it out in the trenches of Tullahoma. Rosecrans is feeling out Bragg and so decides the best way to do that is to send John Wilder's mounted infantrymen, the Lightning Brigade, into the Confederate rear. It's a day-and-a-half, two-day odyssey. They have to swim the horses across some of the creeks because of the flooding rains. They cut the rail line and probe the bridge and the protection there. They raise a lot of havoc and then find out that Bedford Forrest is after them, and Simon Buckner with 3,000 men is coming up by train through Cowan. They get back at noon June 30, and Wilder walks into army headquarters. Rosecrans is amazed to see him. And Wilder says, "Not only do I have the intelligence that you need, I did it without losing a single soul." Without a single casualty. An incredible odyssey in the Civil War.

On the other flank, by the way, one of the best days the Union cavalry had in the war was the Battle of Shelbyville, where they forced Joe Wheeler to swim for his life on June 27, 1863.

Bragg, at this point, is not worried. The railroads reopen as June ticks down and approaches July. He has a council of war with Polk and Hardee and says, "We're going to fight it out." The corps commanders have reservations about that and start to talk about it, and Polk says, "I thought the railroad was cut."

"The railroad's reopen!" says Bragg. "Great news!"

And then Polk says this: "How do you propose to maintain your communications?"

"Well, they'll reopen, I'll string infantry along the railroad, and we'll be fine."

Polk and Hardee look at each other. "General Hardee," Polk says, "what do you think about this?"

Hardee says, "You can do what you want, but I endorse the merit of Polk's views."

Bragg says, "We're going to fight it out."

Then he changes his mind overnight.

This is June 29, the conversation takes place. June 30, he changes his mind. He says, "We are going to withdraw." On the night of June 30, the quartermasters moved the wagons out of Tullahoma, and that means one thing: retreat. That night, the Confederate army evacuates Tullahoma and crosses the rail bridge. The last rear guard passed out in the morning of July 1, 1863, about the time that John Reynolds was shot outside of Gettysburg.[7]

The Federals enter the area quickly. Rosecrans sets up pursuit, and there's a skirmish at the Elk River bridge on July 2, and again Bragg says, "We are going to fight it out." Buckner, Polk and Hardee say, "You know what, somebody may have to take command of the army from him." Bragg changes his mind, retires, and Rosecrans pursues but then breaks off the pursuit at University Place on July 4, 1863. Two days later, some of Sheridan's troopers blew up the cornerstone of the University of South. Tullahoma is over.

The conquest of middle Tennessee has been amazingly cheap. In eleven days of operations from June 24 to July 4, only 570 Federals were killed, wounded, captured, or missing. Bragg's army never tabulated its losses, but Confederate personnel returns on July 10 show an effective strength nearly

---

7 Union Major General John F. Reynolds was killed on the morning of July 1, 1863 while commanding the I Corps during the Battle of Gettysburg.

5,000 men lower than on June 20. Half of that number, 2,500, covered Morgan's Raiders, who had departed to Kentucky, but that still leaves 2,500 casualties. The Federals captured more than 1,600 prisoners, while Stewart's division lost 181 men at Hoover's Gap and Pat Cleburne sustained 121 casualties at Liberty Gap, for a total of 320 men killed or wounded in Hardee's corps. The balance of the Army of Tennessee's loss, about 600 more, consisted of battle casualties, sick, or deserters.

A lot of those 1,600 prisoners I quoted are Tennesseans from this area or elsewhere, realizing, "I don't want to leave home that far behind." It's a sign of the disintegration of the Army of Tennessee to a certain extent.

When this is reported to the War Department, Edwin Stanton congratulates Rosecrans—but they fire salutes when they get the news of Gettysburg and Vicksburg. And then Stanton says this: "You and your noble army now have the chance to give the finishing blow to the rebellion. Will you neglect the chance?"[8] And this illustrates right here that Tullahoma is obscure even in 1863, as opposed to just today. This is what Rosecrans says in reply:

> I just received the batch announcing the fall of Vicksburg and confirming the fall of Lee. You do not appear to observe the fact that this noble army has driven the rebels from Middle Tennessee, of which my dispatch has advised you. I beg on behalf of this army that the War Department may not overlook so great an event because it is not written in letters of blood. I have now to repeat, that the rebel army has been forced from its strong entrenched position at Shelbyville and Tullahoma and driven over the Cumberland Mountains. My cavalry advances within eight miles of the Alabama line. No organized rebel force within 25 miles of there, nor on this side of the Cumberland Mountains.[9]

Bragg's retreat doesn't stop until they're in Chattanooga. And never

---

8 *O.R.*, I, 23, pt. 2, 518.

9 Ibid.

again, except for that last death ride of the Army of Tennessee in 1864, will the Army of Tennessee penetrate middle or western Tennessee with any hope of sustained success. That makes the campaign a great victory, and when you consider the events of the first week of July 1863—Gettysburg, Vicksburg, Tullahoma, Port Hudson—and you look at the collective body blow that put on the Confederacy, that they never fully recover, that makes this campaign just as important an element of the Civil War as any of the other three names that I just gave you.

And I'll leave you with this: Tullahoma is a huge link in that chain of events that leads from the Ohio River all the way to Savannah on the Atlantic coast. If you consider that the Federal presence in Chattanooga, Tennessee, is the dagger thrust against the vitals of the Confederacy - well, before that, the dagger thrust directly into the vitals of Chattanooga is the Federal army at Tullahoma, which they won over eleven days of hard marching and fighting in the rain and the heat in June and July of 1863. It is not written in letters of blood, Rosecrans was right. But the Tullahoma campaign does not deserve the obscurity it has been placed into.

Looking northwest from Lookout Mountain toward Tullahoma offers an excellent view of the table-topped ridges of central Tennessee that the armies had to pass through. *Chris Mackowski*

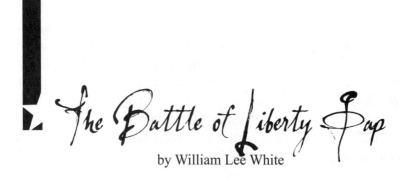

The Battle of Liberty Gap

by William Lee White

The Federal column made its way southward through an afternoon of pouring rain. It was June 24, 1863, and the men of Gen. Richard Johnson's second division of Maj. Gen. Alexander McCook's XX Corps had left their comfortable camps near Murfreesboro, Tennessee that morning as the rest of Maj. Gen. William Starke Rosecrans' Army of the Cumberland fanned out from its winter camp. Some went west, some east, and others directly south—all part of a massive move designed to thoroughly confuse their opponent, Gen. Braxton Bragg and his Army of Tennessee.

This campaign would come to be known as the Tullahoma campaign, named for the little town, about 35 miles south and east of Murfreesboro on the Nashville and Chattanooga Railroad, where Bragg and his army had arrived in the aftermath of their defeat at Stones River the previous January.

Though the area immediately around Tullahoma was relatively flat, to the south and east rose ominously the formidable Cumberland Mountains. A few miles to the front was a belt of steep hills known as the Highland Rim, which offered Bragg a strong line of defense on his nearly twenty-mile front, with only three gaps that needed to be guarded. The roads and railroad ran through these gaps, and it was toward one of them—Liberty Gap—that Johnson's men made their way.

Liberty Gap was the middle of the three, and through it ran the aptly named Liberty Pike, which then led to the little towns of Bell Buckle, Wartrace, and Tullahoma itself. The gap consisted of a nearly quarter-mile-long passage that then opened into a small interior valley of farmland, with another series of hills at the south end, a short distance north of Bell Buckle.

An attack there, feared the Confederates, could split their army in two. But that was not the Union goal. Farther to the east was Rosecrans's main effort, where he hoped to flank and then drive to the south into Bragg's right rear, making Bragg's hold on the region impossible. Johnson's men would play an important role in this grand scheme, but as a diversion.

By 2 p.m. Johnson's lead brigade, Brig. Gen. August Willich's, neared the gap when a smattering of gunfire erupted from his advance guard, five companies of Col. Thomas Harrison's 39th Indiana Infantry. The 39th was mounted that spring and one of several units in the army able to procure Spencer repeating rifles. As the Hoosiers neared the mouth of the gap, they encountered a few Confederates detailed to gather wheat in the surrounding fields. They surprised the Rebels and captured them. From them they learned that to their front was a small detachment of the 1st and 3rd consolidated Kentucky cavalry, backed up by an advanced guard of two regiments of Brig. Gen. St. John Liddell's 1st Arkansas Brigade, part of the division of County Cork, Ireland, native Maj. Gen. Patrick Cleburne.

With this information, Harrison pressed forward with his Indianans, soon engaging the main line of Confederate pickets. With this contact, Willich ordered Harrison to stop his advance while he brought up the rest of the brigade. Willich looked forward to the fight, having just been exchanged after being captured at Stones River. The Prussian-born former revolutionary had returned to his command with many ideas, which he quickly began instilling in his men. One tactic, called "advance firing," and another, the use of Prussian bugle calls, were two innovations unknown to the Confederates, and the bugle calls came into play now. The Confederates soon heard unfamiliar bugle calls echoing to their front as the "Bugle brigade" went into action.[1]

Willich deployed his brigade, with the 15th Ohio to the west of the pike and the 49th Ohio to the east, both assigned as skirmishers, while the 89th Illinois and his old regiment, the all-German 32nd Indiana, were positioned as support. Behind them, the crew of Capt. Wilbur Goodspeed's Battery A, 1st Ohio, unlimbered two Napoleons and four James rifled cannons and went into action, sending several shots howling into the Confederate positions "to

---

1 For more on General Willich see David Dixson's excellent biography, *Radical Warrior: August Willich's Journey from German Revolutionary to Union General* (Knoxville, 2020).

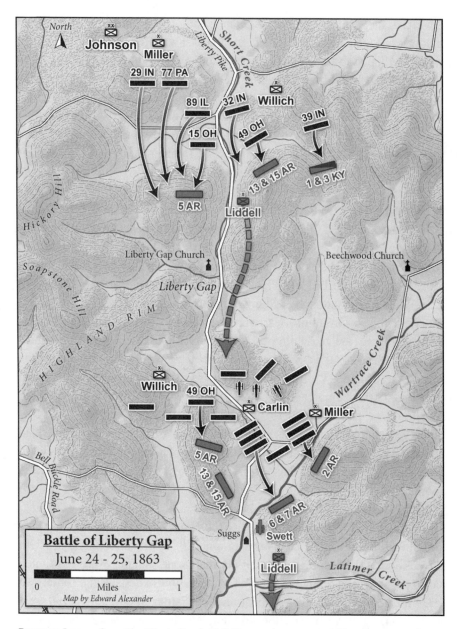

BATTLE OF LIBERTY GAP—The Liberty Gap battlefield was a long narrow defile with a range of steep hills in front, side, and back. Union forces were able to effectively deploy and fight through this difficult terrain, driving back their opponents from several strong defensive positions.

draw the fire of the enemy's batteries. . . ."[2] But no return fire came, and soon Willich's bugles were sounding the advance. Willich's men trudged forward through the muddy rows of wheat as the fire of the skirmishers on both sides escalated. "On my advance, the enemy's skirmishers fell back on their reserves, which were posted on the crest of the hills forming the northern entrance of Liberty Gap," Willich reported. "There the enemy had a very strong, and, in front, easily defended position. The hills are steep, to half their heights open, then rocky and covered with woods. I felt the enemy in front to ascertain whether he would make a decided resistance, and found him in force and determined."[3]

With mounting opposition, Willich paused and reformed his men, with all regiments on line except the 89th Illinois, still in reserve. Meanwhile, he ordered his skirmishers to further develop the Confederate position.

Watching Willich from above was Col. Lucius Featherston and 540 men of the 5th, 13th, and 15th Arkansas Consolidated Regiments. They hurriedly prepared their defenses, piling up rocks and logs on the steep slope. The Union advance had caught them by surprise. Col. Featherston recalled:

> I was sitting down to dinner, a courier arrived from the front and announced that there was a heavy cavalry engagement going on near Old Millersburg, and between that and the McMinnville road. I sent the courier direct to General Liddell, commanding at Bell Buckle, This courier had not gotten out of sight before a second arrived announcing that the enemy were directly in front of Liberty Gap. He too, was sent to the former. I immediately formed my regiment, and sent Colonel Josey orders to turn out his command and dispose of it as had been agreed by him and myself in case we were attacked. I sent Liet. Col. J.E. Murray, with the left wing of my regiment to take position of the Bald Knob Gap and to protect the brow of the hill between that gap and Liberty Gap with skirmishers. . . . I rode out to my pickets; found

---

2   United States War Department, *The War of the Rebellion: A Compilation of the Official Records of the Union and Confederate Armies,* 70 vols. in 128 parts (Washington D.C.: Government Printing Office, 1880-1901), Series I, volume 23, part 1, p. 486 (hereafter cited as *O.R.,* I, 23, pt. 1, 486).

3   Ibid.

all the cavalry behind them. I gave them instructions to deploy as skirmishers on the brow of the hill east of Liberty Gap Pass, and, with such of the cavalry as would go (about 10), I proceeded up the road. On reaching Clark's house, 200 or 300 yards beyond my advance post, I was suddenly fired upon by a regiment of infantry. Satisfied that I had infantry to contend with, I sent a courier to inform Colonel Murray of that fact, and the cavalry to the narrow pass east of the gap, with instructions to dismount and fight at that point as skirmishers. I returned to the church, and there met Colonel Josey, who had disposed of his forces as follows: Three companies as skirmishers on the heights east of the gap; one company as a reserve for the battery, and three companies as skirmishers on the brow of the hill immediately west of the gap. These dispositions had scarcely been made before the firing along the entire line became heavy. . . .[4]

Meanwhile, to their rear at Bell Buckle, General Liddell received the messages from Featherston and immediately sent word south to General Cleburne at Wartrace. He then turned to the brigade bugler and had him sound the assembly for the brigade to form up. One of his men, Stan Harley of the 6th and 7th Arkansas Consolidated, remembered, "The Masons in our brigade were celebrating St. John's Day with a barbecue and speeches. It was a rainy day . . . . About the time dinner was eaten and someone was speaking, a courier dashed up . . . . We were soon on our way at double-quick to the relief . . . ."[5]

As reinforcements made their way to the front, Union pressure increased in response to a furious fire from both sides of the Liberty Pike. The defenders checked Willich's advance, though, as he determined that a frontal assault would be too costly. He sent word back to Johnson, who immediately ordered the rest of his command into the fight. Colonel John Miller brought up his second brigade to aid Willich, slogging forward to add the weight of his men to the assault, reinforcing Willich's line, but also extending the line, hoping to turn the Confederate flank.

The Federals advanced again with the added power provided by Miller's

4   *O.R.*, I, 23, pt. 1, 594.

5   Stanley C. Harley, "Battle of Liberty Gap," *Arkansas Democrat* (Little Rock) June 27, 1903.

men. Two of Miller's regiments, the 29th Indiana and 77th Pennsylvania, overlapped Featherston's line to the west, while Willich's own 39th Indiana swept the Confederate cavalry to the east and south. Miller's two regiments were unopposed as they scaled the steep hillside. "We were obliged to scramble up by laying hold of bushes and saplings to effect progress," Col. Thomas E. Rose of the 77th noted; "in fact, it was equal to the scaling the Heights of Abraham. . . ."[6]

The Confederate position was now becoming untenable. "Thus affairs continued for a considerable length of time, fighting hard all the time and at short range," Colonel Josey later reported. "Owing to exposed position of my flank . . . I ordered the command back to the encampment, a few hundred yards east of south of the southern entrance of Liberty Gap."[7]

Coming up the hill in front of Josey, a soldier in the 49th Ohio gave his perspective:

> [W]e had nearly gained the hill the rebels made one more effort to drive us back and for a moment our line in the center wavert [sic] but just then our gallant Adjutant dashed forward and urged the men onward. . . . [T]he move was successful. . . . [O]ne more dash and the Hill was ours and a hearty cheer told us that we were gaining. . . . [W]e again moved forward on this side of the hill we found the Camp of the 15th Arkansas regiment whome we had been fighting on the hill. . . . [T]hey had left most of their Tents sitting and many knapsacks were left . . . a table was left sitting that was set for supper. . . . [8]

Another of Willich's men added, "their tents and much of the camp equipage which we found very convenient that night."

With the rain pouring in torrents and nightfall approaching, Liddell ordered his men to fall back about a mile, across the interior valley and reform on the hills on the southside near where the spot where Capt. Charles

6 *O.R.,* I, 23, pt. 1, 498.

7 Ibid., 599.

8 Ralph E. Kiene, Jr., ed., *A Civil War Diary: The Journal of Francis A. Kiene, 1861-1864: A Family History* (Privately Published, 1974), 157-158.

Swett's Mississippi battery had deployed. There, the rest of their brigade joined them, reforming on another set of steep hills.

Johnson halted Willich and Miller and pushed forward with his remaining brigade under the command of Col. Philemon Baldwin. Baldwin pushed on to the vicinity of the little Liberty Church as darkness and gloom claimed the field. The brigade then deployed as pickets. "Thus we passed the night," wrote Col. Hiram Strong of the 93rd Ohio in a letter to his wife, "and a sorry night it was too for the rain poured down continuously as indeed it had done all day. We had to stand at arms all night or while one slept in the mud and water the others watched."[9]

The rest of the division went into camp near the mouth of the gap, some of them enjoying the fruits of their victory and taking advantage of the abandoned camps while the rest set up their shelter tents and bedded down for the night. Lyman Widney of the 34th Illinois described the night:

> Our brigade bivouacked on a hillside, minus every article of baggage not carried on our backs. Rain fell incessantly, and wood being scarce kept our fire alive with difficulty. It was my good fortune to secure a boulder partially embedded in the mud near our fire, where I might sit with my chin resting on my knees—lying down was out of the question. A rubber blanket partially protected me from the cold rain.[10]

Early the next morning, Willich's brigade moved forward and relieved Baldwin's tired soldiers, establishing a new skirmish line. To the south, Pat Cleburne arrived on the scene and informed Liddell that Brig. Gen. Sterling Alexander Martin Wood's Alabama and Mississippi brigade was close by to support him. Liddell then informed Cleburne of his dispositions and the situation that confronted them.

Liddell's skirmish line aggressively advanced into the morning mists, and soon the roar of gunfire echoed across the valley and hills. Johnson's men

---

9   Hiram Strong, *The Civil War Letters of Col. Hiram Strong, 93rd Ohio*, Letter of June 26, 1863.

10   Lyman S. Widney, *Campaigning with Uncle Billy, The Civil War Memoir of Lyman S. Widney, 34th Illinois* (Victoria, CN: 2008), 150-152.

were still there. The skirmishers, in a heated fight, were forced to withdraw back across the muddy fields to the base of the hills they started from.

Johnson received reinforcements from Brig. Gen. William Carlin's brigade of Brig. Gen. Jefferson C. Davis's division, and that afternoon once again ordered his men to press forward. Jumping off from the hill occupied by Baldwin's brigade the night before, Goodspeed's Battery A, 1st Ohio and Capt. Edward Grosskopff's mostly German 20th Independent Ohio Battery with a section of 3-inch Ordnance rifles went into action to support the advance. This time Miller's brigade took the lead, advancing to the east of the pike with Willich pushing forward to the west. Willich told Col. William Gibson to take his 49th Ohio and use the advance firing technique as they pushed uphill against Featherston's and Josey's regiments to drive them back under a nearly constant hail of gunfire. "Lord Almighty, who can stand against that!" proclaimed one dazed Arkansan sergeant who was captured. "Four lines of battle and every damn one of them firing!"[11]

Miller's brigade moved steadily forward across the rolling cornfield to his front, filling the small valley with a sea of muddy blue coats. Only part of Liddell's brigade opposed them: the 2nd Arkansas directly in front of and along the edge of the cornfield, the 6th and 7th Arkansas Consolidated Regiment on a hillside, and Swett's Mississippi battery further back near the road. Swett's guns opened fire, raining shrapnel down upon the heads of Miller's men. Lyman Widney recounted the experience:

> It wasn't our purpose to waste time in making a show, so before we had time to consider what were our surroundings the order was given and over the fence we clambered into the midst of the young corn, which toppled over before us as grain before the reaper, while behind us it lay crushed into the soft mud that reached over shoe tops. Not tinder stalks of corn alone toppled over us we advanced-blue forms here and there were seen to fall and rich red blood added its color to the picture of desolation into which that peaceful cornfield had been speedily transformed. We gave little heed to the doleful picture at our backs as we struggled forward. Our eyes were fixed upon the brush beyond the field,

11 "The 49th at Liberty Gap," *The Tiffin Tribune*, 28 August 1863.

where the flash and smoke of musketry disclosed the danger line. The sooner we reach it and dislodge the enemy the fewer of our number will be left writhing in the muddy field. As we emerge from the field the smoke clears away before our eyes and we enter the cover unopposed. The enemy is retreating toward the southern end of the Gap. . . .[12]

Watching the advance from nearby, young Philp D. Stephenson remembered:

> Up and down it we could look, and the order was pretty good, the line only a little "wobbly" and their flags like square flames of crimson (I never saw the Stars and Stripes look so beautiful before or since). They got a little way into the valley and then started on the charge with a cheer. Not a sound from our side! Only when they got across the valley and little way up the base of the . . . knob, then came the crash of musketry from the hill. Like loud increasing crackling of a conflagration in the woods, it continued and continued.[13]

Colonel Miller directed his men onward under the storm. Suddenly he reeled in the saddle, seriously wounded, shot through his left eye. Command now passed to Colonel Rose of the 77th Pennsylvania even as Carlin's brigade of Davis's division came forward to support the attack. The Union line continued to roll forward. Colonel Rose later described what was the final Union assault of the battle:

> keeping up a terrific fire on the enemy, causing their first and second lines to break toward the top of the hill like a flock of sheep,

---

12 Widney, 152.

13 Philip Daingerfield Stephenson, *The Civil War Memoir of Philip Daingerfield Stephenson* (Baton Rouge), 114. St. Louis native Philip D. Stephenson was underage and not permitted to enlist in his brother's regiment, the 13th Arkansas, but he tagged along anyway, serving as an errand boy for his brother and friends. When he turned of age in early 1864 he enlisted in the 5th Company, Washington Artillery.

but we were still exposed to a terrific fire from their third line, and the exhausted state of the men, caused from double quicking through the mud, seemed to preclude the possibility of advancing my line any farther, but springing forward myself, crossing the stream and waving them on, acted like a charm and on came my line with a yell, dashing through the creek gaining the base of the hill, where we were tolerably secure from the fire of the enemy, while our fire told upon them with admirable effect. The rebels were, for a long time, determined to hold their ground and drive us back. My ammunition was becoming rapidly exhausted and I sent for reenforcements...The Thirty fourth Regiment Illinois Volunteers, of my brigade, came up in gallant style, and suffered very heavily from the enemy's fire. At the same time the Thirty eighth Indiana, of General Davis' division, which also, suffered severely in crossing the plain, came up. The firing of the enemy, as this time, ceased, except a few straggling shots, as their lines had been broken. . . . . [14]

Colonel Daniel Govan of the 2nd Arkansas reported "Three forths [sic] of my regiment were now by this time out of ammunition. The enemy . . . advanced again to the charge, and succeeded this time in reaching the foot of the hill. About this time the Sixth Arkansas Regiment came to my assistance, but too leter [sic] to render any effectual resistance. My ammunition was now entirely exhausted. Exposed to a heavy fire being able to fire without being able to inflict any punishment on the enemy . . . my regiment retired. . . . "[15] One final indignity befell the Arkansans. As the men of the 38th Indiana moved up the hill, one shot struck and killed the color-bearer of the 2nd Arkansas, who fell and rolled down the slope into the Hoosiers' ranks, still clutching the regiment's Hardee Corps battle flag, which was then taken as a trophy.

Liddell's right crumbled under the pressure and joined Featherston's and Josey's retreating men. They withdrew back to where Wood's brigade was formed at the south end of the Gap. Johnson did not push on, though, holding on to the newly gained position through the night.

14   *O.R.*, I, 23, pt. 1, 500.

15   Ibid., 593.

The next morning, long-range skirmishing continued but neither side pushed to attack as the day before, though Cleburne brought up Brig. Thomas Churchill's Texas and Arkansas brigade to replace Liddell's tired command. Cleburne summed it up well in his report of the engagement, "The enemy kept up a constant fire all day, the 26th . . . . I had no ammunition to spare, and did not reply to the continual fire of the enemy except with five Whitworth rifles, which appeared to do good service. Mounted men were stuck at distances from 700 to 1,300 yards."[16]

That night, Cleburne would learn of the Union victory at Hoover's Gap and that the Confederate line was flanked. He withdrew his command to Tullahoma, giving the field to the Union forces, which they held until the night of the 27th. Johnson and Davis pressed no farther, though, and they eventually withdrew back to the north and marched eastward to join the rest of the army as it moved toward Manchester. Their mission at Liberty Gap had worked like a charm, keeping Bragg's attention focused there while Thomas's and Crittenden's men turned the Confederate flank to the east and moved on toward Manchester, far to Bragg's rear, threatening to cut his line of retreat. Bragg now saw no options other than to withdraw to Chattanooga, and in one fell swoop Rosecrans and the Army of the Cumberland achieved a great victory with very little loss of life.

Indeed, there had been three battles, all fought at gaps in the Highland Rim, with Hoover's Gap being the best known because it opened Thomas's advance toward Manchester but also because it was largely fought by Col. John Wilder's "Lightning" Brigade. Liberty Gap, though, still had played an important role. By pressing so aggressively into the gap, the fighting occupied Cleburne and his division and kept Bragg focused on the threat there, obscuring Rosecrans's real move further to the east. Though small in scale, it was a fight of great intensity and, despite Rosecrans later noting that the campaign was "not written in letters of blood," Federal casualties were reported at over 260. Cleburne reported he lost 121 men, with almost half coming from the 2nd Arkansas. There was still plenty lost at Liberty Gap.

16 *O.R.*, I, 23, pt. 1, 587.

"At Liberty Gap... Every Man is a Hero": The Story of an Ohio Soldier

by Jon-Erik Gilot

Originally published as a blog post at Emerging Civil War on April 29, 2021

While I have spent many years collecting Civil War artifacts and photographs, at some point I made a conscious decision to limit the scope of my collection to only those items from a specific geographic area, namely southeastern Ohio and the northern panhandle of West Virginia. I have managed to collect dozens of photographs, letters, and other artifacts from several of the area's hardest-fighting regiments, including the 15th, 52nd, and 98th Ohio Infantry regiments. Once word gets out that you collect Civil War, the material often seems to find you.

That is just what happened several years ago when I received a call that a set of wooden crutches had been discovered in a house slated for demolition in nearby Belmont County, Ohio. They were in remarkable condition, with octagonal shafts and attractive brass keepers on the bottom. As an added bonus, they were just my size in the event I needed to use them after telling my wife I was bringing home a set of antique crutches.

What was most unique about the set was the handsome block letters carefully carved into each crutch, the first reading "Marquis de Lafayette Hess," and the second reading "M.D.L.F. Hess, Co. F 15th Regt. O.V.I."

These crutches are a visceral connection to not only a forgotten local soldier with an outstanding name, but the forgotten battle that necessitated their use. Naturally, I had to have them.

As evidenced by his name, Marquis de Lafayette Hess was born into a patriotic family in Washington Township, Belmont County, Ohio. Hess's father, Jeremiah Hess, was born in Pennsylvania in 1775 and served in the War of 1812 before moving west to Ohio. By 1860, Lafayette was living with his older brother, George Washington Hess, and his sons James Monroe and Cassius Marcellus, the family working a farm in the neighborhood of Armstrongs Mills along bucolic Captina Creek.

The outbreak of civil war was a significant concern for Belmont County farmers like the Hess family. A primarily agrarian county, for decades Belmont farmers had utilized the Ohio River to ship crops and goods to markets as far as New Orleans. As such, business interests in Belmont were more closely aligned to the south and west than to the north and east. Located immediately adjacent to the northern panhandle of Virginia, there was a preponderance of Virginia scrip in circulation in Belmont County. One Belmont County resident wrote of a near panic in the county in 1861 following Virginia's secession, noting that "money is spent by the market folks as soon as they get it fearing that it may become worthless on their bonds."[1] As such, antiwar sentiment remained strong in Belmont County throughout the war, with the county seat home to the *St. Clairsville Gazette*, one of the most outspoken Copperhead newspapers in the state.

In the 1860 presidential election Abraham Lincoln lost Belmont County by more than 1,200 votes. Lafayette Hess bucked this trend and instead became an active Republican, serving as a delegate to the county's "Unconditional Union Convention" in August 1861.[2] The following month he enlisted as a corporal in Company F of the 15th Ohio Volunteer Infantry, a recently returned 90-day regiment that was reorganizing for a three year enlistment. The regiment would winter in Kentucky before seeing hard fighting at Shiloh and Corinth.

---

1   Caleb H. Cope to Alexis Cope, 6 June 1861, Cope Family Papers, Historical Society of Mount Pleasant, Ohio (HSMP).

2   *Belmont Chronicle*, 8 August 1861.

In late December 1862 the 15th Ohio moved south as part of Gen. William S. Rosecrans's Army of the Cumberland during the advance on Murfreesboro. Situated on the extreme right of the Federal army at the battle of Stones River on December 31, 1862, the 15th Ohio was hit in a crushing attack by two divisions of Confederate Gen. William J. Hardee's Corps of the Army of Tennessee. Alexis Cope, regimental historian for the 15th Ohio, recalled "our men began to fall and after delivering one volley, seeing the enemy in close proximity, three lines deep, with no supports near us, we were ordered to fall back. A high rail fence was close in our rear...this fence proved to be a fatal obstruction to anything like an orderly retreat. It was in this field and at or nearby this fence that we suffered our chief losses of the four day's battle."[3]

The 15th Ohio suffered grievous losses at Stones River, including 19 men killed, 80 wounded, and more than 100 captured, Lafayette Hess among the latter. Hess and his comrades were transferred to Libby Prison in Richmond in January 1863, remaining in captivity for more than a month before being exchanged at City Point. From there the men returned home before returning to the regiment in early June 1863, just in time for one of the most significant, if unheralded, campaigns of the war.

The hallmark of General Rosecrans's Tullahoma campaign was the skillful maneuvering of four Federal infantry corps, utilizing multiple road networks and feints to confuse the location of the decisive thrust south towards Chattanooga. The 15th Ohio moved out of Murfreesboro on June 24 as part of one such feint, due south towards Liberty Gap, one of three vital passes through the Highland Rim. While Lee White capably covers the Battle of Liberty Gap in the previous essay, it's worth examining the 15th Ohio's contributions at this engagement.

Arriving at Liberty Gap on the afternoon of June 24 and finding the pass lightly guarded by two Arkansas infantry regiments, the Ohioans were deployed as skirmishers, pressing the right flank of the 5th Arkansas. Lieutenant Colonel Frank Askew of the 15th Ohio wrote "the whole line moved forward across the open field and up the steep face of the hill at a double-quick pace."[4] In a driving rain the Confederates stubbornly contested

3 Alexis Cope, *The Fifteenth Ohio Volunteer and Its Campaigns, 1861 – 1865* (Published by the Author, 1916), 235 – 236.

4 Cope, *The Fifteenth Ohio*, 288.

the pass before ultimately withdrawing one mile to the south, intent on further delaying the assumed main Federal thrust.

The following morning, as scattered skirmishing echoed along the hillsides of Liberty Gap, the Confederate commander, Brig. Gen. St. John R. Liddell, mistakenly believed the Federal troops were withdrawing. Sensing an opportunity, Liddell threw his Arkansas regiments against them, renewing the battle of the day prior. The 15th Ohio had been held in reserve through the morning, but by 3:00 p.m. were called into the fight to support the 32nd Indiana. Askew's report of the battle noted that the regiment "encountered a very spirited attack . . . designed to drive us from the summit of the hill," which the Buckeyes "gallantly met and repulsed," driving the Confederates across the valley and to the hill beyond.[5] From their vantage point, the 15th likely witnessed their sister regiment in Willich's Brigade, the 49th Ohio, utilize advance firing to beat back another Confederate attack. A tactical innovation imparted by their brigade commander, August Willich, the advance firing maneuver entailed a battle line of four ranks, each rank advancing alternately and firing while the others stopped to load. The "rolling wall of continuous fire" proved too much for the Confederates, who continued to pull south, leaving Liberty Gap to the Federals.[6]

Reports of the battle and the regiment's involvement were glowing. Willich noted that "the highest ambition of a commander must be satisfied by being associated with such men," while division commander Brig. Gen. Richard W. Johnson believed that "the affair at Liberty Gap will always be considered a skirmish, but few skirmishes ever equaled it in severity."[7] In his report of the battle, Lieut. Col. Askew recalled Liberty Gap as "where every one did his duty fearlessly and faithfully, where every order was obeyed with alacrity and enthusiasm, where men advanced under such showers of death dealing missiles upon an enemy posted with all the advantages which our adversaries had."[8]

Company F accounted for 8 of the 32 casualties suffered by the 15th

---

5   Ibid.

6   David A. Powell and Eric J. Wittenberg, *Tullahoma: The Forgotten Campaign that Changed the Course of the Civil War, June 23 – July 4, 1863* (Savas Beatie, 2020), 156.

7   Cope, *The Fifteenth Ohio*, 291 - 292.

8   *Belmont Chronicle,* 6 August 1863.

Ohio during the battle of Liberty Gap, the regiment sustaining more than a third of the casualties in the entire first brigade. Among the wounded in the fighting on June 25 was Lafayette Hess, only recently returned to the regiment following his capture and confinement. Hess suffered a painful lower leg wound, described by his company captain, Amos Glover, as severe, but not mortal. Once again, Hess was sent home on leave to recuperate. It was during this time that Hess used these crutches.

Hess would remain home through the remainder of 1863. In his absence the 15th Ohio was engaged at Chickamauga, Chattanooga, and Missionary Ridge, before they themselves returned to Ohio on a veteran's furlough. The regiment regrouped at Columbus, Ohio on March 18, 1864, poised to return to the front. Lafayette Hess returned with the regiment, rested and healed from his Liberty Gap wound. Hess also returned as a married man, having wed Lydia Ann McFarland of Belmont County exactly one month earlier. In April 1864, he was promoted to the rank of sergeant, a testament to the esteem in which he was held despite two extended absences from the regiment following his capture and wounding.

As part of Maj. Gen. Oliver O. Howard's IV Corps, Army of the Cumberland, the 15th Ohio would be engaged throughout the Atlanta Campaign, notably at Rocky Face Ridge, Resaca, and Pickett's Mill. At Kennesaw Mountain, the regiment was positioned near the center of the Federal line. On June 21, General Howard ordered the 15th Ohio to attack and hold Bald Knob opposite the Federal line, mistakenly believing he was issuing orders to an entire brigade rather than a single regiment. The 15th Ohio surged ahead "as resolute as Pickett's charge...as unique as Jackson's onset at Chancellorsville," capturing the Confederate works on Bald Knob and taking several dozen prisoners.[9] The engagement cost the regiment 55 casualties, General Howard remarking that "no adventure has ever thrilled me like that spirited charge of the Fifteenth Ohio."[10]

The regimental historian for the 15th Ohio recalled that picket duty on Bald Knob was "more than usually hazardous," the men on duty day and night through constant firing along the line. On June 23, the regiment

9 Cope, *The Fifteenth Ohio*, 498-499.

10 Ibid, 500.

The crutches of a hero. *Jon-Erik Gilot*

was advanced from their line as skirmishers in support of skirmishers from Brig. Gen. William B. Hazen's brigade. The advance was mismanaged and Hazen's men failed to move forward, exposing the 15th Ohio to a devastating enfilade fire. The regiment lost sixteen men killed and wounded in the fighting on June 23. It was here at Bald Knob that Lafayette Hess, having survived his capture at Stones River, confinement at Libby Prison, and wounding at Liberty Gap, breathed his last.

We don't have an account of Hess's death. We don't have his letters or diaries, or even a photograph. He left no children. In 1865 his widow received a pension of $8.00 per month and would later remarry to a veteran of the 176th Ohio. In 1886, veterans from Hess's neighborhood of Armstrongs Mills formed the Lafayette Hess Grand Army of the Republic Post in his honor.

The sheer scope of the Civil War is so vast that it can be easy for the individual soldiers to become faceless. There is no doubt that were it not for these crutches that survived more than a century and a half tucked away inside a dilapidated home, Lafayette Hess would remain one of the hundreds of thousands of seemingly faceless casualties of the Civil War—a casualty of a battle and a campaign too often overlooked in Civil War historiography. When asked to cite instances of personal courage or heroism in his regiment during the fighting at Liberty Gap, Lt. Col. Frank Askew refused, believing that in struggles such as the regiment endured at Liberty Gap, "every man is a hero."[11] These crutches are seemingly our only surviving visceral connection to one such hero who sacrificed his body at Liberty Gap and his life at Bald Knob.

11 *Belmont Chronicle*, 6 August 1863.

Tullahoma Campaign History Written in a Confederate Cemetery

by Brian Swartz

Originally published as a blog post at Maine at War, *an ECW partner, on February 17, 2021, and featured on the Emerging Civil War blog in March 2021.*

About halfway between Chattanooga and Murfreesboro exists a cemetery containing the remains of soldiers killed during the Tullahoma campaign.

And, as I learned, few cemeteries provide so much information about the fighting that put these men in their graves.

Headed to Murfreesboro from Chattanooga on Interstate 24, my son, Chris, and I came through Hoover's Gap and approached Exit 97, which accesses Beech Grove and Route 64. Exit 97 is a quarter-cloverleaf, removing and adding northbound traffic within a short distance, so I was watching other vehicles and just glimpsed a Confederate flag dangling next to a cemetery near the highway.

I also spotted the cannon near the flagpole. Figuring the cemetery had a Civil War connection, we got off at Exit 89, re-entered southbound, and got off at Exit 97. We turned into Beech Grove Confederate Cemetery and Park, as the sign identifies this place.

Beech Grove Cemetery opened during pioneer times; one restored headstone honors Joseph Carney, born in January 1730 and died in June 1811. Another headstone belongs to Isaac Eoff, a private in the "Continental Line" during the American Revolution. Born in 1761, he died in 1841.

Piled stones (perhaps limestone or granite) mark some older graves.

Unaware of any major battles fought out here, I wondered why this Confederate cemetery existed. We started reading the information panels and "discovered" the Tullahoma campaign.

Mainers immersed in Gettysburg and Vicksburg seldom hear about this campaign, and Chris and I learned a lot about it by the time we left the cemetery. I later got a better education with Christopher L. Kolakowski's book, *The Stones River and Tullahoma Campaigns.*

The sign for Beech Grove Confederate Cemetery and Park faces nearby Interstate 24, where Chattanooga-bound trucks head toward nearby Hoover's Gap, site of a major battle during the Tullahoma Campaign.. *Brian Swartz*

Planned by Maj. Gen. William S. Rosecrans and brilliantly conducted by his Army of the Cumberland (some 70,000 troops), the Tullahoma campaign took place in late June 1863. Focused on Vicksburg, Ulysses S. Grant, Robert E. Lee, and the Army of Northern Virginia running amok in Pennsylvania, the Union press largely ignored Rosecrans's campaign, which pried central Tennessee from Southern hands and opened the road to Chattanooga.

Expecting Rosecrans to move against the city, Confederate Gen. Braxton Bragg had spread his smaller Army of Tennessee (about 43,000 men) across the roads leading into the Cumberland Plateau. A rugged region rising in Alabama and running northeast across Tennessee to eastern Kentucky, the plateau "today is a labyrinth of rocky ridges and verdant ravines" and deep

Confederate veterans repurposed an existing pioneer cemetery as the final resting place for comrades killed in the June 1863 battle of Hoover's Gap. *Brian Swartz*

gorges, according to The Nature Conservancy.

In mid-1863, the Tennessee River provided the easiest access into the Cumberland Plateau. Few roads penetrated it between Murfreesboro, where Rosecrans was headquartered, and Chattanooga, vital to the South. Among the existing roads is modern Route 41, which hugs the Tennessee River shore beneath Lookout Mountain before running through the mountains toward Murfreesboro.

Bragg had to defend every possible point where Yankees could punch onto the plateau. Advancing his much better-armed troops in four columns, Rosecrans prevented Bragg from shifting units to meet every threat.

Route 41 (called the Manchester Pike at Beech Grove) was "the main road to Chattanooga," according to Tennessee Backroads Heritage, and southeast along this road marched a column commanded by Maj. Gen. George Thomas, the future "Rock of Chickamauga." Rain fell and all the Yankee-used roads turned to slop, but Rosecrans kept his men advancing.

By capturing Manchester southeast of Beech Grove, Thomas could block Bragg from retreating to Chattanooga. The Manchester Pike passed

Piled stones mark some early graves at Beech Grove Confederate Cemetery and Park in central Tennessee. Beyond these graves rise the headstones of Confederate soldiers killed during the June 1863 Tullahoma Campaign. *Brian Swartz*

through the mountains at Hoover's Gap beyond Beech Grove, toward which Col. John T. Wilder and 2,000 mounted Yankee infantrymen (equipped with the new Spencer repeating rifle) rode on Wednesday, June 24.

Fighting engulfed Beech Grove and Hoover's Gap that rainy afternoon. The 72nd Indiana Infantry Regiment fought inside Beech Grove Cemetery, and Capt. Eli Lilly (think pharmaceuticals) and his 18th Indiana Battery "did considerable damage to the advancing Confederate infantry with double rounds of canister," indicates an information panel provided by the Midwest Civil War Artillery Association.

The Yankees won, the Confederates withdrew, and the war left Beech Grove alone.

In 1866, Maj. William Hume led other Southern veterans seeking Confederates buried from Beech Grove to Hoover's Gap. As at Manassas, Fredericksburg, and elsewhere, the victors—in this case the Yankees— quickly buried their dead opponents in shallow graves.

Hume and his companions found some skeletal remains partially exposed; Union troops marching north to Gettysburg noticed similar graves

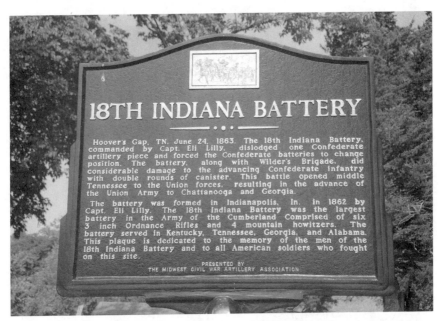

The 18th Indiana Battery and its commander, Capt. Eli Lilly, played a key role during the June 24-26, 1863 fighting at Beech Grove and Hoover's Gap. *Brian Swartz*

while tramping across the Manassas battlefield in June 1863. With a war on, little time was available for proper grave-digging.

According to Tennessee Civil War Trails, Hume's veterans disinterred dead Confederates and buried them at Beech Grove Cemetery, on land that David Lawrence owned (he apparently was a local veteran). A Tennessee Historical Commission information panel indicates these men were "soldiers who fell at isolated places in the Beech Grove-Hoover's Gap engagement, June 24-26, 1863."

Hume later wrote that each soldier was buried in "a nice walnut coffin," with each grave marked by a headboard, "but being unable to put any name, as all were unknown." Some 50 Confederates were laid to rest at Beech Grove, and his veterans "also put a nice paling fence around the graves."

Other Confederate veterans were apparently buried here in later decades, based on some headstones marked with names.

The state of Tennessee restored Beech Grove Confederate Cemetery in 1954. It's a poignant place to learn about the Tullahoma campaign.

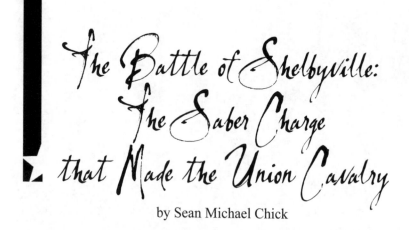

The Battle of Shelbyville: The Saber Charge that Made the Union Cavalry

by Sean Michael Chick

Originally published as a blog post at Emerging Civil War on June 28, 2017

One of the most dramatic and decisive cavalry clashes of the American Civil War occurred at Shelbyville, Tennessee, on Sunday, June 27, 1863. The battle was part of Maj. Gen. William Rosecrans's Tullahoma offensive. Rosecrans needed to force his army through the highland rim of middle Tennessee, held by Gen. Braxton Bragg's Army of Tennessee. Rosecrans paused his army for six months after his victory at Stones River, improving the army's training and expanding its staff. Mostly, he wanted a cavalry force that could compete with the Rebels. By June 1863, Rosecrans decided he was ready.

The bulk of the Army of the Cumberland was sent through Hoover's Gap and Gilley's Gap in an attempt to turn Bragg's right flank. Rosecrans sent Maj. Gen. Alexander McCook's XX Corps to attack Liberty Gap in the center. To the west, Rosecrans sent two divisions to threaten Shelbyville, a town that Bragg had fortified over the winter. One was the cavalry division led by Brig. Gen. Robert Mitchell. The other was an infantry division commanded by Brig. Gen. Absalom Baird. Major General Gordon Granger was the overall commander, although Maj. Gen. David Stanley, the cavalry corps commander, was with Mitchell's division.

Granger's feint began on June 23, striking Brig. Gen. William Martin's division of Maj. Gen. Joseph Wheeler's cavalry corps. Wheeler's two divisions were stretched thin, and he fell for Granger's feint. He did, however, ask Brig. Gen. Nathan Bedford Forrest to move his command from Columbia to Shelbyville.

Around 4:00 p.m. on June 26, Bragg was informed that the position at Hoover's Gap had collapsed. His right had been turned. He ordered Lt. Gen. Leonidas Polk to give up Shelbyville while Wheeler held off Granger. In the early morning, on June 27, the Confederates abandoned Shelbyville. Granger approached with his Reserve Corps, spearheaded by Mitchell's cavalry. Marshall Thatcher of the 2nd Michigan Cavalry was impressed by the scene, writing "The sun burst through the heavy clouds and shone full in the faces of 10,000 cavalry, in two lines, division fronts; banners flying, bands playing and the command marching in as perfect lines as if on a parade. Such a sight was rare in the history of the war."[1]

Stanley, reinforced by Col. Robert Horatio George Minty's cavalry brigade, bolted ahead, leaving behind the wagons and cannons. They encountered Martin's division in Guy's Gap. Stanley brought up his artillery and while the cannons boomed regimental bands played "Yankee Doodle" and "Dixie." Minty's brigade attacked cautiously at first, but then rushed headlong in a mounted charge. Some 200 of Martin's men were captured and many hundreds more were scattered.[2]

Martin's men rallied in the trenches that covered Shelbyville. Wheeler, sensing that affairs were desperate, took personal command. Shelbyville was heavily fortified, but the lines needed a large body of men to be properly

---

1 Dennis W. Belcher, *The Cavalry of the Army of the Cumberland* (Jefferson, NC: McFarland, 2016), 92; Marshall P. Thatcher, *A Hundred Battles in the West* (Detroit: Marshall P. Thatcher, 1884), 133.

2 United States War Department, *The War of the Rebellion: A Compilation of the Official Records of the Union and Confederate Armies*, 70 vols. in 128 parts (Washington D.C.: Government Printing Office, 1880-1901), Series I, volume 23, part 1, p. 539 (hereafter cited as *O.R.,* I, 23, pt. 1, 539); George Steahlin, "Stanley's Cavalry: Minty's Sabre Brigade at Guy's Gap," *National Tribune*, May 27, 1882.

used. Wheeler later claimed a courier assured him that Forrest was on the way and he needed Wheeler to hold so he could cross the rain swollen Duck River. The messenger also indicated that Forrest hoped to strike Stanley's rear. Forrest, for his part, denied that any such promise was made. Regardless, Polk's wagons were not yet out of Shelbyville, and Wheeler had to protect them.[3]

Stanley wanted to avoid a bloodbath, and he did not attack right away. He sent the 3rd Indiana Cavalry on the left to probe. The 4th Michigan Cavalry moved along the lines on the right, through a wooded path until they reached a spot where the lines were undefended. They entered the defenses and then struck the refused end of the Confederate line. As the troopers engaged the left end of the line, Stanley assaulted the front. Wheeler's men were overpowered by overwhelming numbers.[4]

In Shelbyville itself, Wheeler rallied his command for a desperate stand. The last of the supply trains had not yet cleared the town and the "War Child" was determined to protect them. Wheeler formed his men in the Shelbyville square. The excited Wheeler rode about exhorting his men to hold out.[5]

Minty regrouped while the 18th Ohio Artillery shelled the Confederates. All winter and spring Minty had drilled his men in mounted charges. He was about to show that such training had not been in vain. The 7th Pennsylvania Cavalry formed in a column in the streets of Shelbyville, just behind the guns of the 18th Ohio Battery. After a quick barrage, the 7th Pennsylvania emerged out of the smoke with sabers drawn. The Rebel artillery overshot, and only two Federals went down; the rest pressed on. Adjutant George Steahlin wrote that the men made "right cuts, left cuts, front cuts, and rear cuts making thrusts right, left and front – dealing death at every blow." Major Charles Davis, who led the vanguard of the attack, was later awarded the Medal of Honor.[6]

---

3   Belcher, *Cavalry of the Army of the Cumberland*, 93; W.C. Dodson, *Campaigns of Wheeler and His Cavalry 1861-1865* (Atlanta: Hudgins, 1899), 88; Edward G. Longacre, *A Soldier to the Last: Maj. Gen. Joseph Wheeler in Blue and Gray* (Washington: Potomac Books, 2007), 105.

4   Belcher, *Cavalry of the Army of the Cumberland*, 95.

5   Dodson, *Campaigns of Wheeler*, 92; *Harper's Weekly*, June 18, 1898.

6   Belcher, *Cavalry of the Army of the Cumberland*, 94; John Allan Wyeth, *With Saber and Scalpel* (New York: Harper & Brothers, 1914), 214.

The charge broke the Confederate defense. In the chaos, two cannons were captured. The Rebels fled across the Duck River. One cannon's wheels broke on the Skull Camp Bridge, partially blocking the way and creating more panic. Once across, Wheeler was informed that Forrest was approaching with his command from Columbia. Forrest wanted to know if he could cross using the Skull Camp Bridge, which had just then fallen into Union hands. Wheeler called for volunteers and counterattacked. He briefly retook the bridge but found himself cut off.[7]

Wheeler with sixty men charged the Union cavalry with his sword out and his hat in hand. The Rebels broke through and were pursued. Wheeler plunged into the river from a fifteen-foot height. Martin brought his horse in less dramatically. Of the sixty men Wheeler led in his escape, only thirteen had survived. In total, Wheeler's losses were around 900 men and three cannon. Stanley's losses were likely around fifty [8]

The battle of Shelbyville was a turning point. Rebel cavalry in the west would have other fine showings in its future; they were, even as late as December 1864, a force to be reckoned with. Wheeler's last-minute heroics allowed him to remain popular within his command. However, Shelbyville was the resounding signal that their days of dominance would never return. The Union had achieved parity, if not superiority, in the Western Theater. After the victory and in honor of their charge, Minty's outfit became known as the "Saber Brigade." Never again would the Union cavalry be the laughingstock of the Army of the Cumberland.[9]

---

7 Dodson, *Campaigns of Wheeler*, 93; *Harper's Weekly*, June 18, 1898.

8 Dodson, *Campaigns of Wheeler*, 90; John Witherspoon DuBose, *General Joseph Wheeler and the Army of Tennessee* (New York: Neale Publishing, 1912), 176; William F. Fox, *Regimental Losses in the Civil War 1861-1865* (Albany: Albany Publishing, 1889), 545; *Harper's Weekly*, June 18, 1898.

9 Larry J. Daniel, *Days of Glory: The Army of the Cumberland 1861-1865* (Baton Rouge: Louisiana State University Press, 2004), 272; Christopher L. Kolakowski, *The Stones River and Tullahoma Campaigns: This Army Does Not Retreat* (Charleston: History Press, 2011), 129.

Battle at Bethpage Bridge

by Dave Powell

*From a blog post originally published at Emerging Civil War
on September 25, 2020*

On the morning of July 2, the 104th Illinois Infantry led Maj. Gen. James S. Negley's division of the 14th Army Corps to the site of Bethpage Bridge over the Elk River, pursuing Bragg's retreating Rebels. With the Elk in flood stage thanks to the recent rain, any fords were largely unusable, rendering the handful of existing bridges over the river as highly desirable military targets. When Federal brigade commander John Beatty realized that the Bethpage Bridge was still standing, guarded by an occupied Rebel stockade on the north bank, he decided to try and seize both structures. However, the stockade was solidly built, with good fields of fire; moreover, Confederate dismounted cavalry and artillery supported the stockade from the south bank, prepared, said Beatty, to "open on us whenever the head of our column should make its appearance in the turn of the road."

Any Federals moving against the stockade would be subject to a galling fire, leaving Beatty to conclude that "it would be useless to expose my infantry" without support. Instead, he called up two batteries, and once emplaced, ten Union cannons opened up against both the Confederate guns and the stockade. Within "forty minutes," the Rebel artillery was overwhelmed and fell back, allowing Beatty to push a skirmish line forward. There was still the matter of the stockade, however.

During the action, the Rebels managed to set the Bethpage Bridge alight, which added urgency to Beatty's mission. Losing the bridge would greatly delay any Union pursuit across the Elk for a day, maybe more, buying yet more time for Bragg to escape over the Cumberland Plateau. In response, Beatty ordered Col. Absalom B. Moore to try and capture the bridge. That couldn't happen, however, until someone dealt with the Confederate sharpshooters garrisoning the stockade.

Moore turned to Sgt. George Marsh of Company D, asking Marsh "to lead a squad to reconnoiter, and if possible, take the stockade." Marsh, in turn, called for volunteers: "all who are not afraid, fall in!" He "took the first 10 who stepped forward."

Deploying his small band, once they were ready, Marsh led the way down towards the enemy "at a double-quick." They did so, the Sergeant recalled, "under a heavy fire of musketry and artillery" from both the south bank of the river "and at first from the stockade." Amazingly, all eleven Yankees survived the dash to reach the stockade wall, unwounded.

Here, the next surprise occurred. Marsh and his compatriots had so far not fired a shot. They now, according to Marsh, "forced an entrance into the stockade . . . [and] emptied our rifles into the Confederates" inside. This fusillade did the trick. "Upon seeing us enter the fort," said Marsh, the Rebels "climbed the stockade['s]" opposite wall "and ran up the bank."

The 104th's regimental history noted that the dozen rebels left to hold the stockade, "seized with a panic at the bold action, left in confusion, swimming the Elk, took to the woods, from which they sent back a few shots. The [assault] party was soon after ordered back and received the personal thanks of the General [Beatty]. Captain [George W.] Howe, with Company B, was then sent down with a detail to put out the fire at the bridge." Howe and his men extinguished the flames and saved the bridge in sound enough condition to be used to cross the infantry.

Marsh's dramatic charge was observed with enthusiasm by Beatty, Colonel Moore, and numerous other Federal observers. They never forgot it, and, in 1897, Sergeant Marsh and his companions were each awarded the Medal of Honor. Of those ten men who made the charge, only seven could be named in 1897, and are recorded for posterity. In addition to Marsh, they were John Shapland, Oscar Slagle, Reuben Smalley, Charles Stacey, Richard J. Gage, and Samuel F. Holland. Marsh's citation reads: "for having led a small party at Elk River July 2, 1863, captured a stockade and saved the bridge."

"All In Our Favor": A Federal Officer in the Midst of the Tullahoma Campaign

by Daniel A. Masters

Originally published as a blog post at Emerging Civil War on June 28, 2021

After four days of marching in nearly constant rain and sticky Tennessee mud, Capt. Wesley Porter Andrus of the 42nd Illinois spent Sunday, June 28, 1863, in camp attending to one of a soldier's most mundane tasks: washing his muddy clothes in the Duck River. It being a Sunday and his activities reminding him of domestic life, Andrus thought of his mother, Lucina, back in his home state of New York. After reveille that night, he sat down by candlelight and wrote her the following letter.

Captain Andrus and the 42nd Illinois had already seen much hard service. Andrus (also spelled Andrews) was born in 1834 in Yates County, New York, and had moved to Illinois with his younger brother, Samuel, before the war. Mustering into service as first lieutenant of Company I in July 1861 (Samuel enlisted as a sergeant), Andrus followed the fortunes of the regiment in the Western Theater. The regiment spent its first winter in Missouri and earned praise for its actions in securing Island No. 10 on the Mississippi River in April 1862. As part of Sheridan's division at Stones River, the 42nd Illinois held a critical point near the Wilkinson Pike, suffering more than 200 casualties before being driven back. Sheridan's division emerged from Stones River with a reputation as one of the best fighting divisions in the Army of the Cumberland, a reputation Andrus was determined to preserve. He was promoted to the rank of captain in April 1863 and given command of Company H.

As the Civil War approached its turning point at Gettysburg and Vicksburg, Captain Andrus and his comrades of the Army of the Cumberland were also doing their part to turn the fortunes of the war in favor of the Union.

In bivouac near Tullahoma, Tennessee
June 28, 1863, 10 p.m.

Dear mother,

I intended to have written you before I left camp, but I did not find time to do so. I therefore seize this, my first opportunity, to perform that pleasant task. The grand advance of the Army of the Cumberland commenced on the morning of the 24th instant; we moved in three columns with McCook's corps (ours) on the right, Thomas' corps in the center, and Crittenden's on the left. We have met with more or less resistance along the whole of our front, but nothing as yet approaching to a general engagement. Our division (Sheridan's) has not yet been brought into action, as we are being held in reserve. General Rosecrans has given our gallant little Phil the post of honor as he had shown himself capable of filling at Stones River. The enemy is contesting our advance obstinately and several sharp engagements have taken place, all of which have resulted in our favor.

We have taken a battery and at the least estimate over 1,000 prisoners. Four hundred of Wheeler's cavalry were captured yesterday, and I must say for them that they are the finest looking lot of butternuts I have yet seen. They are nearly all large men and look fleshy and healthy; they have not that gaunt and woebegone look which is the usual characteristic of Rebel troops. I talked a little with some of them. They said that General Wheeler was close by when they were taken and if he was not captured, too, it was because our troops could not distinguish him from the rest of them. They seem sanguine as to their ability to whip us Yankees as they invariably dominate us and establish their independence.

I asked one of them what they thought of our arming the Negroes against them. "We will kill every one of them we can get hold of," was his reply." Will you?" said I. "Good, we have got 400 fine fellows to retaliate with," I very coolly remarked. "Unfortunate foreigner," (he was a Dane) I continued, "you are a prisoner at a very precarious period if your policy shall prove to be that adopted by your government for, mark you, every Negro you kill after surrender or capture, a white Rebel soldier hangs!" I said this quite loud so that as many of the Rebels as possible might hear me. It made the eyes of a good many of them stick out, but not one of them made any reply. The Danish gentleman thereafter subsided.

The country is very hilly and there are a great many gaps and knolls of which the enemy are not slow to avail themselves to check our progress. We are pressing them hard, however, and driving them slowly but steadily. Our effective force is between 50,000 and 60,000 and as good soldiers as there are in the world. This army was never in so good fighting condition as at the present time notwithstanding the drenching rain storms that have soaked us through and through both night and day since we left camp. I would like to be in one battle when it did not rain just to see how it would seem. Nevertheless, great enthusiasm prevails among the men. They are all tried soldiers and eager to smell burnt gunpowder again and listen to the Eolian harp-like music of bullets. They have unbounded confidence in their General and are anxious to avenge the loss of their comrades who fell at Stones River. If we have a general engagement, and I don't see how it can be avoided, it will be one of the most hotly contested of the war for this army will fight, and there is no mistake.

It wounds our pride to think that Lee and his Rebel hordes should have the audacity to treat with such supreme contempt the arms of the Union which is so emphatically manifested by his movement into Pennsylvania, recklessly exposing his communications to the Army of the Potomac. The audacity of that movement has no parallel in the history of the world. Oh, for a leader like Charles the 12th, Frederick the Great, or Napoleon! But I fear it would do us no good if we had the best general that ever lived; I fear he would be immolated. I do fear it. But I am a soldier and must not talk so. History will pronounce judgment in due time, and "ours is not to reason why, ours but to do and die, freedom's true defenders."

We must leave all to an overruling Providence hoping that all may yet be well. Whatever my fate may be in the approaching contest, my first wish is that our arms may triumph. If I fall, I die in a good cause. *Dulce est pro patria mori.* [Latin: It is sweet to die for your country] I have told you many times in whom I place my reliance and I have not made a new choice of masters.

P.S. If there are any "peace men" up there in New York, give them my disregards and tell them General Lee commanding the C.S.A. in Pennsylvania very respectfully desires their august presence in convention at Philadelphia, Pennsylvania on the 4th of July 1863 to determine upon what terms the states of Pennsylvania and Maryland shall be retained in the Union.[1]

The 42nd Illinois did not see action during the balance of the Tullahoma campaign, the entire brigade only losing one man wounded. Later that year, the 42nd Illinois would find battle again, losing more than half of their number at Chickamauga. Andrus was discharged in May 1864 and returned home. The following year he moved to Michigan, perhaps at the behest of his comrades in Company H, which was comprised entirely of Michiganders. Wesley and his brother Samuel married two sisters (Alice and Ella Thomas) and went into the hardware business together at Cedar Springs, Michigan. Captain Andrus passed away in 1898 and is buried at Elmwood Cemetery in Cedar Springs.

1   Capt. Wesley P. Andrus, Letter, in *Yates County Chronicle*, July 23, 1863, 1.

Forgotten! The Tullahoma Campaign

by Chris Kolakowski and Chris Mackowski

The following is a transcript of the December 18, 2018,
edition of the Emerging Civil War Podcast. The conversation has been
lightly edited for brevity and clarity.

Chris M: Welcome to the Emerging Civil War Podcast. I'm Chris Mackowski.

Chris K.: And I'm Chris Kolakowski. And today, the Tullahoma campaign.

Chris M: Tulla, what?

Chris K.: Exactly. There was more going on in June and early July of 1863 than just Gettysburg.

Chris M.: Today we're talking Tullahoma. It's like talking turkey, but Tullahoma. (laughter) Now we've got to start out with the fun fact about Tullahoma that you shared with me just before we started.

Chris K: Tullahoma . . . first of all, for those of you who may not be familiar, Tullahoma is a town in middle Tennessee about 40 miles southeast of Murfreesboro.

Chris M: So it is not a town well known to us the way like Gettysburg is known to us.

Chris K: Fun fact, by the way, is that it's the only locality in all the world named "Tullahoma."

The origin is unclear, though. There's some question as to exactly where it came from. But, the joke was, 'cause it rained so much during the campaign of Tullahoma—which was June 24 to July 4, 1863—that the Army of the Cumberland joked that it came from the Cherokee word "tulla" meaning mud and "homa" meaning "more mud." (laughter).

Chris M: And so this is a campaign that takes place essentially simultaneously with the Gettysburg and Vicksburg campaigns.

Chris K: Correct.

Chris M: And yet it's not a campaign that rolls off the tongue the way those other two do.

Chris K: That's correct. It's fought between William Starke Rosecrans's army, The Cumberlands, about 70,000 Federals, versus 45,000 Confederates under Braxton Bragg, the Army of Tennessee. It's basically a brilliant campaign, ten, eleven days of maneuver. Rosecrans is able to force Bragg out of the mountains protecting middle Tennessee, or Bragg's area of middle Tennessee, all the way back to Chattanooga at the cost of just a couple thousand casualties. And he'll later write, Rosecrans will later write to the War Department and say "do not overlook this victory because it is not written in letters of blood."

Chris M: So just because there was not a big huge, bloody battle, don't forget about it?

Chris K: Exactly. And yet, it's been forgotten. It was forgotten even then. Even in 1863 it was completely overshadowed by Gettysburg, Vicksburg, and even the fall of Port Hudson on July 9, 1863.

Chris M: Port Hudson, which nobody ever remembers, and yet even that gets more love than Tullahoma.

Chris K: Yeah, exactly.

Chris M: Now, one of the things that I find fascinating by this, and, of course, you've written a book about the Stones River campaign and the Tullahoma campaign, which I thought was just a fantastic book. [*The Stones River and Tullahoma Campaigns: The Army Does Not Retreat* (History Press, 2011)]

Chris K: Thank you.

Chris M: It's so illuminating that here you have one of the principle Union armies gobbling up a huge chunk of real estate in a strategically vital state, so it's really an achievement on par with what the other Union armies are doing at Vicksburg and Gettysburg.

Chris K: Yeah, that's true. It's, if you put the four together—Gettysburg, Vicksburg, Tullahoma, Port Hudson—it is a body blow to the Confederacy that they never fully recover from. They never recover from the loss of middle Tennessee. Once the Federal army occupies that terrain at the end of the Tullahoma campaign, the Confederates never return. And without Tullahoma, you don't get Chickamauga, Chattanooga, Atlanta, the March to the Sea, none of that. This is an essential link in that chain of campaigns that leads all the way to Savannah, Georgia, at the end of the year, at the end of 1864.

Chris M: I suspect the Army of the Cumberland probably wasn't glad to get Chickamauga, as you rolled that list off.

Chris K: Well, this is true. They were happy to take the City of Chattanooga. I always point out that, even though they lose the battle of Chickamauga, they win the campaign because the fruits of the campaign are to take the City of Chattanooga.

Chris M: Right, right—although you say "fruits," and they run out of fruits, vegetables, bread, meat and pretty much anything else by the time.

Chris K: They were practically eating the horses by the time relief arrives, yes.

Chris M: But that's huge, though, essentially capturing all of Tennessee like that.

Chris K: Basically, Bragg's front line moves, in those eleven days, from an area known as the Highland Rim, which is a chain of hills roughly 1,500 feet high. For those of you who may be familiar with South Mountain or some of the Catoctin Mountains or some of the mountains in the Shenandoah Valley, it's along those lines. And there are several passes that have to be defended. The front line maneuvers from there more than 80, 90 miles, all the way to the Tennessee River at Chattanooga.

Chris M: Which today you can follow on a nice big highway.

Chris K: Yeah, you can drive I-24—it takes you right down there.

Chris M: But that wasn't quite the avenue the armies took back then.

Chris K: No.

Chris M: So what made this campaign so brilliant?

Chris K: Maneuver. The big thing was maneuver, but it was also the skill of the Federal army. For example, one of the things Bragg's army had done was they had deployed with cavalry pickets in front of the gaps as a warning. But the Federals had reorganized and created the Lightning Brigade, as it would soon be known because of its actions. It's a bunch of mounted infantrymen with Spencer repeating rifles, and as they march out and make contact with these on the main, the Manchester Pike, which is today U.S. 41, they smash right through the pickets so fast that they reach the mountains, they reach the hills at the gap—it's a place called Hoover's Gap—before the Confederates can even react.

And the commander's like, "Hey, you know what, I can take those fortifications when they're empty. Before the infantry shows up, let me get through." And so they do, and by the time the Confederate infantry shows up, the Lightning Brigade is ready for battle under a guy named John Wilder.

They're outnumbered by the Confederates, but their firepower makes the difference. And then as the Confederates are falling back, here comes the XIV Army Corps under George Thomas to secure the position.

And that action on the first day is emblematic of the entire campaign, where the Army of the Cumberland is just maneuvering constantly, from that point on, and it has Bragg and his men completely off balance. Bragg is just reacting to what Rosecrans is doing, and Rosecrans continually threatens Bragg's rear. He forces Bragg to retreat to Tullahoma first. Bragg decides to hold in the city. At the last minute he realizes, as the Federals are beginning to work their way around to the east of Tullahoma to his line of retreat back to Chattanooga, "I think we better get outta here." Polk and Hardee, his two corps commanders, come to him and say, "We need to get out of here." And so they evacuate.

But Rosecrans, he does all this through guile and maneuver. I mean, there are a few significant scraps, significant engagements, but nothing on the scale of a major battle like what's happening in Pennsylvania at the same time, you know, Gettysburg. But even so, it still does the job. It's a masterpiece of maneuvering and logistics.

Chris M: It's a great example of Rosecrans just out-generaling Bragg.

Chris K: Agreed. One of the things I've learned having studied the generalship of Braxton Bragg is he could never think more than one move ahead. You know how you talk about how leaders of many types, strategic leaders of any organization, have to think several moves ahead, have to consider different factors. Bragg never could quite do that; he could always think one move ahead, but he could never think two, three, four. Rosecrans understands; he's already fought. He's got about three or four contingencies, he'll see how it goes, and then he'll activate whatever contingency needs to be made.

Chris M: So let's back this up just a little bit to sort of set the campaign up because the two armies had squared off right around the turn of the year at Stones River. Rosecrans's army was severely bloodied, and yet Bragg leaves the field. So, essentially, Rosecrans gets the win 'cause he's holding the field, but it's one of those victories that leaves him so bruised that he can't really do anything for a while.

Chris K: People forget that Stones River is the bloodiest battle by percentage of loss in the war. The 27 to 28% of the men on both sides that fight there fall killed, wounded or missing. So these armies are mangled in a way that they're not mangled in any other battle by percentage.

The other thing that needs to be pointed out about Rosecrans is not only is his army in very bad condition, but where's his supply base? It's Nashville. He's got three weeks of rations in there, and guess what? It's January, and a huge snowstorm hits right after they occupy Murfreesboro on January 5, 1863. But he's got a bigger problem, because what feeds his supply base at Nashville? It's the railroad to Louisville. And what has just happened to the railroad at Louisville? John Hunt Morgan has been up there and has cut it. In fact, that railroad between Louisville and Nashville is only open for the year from June 30, 1862 to June 30, 1863. It's only open, fully operational, for seven months and twelve days.

Chris M: Not a lot of time.

Chris K: No. And so, that's one of the things people forget is when they look at Rosecrans, why does he pause all this time between campaigns? It's because not only has his army been mangled, it's because he has to stop and not only fix the railroad he just conquered. He's gotta fix the railroad all the way back into Kentucky. And if it's not John Hunt Morgan and his cavalry messing with it, it's Confederate banditos up there messing with it.

Chris M: So not just repair, but then protect.

Chris K: Exactly. The Army of the Cumberland consistently throughout the war has the longest and most vulnerable supply lines of any of the major Federal armies.

Chris M: And I know some people sort of second guess and say, "Well, look, Sherman lived off the land during his march to the sea," and etc., but Sherman hadn't had the chance to learn that yet by this point in the war.

Chris K: Correct.

Chris M: So Rosecrans really doesn't have that kind of experience to try to figure that out.

Chris K: And by the way, the middle part of Tennessee between Murfreesboro and Chattanooga is known as "the barrens," and it was very sandy soil. So what do you think the prospects of living off the land were? And, actually, I'll point out to you as well, until the Nashville and Chattanooga Railroad was punched through that area, most of those towns did not exist until the 1850's.

Chris M: Wow.

Chris K: There were three or four towns in that area—Manchester, Shelbyville—and then everything else, all the other settlement comes in in the 1850's with the N & C Railroad that comes through. Tullahoma came up from the railroad.

Chris M: So by the time Rosecrans gets himself into position to make a move, he's had the chance to think this through. Why hasn't Bragg taken the time to think through his defense?

Chris K: Because Bragg is busy fighting with his generals. And one of the things that has happened is immediately after Stones River, Bragg was excoriated in the Confederate press for losing the battle. He had reported at the end of the first day that it was a great victory, which from the prospective of just that one day, it probably was. I mean, the Confederates had nearly destroyed the Army of the Cumberland, but he ends up withdrawing, and it creates a problem for Bragg. He feels very insecure, and he actually goes to his commanders and his generals all the way down to brigade and regiment, and says "I want a statement from you that you supported me and you continue to support me, and if I find out that I have lost the good name of my generals, I will retire without a murmur."

Well, most of them come back and say "you need to go." But he stays in command. And in my book, I devote a whole chapter to that, called "Corrosion of an Army," because what happens is you now have a referendum on Bragg. Bragg now knows who his enemies are.

Chris M: It's very Nixonian. Like, he says he has an enemies list.

Chris K: It is. He has an enemies list. Exactly. And so now it's time to do the Stones River reports. And what do you think: these battles now spill into the paper. One of the few times, actually the only time, I've ever seen it in the official records is when there's a report by John Breckinridge, and Bragg writes an addendum to it, basically telling, saying that Breckinridge is a liar for what he did at Stones River.

So this is the atmosphere. Just when the atmosphere is starting to calm down once the reports are in, they start catching up on paperwork and that brings up the Kentucky campaign. And if you go into the Kentucky campaign official records, you'll notice about half of those are written from Tullahoma, Tennessee, in the spring of 1863. And one of them contains a letter from one of Bragg's corps commanders to the other saying, "I see what you mean when you say this is as necessary to watch Tullahoma," i.e., army headquarters, "as it is to watch Murfreesboro," i.e., the enemy.

So what do you think that does to the atmosphere of the Army of Tennessee, and what do you think that does to any planning that they're doing? They have no planning.

I contrast it to Robert E. Lee before the 1864 campaign, where he and his staff have met and have planned and said, "If the Yanks do *this* coming out of Culpeper, we go here, and if they do *this*, we're going here, and if they do *this*, we're going to do this." I have seen none of that in the Army of Tennessee in 1863.

Chris M: Instead, it's the first of a number of finger-pointing episodes that basically corrupts the army. It ruins the army.

Chris K: It destroys it from within. That's exactly right.

Chris M: So Rosecrans, he's setting up his plan. I've heard that James Garfield, who is serving as his chief of staff, played a role in planning Tullahoma, but Garfield's role is controversial.

Chris K: James Garfield was an interesting character. I think he respected Rosecrans to a certain extent from a military ability standpoint, but disliked the man. And he didn't like working for him. They had very different personal habits, and that created some friction. And by the time they get to the fall campaigns, he is actively undermining Rosecrans. But at the same time, from a logistics standpoint, from a coordination standpoint, and from just communicating over a wide range of geographic distance, Garfield is essential to the prosecution of the campaign.

Chris M: Some of Garfield's biographers have said that he actually did the planning of the campaign, and they minimize Rosecrans's role in that.

Chris K: I don't buy that. I don't buy that.

I do think that they worked together on it, but at the same time, it was Rosecrans's operation. Rosecrans called the shots. You can find it all in the Official Records, and you can see the staff structure, you can see the things like that. A lot of the campaign, Garfield had managed and helped set up, but the impetus for a lot of it and the vision for a lot of it comes from Rosecrans. Rosecrans was a great strategic thinker.

If you look at how he maneuvers his armies in his various campaigns, you can see that he can think well. He's got a good sense of the objective, and a good sense of how to get there, but at the same time, he needs that good staff person to help manage and translate his ideas and his concepts into the details and the action necessary.

Chris M: So, let me go back to something you talked about earlier with the Lightning Brigade. Mounted infantry. With Spencer repeating rifles.

Chris K: Correct. Which were originally paid for by the men, later reimbursed by the army.

Chris M: How much of that action may have affected Phil Sheridan's thinking about how cavalry should be used, when Sheridan eventually becomes cavalry commander in the east?

Chris K: Oh, I definitely think that's part of it, because the Lightning Brigade has two great moments in this campaign—and I'll come back to Phil Sheridan's role here in just a minute. The Lightning Brigade has two great moments. The first great moment was Hoover's Gap. But the second great moment is a couple of days later when they spend a day and a half going into the rear of Bragg's army and threatening his line of retreat to Chattanooga, including the bridges over the Elk River, which are a key place. And they raise all kinds of havoc. And then they return without losing a person. Without loss.

Chris M: That's amazing

Chris K: What happened, though, was that they had attracted all kinds of infantry; they had attracted Bedford Forrest's cavalry; they had attracted Joe Wheeler's guys. They had a lot of people chasing each other—which is what Sheridan thinks about in 1864 when the Army of the Potomac is heading toward Spotsylvania: "Let me go after the Confederate cavalry, let me get into the rear and create all this havoc, and I will be able to impact the operations of the main army."

Chris M: That was a very different way of thinking about how to use cavalry in the east, where it was sort of, "Do some scouting, protect your supply lines, guard the flanks." And Sheridan's like, "No, we're gonna use these guys as a strike force and send them out and be on the offensive and be aggressive and get to the rear."

Chris K: Exactly. And see, Phil Sheridan sees that 'cause he's left over on the right wing. He's the last guy to pull out of the right wing of the army and is kind of the right wing flank protection with the cavalry corps of the Army of the Cumberland. And they spend time skirmishing with the Confederates and putting up a bold front during the Tullahoma campaign, but he sees what the Lightning Brigade has done, he sees what the cavalry has done, and he realizes, you know, this is an opportunity.

Jeff Wert, I think, sums it up very well: he says that Sheridan understood that cavalry could be used in many ways, and the twentieth-century equivalent would be armor, as a mobile, powerful strike force to deliver firepower on the battlefield and be able to get somewhere quickly and be able to hit hard because he's seen it. That's how the Lightning Brigade gets its name. It's because of its lightning-quick maneuvers during the Tullahoma Campaign.

Chris M: Like a blitzkrieg.

Chris K: I know, right? Yeah.

Chris M: Look at me. As a couple Polish guys, I don't know if I should be bringing up the German army. (laughter)

So, the big question for me, is why this campaign gets overlooked. It really rivals in impact the outcome of Gettysburg and Vicksburg. Why is it so overlooked?

Chris K: I think it comes back to what Rosecrans tells the War Department a few days after, when they write and say, you know, "Great victory; will you be able to finish the rebellion at this point?" That's basically what they say. "Will you neglect the chance?" And Rosecrans writes back and says, "I beg to inform you," and he lists all the things that the army has done, and he says, "I beg you not to overlook this victory because it is not written in letters of blood." When you compare it to the much more hotly contested actions. . . .

Chris M: Gettysburg is a huge, dramatic victory on Northern soil, you know?

Chris K: Yeah, and to me that's the difference. It was overlooked even in July of 1863. It continues to be overlooked today.

Chris M: And, you know, when Grant captures Vicksburg, opens up the Mississippi, and then Port Hudson. I mean, huge, huge tangible results from Vicksburg and Gettysburg in very dramatic fashion.

Chris K: Correct. And there are huge, tangible results in middle Tennessee but with less drama. And therein lies the rub.

Chris M: Oh boy. Poor Rosecrans. So, what's the result of Tullahoma?

Chris K: Without Tullahoma, you don't get Chickamauga, Chattanooga, March to the Sea, Atlanta Campaign.

Chris M: You gotta have Chattanooga. Tullahoma gives them that.

Chris K: Correct. If you think about a chain, links in a chain that the Federal army has to conquer as they advance south from Louisville, Kentucky in 1862 all the way to Atlanta and beyond, this is a vital link in that chain. And so they're progressing down that chain, which will eventually lead them to Atlanta.

Chris M: So for someone who wants to study the Tullahoma campaign more closely, what recommendations do you have for them?

Chris K: The two things that I would recommend. First of all, I've written a book called *The Stones River and Tullahoma Campaigns: This Army Does Not Retreat.* It came out in 2011 by The History Press.

Chris M: Fantastic book.

Chris K: Thank you. Thank you. And, uh, the other thing is *Blue and Gray* a few years ago came out with an outstanding driving tour of the Tullahoma campaign sites, and so as a good kind of introduction. Those would be the two things I'd look at.[1]

Chris M: Excellent, excellent. Thanks so much for talking about this forgotten campaign, which is fascinating.

Chris K: Well, thanks for having me.

---

1   Since this interview was first broadcast, our ECW colleagues David Powell and Eric Wittenberg have published a book, *Tullahoma: The Forgotten Campaign that Changed the Civil War* (Savas Beatie, 2020), which won the 2020 Tennessee History Book Award. We highly recommend it!

Not Written in Letters of Blood, Redux

by Dave Powell

Adapted from a blog post originally published at Emerging Civil War on September 25, 2020

On July 7, 1863, Union Maj. Gen. William S. Rosecrans, in reply to a telegram from Secretary of War Edwin Stanton, wrote: "I beg in [sic] behalf of this army that the War Department may not overlook so great an event because it is not written in letters of blood."[1] Rosecrans was referring to the recent operations of the Army of the Cumberland in late June and early July 1863, more commonly known as the Tullahoma campaign.

The Tullahoma campaign is, by and large, still undiscovered country for most students of the Civil War. Many people know *of* Tullahoma, I have found, but not many know much *about* Tullahoma.

There are at least three overriding reasons for this obscurity. First, neither the Union nor Confederate commanders were top talent. Immediate draws of the likes of Grant, Lee, Sherman, or Stonewall Jackson were not present in Middle Tennessee. Second, the campaign lasted slightly more than one week and ended without a climactic battle. Today, no national or even state

---

1   United States War Department, *The War of the Rebellion: A Compilation of the Official Records of the Union and Confederate Armies,* 70 vols. in 128 parts (Washington D.C.: Government Printing Office, 1880-1901), Series I, volume 23, part 2, p. 518.

park exists to preserve its story. Third, Tullahoma is overshadowed by two other great events that happened simultaneously: Gettysburg and Vicksburg, both of which overpowered news of Tullahoma even as it was happening.

Despite that obscurity, Tullahoma has another reputation, passed as if by word-of-mouth, as one of the truly remarkable examples of military movement in the Civil War. For over the course of roughly eleven days, from June 23 to July 4, 1863, Rosecrans unleashed a campaign of deception and maneuver that so baffled his Confederate opponent, Braxton Bragg, that the Rebels were driven completely out of middle Tennessee, surrendering a huge swath of the state to Federal control as they retired to Chattanooga, in the very southeast corner of the state.

Faced with extensive Confederate earthworks and the daunting real estate of the highland rim, Rosecrans repeatedly eschewed frontal assaults and leveraged Bragg out from behind works at Shelbyville, Wartrace, and the Confederate supply base at Tullahoma. Rosecrans orchestrated a successful campaign, remarkably devoid of endless casualty lists flooding hometown newspapers, won at a cost of less than 600 Federal soldiers. Bragg's losses were heavier, but mostly in deserters and captures; none of the actions fought over the course of those ten days were particularly bloody.

In the end, Bragg's army escaped to fight another day, avoiding disaster by the thinnest of margins, thanks in part to the abnormally heavy rains that fell during that ten-day stretch. Bragg's escape provides yet another reason why Tullahoma has been overlooked. It feels like a prelude, not a decisive stroke in its own right. Two months later Rosecrans and Bragg faced off again, this time for control of Chattanooga, and that confrontation did result in an epic collision: Chickamauga, the second-bloodiest battle of the entire war.

Contributors Notes

Emerging Civil War is the collaborative effort of more than thirty historians committed to sharing the story of the Civil War in an accessible way. Founded in 2011 by Chris Mackowski, Jake Struhelka, and Kristopher D. White, Emerging Civil War features public and academic historians of diverse backgrounds and interests, while also providing a platform for emerging voices in the field. Initiatives include the award-winning Emerging Civil War Series of books published by Savas Beatie, LLC; the "Engaging the Civil War" Series published by Southern Illinois University Press; an annual symposium; a speakers bureau; and a daily blog: www.emergingcivilwar.com.

Emerging Civil War is recognized by the I.R.S. as a 501(c)3 not-for-profit corporation.

* * *

Edward Alexander is a freelance cartographer at Make Me a Map, LLC. He is a regular contributor for Emerging Civil War and the author of *Dawn of Victory: Breakthrough at Petersburg* in the Emerging Civil War Series. Edward has previously worked at Pamplin Historical Park and Richmond National Battlefield Park. He has written for the Emerging Civil War blog since March 2013.

Paige Gibbons Backus has a bachelor's degree in Historic Preservation, and a master's degree in Applied History. She has been in the public history field for close to ten years focusing on educational programming and operations working at several historic sites in Northern Virginia. Her research interests include social and women's history, as well as the more morbid side of history such as death, disease, medicine, murder, or scandal. She started writing for the Emerging Civil War blog in July 2017.

Sean Michael Chick is a New Orleans native. He holds an undergraduate degree from the University of New Orleans and a Master of Arts from Southeastern Louisiana University. He is currently a New Orleans tour guide, giving one of the only guided tours of the French Quarter concentrating on the American Civil War and slavery. His first book was *The Battle of Petersburg, June 15-18, 1864*. He joined the Emerging Civil War blog in the summer of 2017 after making several guest contributions to the blog.

Caroline Davis grew up in Indiana, with her passion for history starting at a young age. She earned her bachelor's degree in American History from Ball State University and her Master's in Historical Preservation with a concentration in Public History at Georgia State University. She has worked at Fredericksburg and Spotsylvania NMP, Vicksburg NMP, Stones River NB, and C&O Canal NHP. She hopes to continue a career with the National Park Service. Caroline started writing with ECW in June 2013.

Meg Groeling received her Master's degree in Military History, with a Civil War concentration in 2016 from American Public University. She is the author of *Aftermath of Battle: The Burial of the Civil War Dead* and *First Fallen: The Life of Colonel Elmer Ellsworth*, both published by Savas Beatie. She and her husband live, with three cats, in a 1927 California bungalow covered with roses on the outside and books on the inside. Meg started writing for the blog in 2011.

In 1990, **Chris Heisey** began photographing American battlefields. He has published images in more than 250 worldwide publications and media venues, and his images have garnered numerous awards including four national merit awards. He has collaborated on three previous books: *In the Footsteps of Grant and Lee* with Gordon Rhea; *Gettysburg: This Hallowed Ground*; and *Gettysburg: The Living and The Dead* with Kent Gramm. He started writing and contributing photography with Emerging Civil War in June 2020.

Dwight Hughes is a retired U. S. Navy officer, Vietnam War veteran, and public historian who speaks and writes on Civil War naval history. He is the author of two books and a contributing author at the Emerging Civil War blog. Dwight has presented at numerous Civil War roundtables, historical conferences, and other venues. You can find out more about Dwight's works at https://civilwarnavyhistory.

com. His first guest post on the ECW blog was in December 2014, and since that time has contributed over 66 posts.

Christopher L. Kolakowski is ECW's Chief Historian. He has spent his career interpreting and preserving American military history, and is currently Director of the Wisconsin Veterans Museum in Madison, Wisconsin. He has written and spoken on various aspects of military history from 1775 to the present, including four books on the Civil War and World War II. He started blogging for Emerging Civil War in May 2013.

Chris Mackowski, Ph.D. is the editor in chief and a co-founder of Emerging Civil War, and he's the managing editor of the Emerging Civil War Series published by Savas Beatie. Chris is a writing professor in the Jandoli School of Communication at St. Bonaventure University, where he also serves as the associate dean for undergraduate programs, and is the historian-in-residence at Stevenson Ridge, a historic property on the Spotsylvania Court House battlefield.

Andrew Miller is a graduate of the State University of New York at Cortland where he earned both his bachelor's and master's degrees. He has worked at numerous National Park Service sites including Stones River NB, Shiloh NMP, and Fort Pulaski NM. Andrew's current duty station is Vicksburg NMP. Andrew and his wife, Emily, have a daughter, Georgia, and two dogs: Sherman and Melly Wilkes. He has been a writer with Emerging Civil War since December 2017.

David A. Powell is a graduate of the Virginia Military Institute (1983) with a BA in History. He has published numerous articles and more than fifteen historical simulations. For the past fifteen years, David's focus has been on Chickamauga, and he is nationally recognized for his tours of that important battlefield. David, his wife Anne, and their three bloodhounds live and work in the northwest suburbs of Chicago, Illinois. He started blogging with ECW in September 2017.

Angela Riotto received her Ph.D. from the University of Akron. Her research examines the ways in which both Union and Confederate former prisoners of war discussed their captivity between 1862 and 1930. She currently works as a historian with the Army University Press Films Team at Fort Leavenworth, Kansas, developing documentaries to teach U.S. Army doctrine and military history. She has written for ECW since April 2020.

Raised on Chamberlain Street in Brewer, Maine, **Brian F. Swartz** has worked as a newspaper reporter, editor, and photographer for 34 years and has published several books, including *Passing Through the Fire: Joshua Lawrence Chamberlain in the Civil War* for the Emerging Civil War Series. He writes the *Maine at War* blog post, published weekly at www.maineatwar.bangordailynews.com. He has been collaborating with ECW since March 2019.

Kristen M. Trout is the Museum Director at the Missouri Civil War Museum in St. Louis. She received her BA in History and Civil War Era Studies at Gettysburg College, and her MA in Nonprofit Leadership from Webster University. Trout has worked with the American Battlefield Trust, the Civil War Institute, the Gettysburg Foundation, and the National Park Service. A native of Missouri, Trout's focus of research is the Civil War in Missouri. She has been a contributor with Emerging Civil War since July 2018.

Kristopher D. White is the senior education manager at the American Battlefield Trust, and the co-founder of Emerging Civil War, the Emerging Civil War Series, and Engaging the Civil War Series. White is a graduate of Norwich University with an M.A. in Military History, and a graduate of California University of Pennsylvania with a B.A. in History. For nearly five years he served as a ranger-historian at Fredericksburg and Spotsylvania National Military Park.

William Lee White is a park ranger at Chickamauga and Chattanooga National Military Park, where he gives tours and other programs. He is the author of *Bushwhacking on a Grand Scale: The Battle of Chickamauga, Let Us Die Like Men: The Battle of Franklin*, both part of the Emerging Civil War Series, as well as several articles and essays on topics related to the Western Theater. He also edited *Great Things Are Expected of Us: The Letters of Colonel C. Irvine Walker, 10th South Carolina Infantry CSA*. He has contributed to Emerging Civil War since 2013.

 *Postscript*

To the Good People of Vicksburg:

I know I have been delayed in moving to the salvation of your fortified city, but please accept my assurances that I am on my way. Finally.

Even now, I finish the final preparations I have been making to amass an Army of Relief large enough to ensure success against the enemy forces besieging the city. Coming to your aid before this army was fully reinforced and equipped—before I could wholly ensure its complete and total stunning victory—would have only doomed the army and city alike. The delays that have thus far prevented my movement have been all but overcome, almost.

But on my honor as a soldier and my word as a gentleman, accept my assurance that I am nearly ready and shall soon move with all possible haste as circumstances and the probability of victory allow, immediately if not sooner. Expect alacrity and boldness, tempered only by wise caution.

Joseph E. Johnston, General Commanding
Department of the West
July 2021

P.S.: I have heard distressing rumors that Vicksburg has fallen already, but have not yet been able to confirm. Please continue to hold out—and hold out hope—as I work to investigate this news.

I pray I am not too late!

Dan:

A reader sent this purported correspondence from Joe Johnston for us to look at.
He claimed the handwriting matched up with a member of Johnston's staff.
I have doubts about its authenticity, but check out the timing—
for Old Joe, that sounds about right!

– Chris

Index

2nd Texas Lunette, 6, 131

3rd Louisiana Redan, 32, 136, 139, 140

Abraham (enslaved man), xx, 136-149, *138*, 195

Adams, John (Founding Father), 154, *156*, 156-157, 160

Adams, Brig. Gen. John, 86-87

Adams, Henry, 210

African Brigade, 196

Alabama, 61, 172, 240, 260; Mobile, 100, 172, 176; Selma, 61

Alabama troops, 98, 248
30th Infantry, 98
65th Infantry, 100

Alexander, Pvt. Wallace, 70

American Battlefield Trust, 1

American Revolution, 260

Andrus, Sgt. Samuel, 270, 273

Andrus, Capt. Wesley P., 270-273

Antietam National Battlefield, 212

Appomattox Court House, 82

Archinal, Pvt. William, 110

Arkansas Post, 55, 65, 130, 132

Arkansas River, 55, 65

Arkansas troops, 243, 252, 255, 256
2nd Infantry, 249, 251, 252
5th Infantry, 255
5th, 13th, and 15th Consolidated, 245, 247
6th and 7th Arkansas Consolidated, 246, 249, 251

Army of Northern Virginia, 173, 187, 260

Army of Tennessee, 187, 215, 218, 222, 223, 226, 227, 229, 233, 237, 240, 241, 255, 260, 275, 281
Hardee's Corps, 240
Wheeler's Cavalry Corps, 265

Army of the Cumberland, xix, 187, 218, 219, 222, 227, 228, 229, 232, 238, 255, 260, 275, 276, 278, 279, 280, 283; at Murfreesboro, 215
IV Corps, 257
XIV Corps, 222, 232, 268
XX Corps, 264
XXI Corps, 219, 222, 232
Cavalry Corps, 232, 283
Reserve Corps, 222, 232, 265

Army of the Potomac, 173-175, 176, 212, 273
IX Corps, 179

Army of the Tennessee, 2, 36, 60, 72, 74, 81-82, 91, 108, 149, 171
XIII Corps, 6, 10, 13, 64, 93, 130-132
XV Corps, 5, 6, 10, 20, 66, 85, 92-93, 108
XVI Corps, 61
XVII Corps, 6, 10, 17, 92-93, 139, 149

Arnold Air Force Base, 221

Ascension Day, 170

Askew, Lt. Col. Frank, 255, 258

Bachelder, John, 214

Baird, Brig. Gen. Absalom, 264

Bald Knob, Battle of, 257

Balfour, Emma, 162-164

Banks, Maj. Gen. Nathaniel, 76-82, *77*, 127, 211

Barksdale, Brig. Gen. William, 185

Barnum, P.T., 138, 146-147, *148*

Battlefield Park (Jackson), 18-20, *19*

Beatty, Brig. Gen. John, 268, 269

Beauregard, Gen. P. G. T., 151, 182, *183,* 184, 186, 189

Beech Grove, Battle of, 236, 237, 262, 263

Beech Grove Confederate Cemetery and Park, 259-262, *260*

Beech Grove, TN, 219, 238, 259, 261-262

Belmont, Battle of, 128, 132

Benton, Gen. William P., 68-69

Big Black River, 4, 5, *8*, 9, 69, 82, 96, 105, 209

Big Muddy, 36

Black River, 61, 70

Blair, Maj. Gen. Francis Preston "Frank," 16, 66-67, 108, 109, 114-115, 116-117, 118, 122

bombardments, 6, 26, 41, 114, 169

Bowen, Maj. Gen. John S., 22, 96, 97, 150, 151, 152, 153

Bowen, Mary, 153

Bragg, Gen. Braxton, 187, 218, 219, 222-227, 230-232, 236-240, 260-261, 264, 269, 275, 277, 278, 281, 283

Brickell, Surgeon Daniel Warren, CSA, 171

Breckinridge, Maj. Gen. John, 26-27, 225, 281; statue of, *27*

Bruinsburg, 2, *8*, 9, *9*, 10, *10, 11*, 12, 14, 47, 55, 62, 59, 75, 79-80, 181

Buckland, Brig. Gen. Ralph, 88, 89, 93

Buckner, Maj. Gen. Simon B., 238, 239

Burma, 73, 74

Burnside, Maj. Gen. Ambrose, 27, 118, 174, 179-180

Butler, Maj. Gen. Benjamin, 127

Calhoun, John C., 159

Camp Forrest, 221

Camp Randall, 103

Carney, Joseph, 259

Carr, Brig. Gen. Eugene, 68

Cash, Johnny and June Carter, 7

Catholic Church, xix, 15, 168, 171

Catton, Bruce, 212; *Grant Moves South,* 212

caves, 6, *163*, 164-166, 170

cemeteries, 15, 33-34, *34*, 153, *198*, 235, 259-261

Champion Hill, Battle of, 3-4, 20-23, *22, 23*, 82, 93-94, 95-100, 105-106, 131, 209, 212

Champion, Matilda and Sid, 4

Chancellorsville, Battle of, 82, 185, 187, 190, 204, 205

Chattanooga, Battles around, 211; as national park, 212

Cheat Mountain, xix

Chicago Daily Tribune, 140, 144

Chickamauga, Battle of, 204, 273; as national park, 212

Chickasaw Bayou, Battle of, xix, 1, 36, 55, 130, 209

Chippewa River, 103

Civil War Trails, Tennessee, 262

civilians, 62, 162-167, 168, 170, 192

Cleburne, Maj. Gen. Patrick, 231, 234, 240, 243, 246, 248, 252

Cockrell, Col. Francis, 5, 112, 114, 115

Coddington, Edwin, 212

Collins, Pvt. Bernard, 135

Colquitt, Col. Peyton, 86-87

Commission to Ascertain and Mark Positions of Illinois Troops at the Siege of Vicksburg, 196

Confederate flag, 27, *28*, 91, 104, 161, 206, 259

Congress, 102, 118, 194, 202

Connecticut troops
9th Infantry, 30-31; monument, 30-31, *30*

Continental Line, 259

Cook, Major, 170

Cope, Alexis, 255

Cotton trade, 169

COVID-19, 200, 202

Crittenden, Thomas L., 222, 232, 236

Cumberland Plateau, 260-261, 269

Curtis, Samuel, 72-73

Dahlgren smoothbore, 37

Daily Whig & Courier, 133, 135

Davis, Flag Officer Charles H., USN, 50-51, 54, 266

Davis, Jefferson, 26-27, 125, 147, *178*, 182-184, 186, 189-190, 208-209; statues of, 27, *27, 28*

"Declaration of the Immediate Causes which Induce and Justify the Secession of the State of Mississippi from the Federal Union, A," 158-160

Deeds of Valor, 109

Dennis, Brig. Gen. Elias S., 95

Department of South Carolina (CSA), 182, 186

deserter, 133

De Soto Point, 29-30, 44

Douglass, Lt. John C., 95-96

Douglas, Stephen, 128

Drumgould's Bluff, 201

Duck River, 266-267, 270

Dunbar, Capt. Samuel H., 68-71

Edward's Depot, MS, 96, 99

Elk River, 220, 268, 269

Elliott, Lt. Marcus D., 195

Emerging Civil War, xx, 133, 139, 259

Eoff, Pvt. Isaac, 259

Ewing, Brig. Gen. Hugh, 114, 115, 116

electronic explosive device, 36, 201

"Facing Execution with Faithfulness, Triumph Amidst Bloodshed: Civil War Soldiers' Spiritual Victories," 135

Farragut, Flag Officer David G., USN, 54-55, 169

Faulkner, William, 206; *Intruder in the Dust*, 206

Fifteenth Army (Japanese), 73

food shortages, 166-167

Foote, Flag Officer Andrew H., USN, 50-51

Forlorn Hope, 108-110, 111-119 *113*; definition of, 111-112

Forrest, Gen. Nathan B., 229, 231, 238, 265-267, 283

Fort Cobun, 14, 16, 47, 78

Fort Donelson, 11, 50, 129, 139

Fort Henry, 50, 129

Fort Hindman, 55

Fort Pillow, 200

Fort Sumter, 215

Fort Wade, 14, 15, 47, 48

Fortress Rosecrans, 230

Foster, Lt. Henry, 195

Fourteenth Army (British), 74

Fox, Gustavus V., 54

Fredericksburg, Battle of, 214, 261

Fuller, J.F.C, 212

Gaddy, Pvt. James E., 135

Gage, Richard J., 269

Garfield, James, xix, 282

Gettysburg, Battle of, 41, 172-173, 204-207, 220, 260, 272-273; number of books published, 213; on top 10 list of turning point battles, 203-04

Gettysburg, Pennsylvania, 261; as National Military Park, 212; as a park ranger at, 204

Gibraltar, 36, 48

Gilley's Gap, 264

Golden Years, 195

Gorgas, Col. Josiah, 211

Government Printing Office, 135

Graham, George, 128

Grand Gulf, 14-16, *15*, 47, 58-59, 66, 67, 68, 70, 75, 76, 78, 80-82

Grand Gulf Military Museum, 15

Granger, Maj. Gen. Gordon, 222, 232, 264-265

Grant, Maj. Gen. Ulysses S., xviii-xix, xx, 1, 2, 3, 4, 5, *5*, 10, 12, 13, 14, 16, 22, 24, 25, 26, 30, 36, 41, 42, 46, 48-56, 58-59, 60, 61, 62, 64, 66, 67, 72, 74, 75-82, 86, 92-93, 103, 105, 108, 112, 122-123, 133, 135, 145, 148, 150-152, 154-155, 172-176, *173,* 177, 182, 184-185, 187, 189-190, 195, 200, 209, 212, 213, 219, 226, 260, 284; comes east, 208; falling out with McClernand, 128-132; sending troops to Pennsylvania, 175, 215; statue of, *xxviii-xxix,* 25

Grant's Canal, xix, 1-2, 28-30, *29*, 36, 56, 130

Graveyard Road, 5, 6, 105, 110, 113-115, *113, 116*

Greencastle College, 71

Gregg, Brig. Gen. John, 2, 3, 17, 86-87, 90-91, 94

Grierson, Col. Benjamin, xx, 60, 61, *61*, 62, 63, *63*

Groce, John H., 114, 116

Guadalcanal, 73-74

Guion, Capt. Louis, 196

gunboat, 35-37, 51, 55, 56, 58, 170

Guy's Gap, 219, 265

Halleck, Maj. Gen. Henry W., 54-55, 60, 76-77, 79-82, 129-132, 175-176

Hallowed Ground, 1

hand grenades, 116, 195

Hankinson's Ferry, 75, 80-81

hard war, 60, 61, 62

Hardee, Lt. Gen. William J., 222, 239, 278

Hatch, Reuben, 128

Hazen, Brig. Gen. William B., 236, 258

Hébert, Louis, 112

Hess, Lafayette, 253-258

Hickenlooper, Capt. Andrew, 136-137, *137*

Hill, Maj. Gen. Daniel Harvey, *183*

Hills, Brig. Gen. (ret.) Parker, 9-11, 16-18, *17*, 21, 22-23, 31, 81

Hoit, Pvt. Nicholas, 135

Holland, Samuel F., 269

Holly Springs, xix

Homaston, Edward, 105, 107

Home for Little Wanders, 133

Hood, Maj. Gen. John Bell, 178, 185

Hooker, Maj. Gen. Joseph, 180-182, 183, 185

Hoover's Gap, Battle of, 261-262

Hoover's Gap, TN, 219, 220, 259-262

hospitals, 96, 144, 145, 170, 171

hostages, 135

Howard, Maj. Gen. Oliver Otis "Uh-Oh," 149, 257

Howard Mission, 133

Howe, Capt. George W., 269

Howe, Pvt. Orion, 31

Hume, Maj. William, 261-262

Hurlburt, Maj. Gen. Stephen A., 61

Illinois, xix, 211; Cairo, 50-51, 55, 128, 149; Chicago, 215; Galena, xix, 128

Illinois-Vicksburg Commission, 196

Illinois Monument, *xxvi-xxvii*, 26, *26*

Illinois troops, 210
  6th Cavalry, 61
  42nd Infantry, 270-273
  45th Infantry, 148
  81st Infantry, 139, 140, 143
  104th Infantry, 220, 268, 269

Imphal, 73-74

independence, 156

India, 73-74

Indiana, Greenfield, 71

Indiana troops, 210
  1st Artillery, 68
  18th Artillery, 261-262
  3rd Cavalry, 266
  8th Infantry, 68-71
  11th Infantry, 70
  18th Infantry, 69
  23rd Infantry, 195
  32nd Infantry, 256
  59th Infantry, 91
  72nd Infantry, 261

Institute for the Deaf and Dumb (Jackson, MS), 170

Interpretation, 195

Iowa, 211

Iowa troops
  17th Infantry, 93-94
  24th Infantry, 194

ironclads, 35-37, 39, 44, 47, 50, 55, 56

Island Number 10, Battle of, 36, 270

Jackson, MS, xx, 2, 3, 7, 22, 60, 62, 82, 85, *88*, 91, 101, 170, 209

Jackson, Andrew, 159

Jackson, Lt. Gen. Thomas Jonathan "Stonewall" ("Did you see how Mackowski weaseled me into a book about the Western Theatre?"), 184, 186, 189

Jefferson, Lt. Col. John, 92

Jefferson, Thomas, 154, 156-157

Johnny Rebs, 133

Johnston, Gen. Joseph E., 22, 86-87, 92-94, 96, 112, 124-125, 177-178, 180, 182, 184-185, 187, 210

Johnson, Brig. Gen. Richard W., 256

Jones, John B., 189, 210

Kawaguchi, Kiyotake, 73-74

Kennesaw Mountain, Battle of, 257

Kentucky, 215, 260

Kentucky Monument, 26-27, *27*

Kentucky troops
3rd Kentucky Mounted Infantry (CSA), 86-87

Koch, Capt. Charles R.C., 196-97

Kolakowski, Christopher L., 260

Kohima, 73-74

Kountz, William, 128-129

labyrinth, *260*

Lawrence, David, 262

Lee, Gen. Robert E., xix, xx, 173, 177-186, 188-190, 213, 260, 273

Lee, Brig. Gen. Stephen D., 95, 98-100

Leray, Father Francis Xavier, 170

Libby Prison, 255, 258

Liberty Gap, Battle of,

Liberty Gap, 219, 220

Liberty Gap, Battle of, 255-257, 264

Liddell, Brig Gen. St. John R., 256

Lighting Brigade, 234, 236, 238, 277, 278, 282-284

Lilly, Capt. Eli, 261-262

Lincoln, Abraham, xix, 26, 48, 51, 53, 55, 60, 139, 140, 173, 176, 208-209; relationship with McClernand, 127, 129-130, 132; frustration with Meade, 173, 207

Lockett, Maj. Samuel, 136-137

Logan, Maj. Gen. John, 3, 26, 107, 128, 138, 139-140, 145, 146-147, 148, 149, 154-155, 160; monument to, *141;* General John A. Logan Museum, 146

London, England, economic system, 169

long roll, 135, 235

Longstreet, Lt. Gen. James, 181, *183,* 185-188

Loring, Maj. Gen. William W., 96-97

Loughborough, Mary Webster, 164-166

Louisiana, xviii, xix, 28-29; Baton Rouge, xx, 62, 76, 82; New Carthage, 43,47; New Orleans, 1, 53-54, 211

Louisiana Monument, commission, 196

Louisiana troops
9th Infantry, African Descent, 197
11th Louisiana, African Descent, 197
26th Infantry, 196
27th Infantry, 5, 196
28th Infantry, 196

Madison, James, 157

Maine, 133; Bangor, 133

Maine at War, 133

Maine newspapers, 135

Maine troops, 260
1st Heavy Artillery, 118

Manassas battlefield, 262

Manassas, First Battle of, 139, 261

Manchester Pike, 261

Marsh, Sgt. George, 269

Marsh, John B., 133-135

Marsh, Rev. Leonard, 134

Martin, William, 265, 267

Maryland, Baltimore, 168-169; Williamsport, 207

Massachusetts, 168

Matthies, Brig. Gen. Charles, 88, 89
McClellan, Maj. Gen. George, xix, 129

McClernand, Maj. Gen. John A., 10, 13, 25, 26, 48-49, 51-52, 55-56, 68, 77-78, 93, 112, 117-123; as Sherman's "Demon Spirit," 64-67, *66*; falling out with Grant, 127-132

McCook, Alexander, 222, 232, 264

McGinnis, Gen. George F., 69-70

McGinnis, James, 103

McKee, Pvt. Ike, 69

McLaws, Maj. Gen. Lafayette, 185

McPherson, Maj. Gen. James, 10, 13, 17-18, 25, 78, 80, 85, 91-94, 112, 117, 131, 145, 146, 148, 149, 151, 152

Meade, Maj. Gen. George Gordon, 172-175, *173*, 207, 208

Medal of Honor, 31, 116, 220, 266, 269

Melville, Herman, 42, 44-45

Memorial Day, 108

memory, *xv*, 160, 195

Michigan, Cedar Springs, 273; Holly, 195

Michigan troops
    2nd Cavalry, 265
    4th Cavalry, 266
    2nd Infantry, 139
    7th Infantry, 118
    Light Artillery, Eighth Battery, 19

Midwest Civil War Artillery Association, 261

Miles, Pvt. Samuel C., 83-85, *84*, 87, 89-93, 101

Miller, Dorra, 165-167

Milliken's Bend, 10, 14, 30, 79; Battle of, 196-97

mine, 6, 136-137, 140, 140-142, *143*, *144*, 195

Minty, Col. Robert Horatio George, 265-267

Mississippi, 66, 67; Brookhaven, 62; Canton, 86, 91, 171; Clinton, 2, 86-87; Corinth, 54; Edwards, 3, 96, 99, 153; Meridian, 61; Mississippi Springs, 170; Oxford, 170-171, 215

Mississippi Delta, *xix*, xxx, 36, 56

Mississippi troops, 148
    6th Infantry, 148
    36th Infantry, 112, 123

Mississippi River, 1, 2, 9-10, 14,16, 28-29, 36-37, 42,46-47, 51, 54-55, 59, 75, 76, 77, 79, 135, 170, 208; batteries on, xx, 43-45

Mississippi River Squadron, 36, 41, 48-50

Mississippi River Valley, 133

Missouri, 191-193

Missouri troops
    1st Infantry, 112
    5th Infantry, 112
    8th Infantry, 116

Missouri State Memorial at Vicksburg, 191

Mitchell, Robert, 264

Montgomery, Louis, 150-152

monuments, *xvi-xxvii*, *xxviii-xxix*, 25, 26-27, *27, 28, 117,* 191-193; 9th Connecticut, *30*, 30-31; Adams, John, *156*; African-American Memorial, *vi*; Breckinridge, John C., *27*; Champion Hill, *23*; Davis, Jefferson, *27, 28*; Grant, Ulysses S., memorial, *xxviii-xxix, 25*; Guide to the Campaign Trail, A (Raymond), *18*; Hoover's Gap, Confederate Dead of, *235*; Illinois state memorial, *xxvi-xxvii, 26*; Kentucky state memorial, *27*; Logan, John A., *141*; Mississippi state memorial, *xxiii*; Missouri state memorial, 191-193, *192*; Vicksburg Memorial Arch, *24*; Wisconsin state memorial, *21*

Morgan, John H., 229, 231, 240, 279

Moore, Col. Absalom B., 269

Mower, Brig. Gen. Joseph, 85, 88-90, 93, 101, 104-105

Murfreesboro, Battle of, (see "Stones River, Battle of")

Murfreesboro, Tennessee, 215, 222, 227, 228, 229, 230, 231, 232, 234, 237, 238, 255, 259, 261, 274, 279-281

Mutaguchi, Renya, 73-74

My Cave Life in Vicksburg, 164-166

naval artillery, 36, 41

Nature Conservancy, The, 261

Negley, Maj. Gen. James S., 268,

New York City, 133, 169, 215

New York Times, 35

Nixon, Richard, 281

O'Neal, George, 114, 116

Ohio, 134-135; Belmont County, 253-254, 257

Ohio troops
    18th Artillery, 266
    15th Infantry, 253-258
    30th Infantry, 115
    37th Infantry, 115
    43rd Infantry, 135
    47th Infantry, 116
    95th Infantry, 89

Ohio River, 254

Old Abe, the War Eagle, 26, 85, 90, 101-107, *103, 106*

Old Courthouse Museum, *161*

Old Flag, 134-135

Old Tecumseh, 57, 59

Ole Miss: The University of Mississippi, 215

Ord, Maj. Gen. Edward, 132

Palmer, John, 236

Panola County, Mississippi, 135

Parrish, Lt. Col. Charles S., 70

Pea Ridge, Battle of, 72

Pemberton, Lt. Gen. John C., 2, 3, 4, 5, *5*, 6, 10, 22, 62, 79, 86, 96, 99, 112, 125, 150-152, 155, 162, 177-178, 182, 189, 195, 209

Pennsylvania, 260; Chambersburg, 205; Harrisburg, 211; Philadelphia, 211, 273, Pittsburgh, 1

Pennsylvania troops
    7th Cavalry, 266

Perkins, John E., 102

pharmaceuticals, 261

Pickett, Maj. Gen. George, 178, 180, 183, 184, 187-188, 190

Pitzman, Julius, 88-89

plantation elite, 169

Plum Point, 200

poetry, 42

Polk, Lt. Gen. Leonidas, 222, 224, 227, 230-232, 236-239, 265, 278

Pope, Maj. Gen. John, xx

Port Gibson, MS, 2, 12, 14, 22, 70, 68-71, 80-81, 94, 131, 209

Port Hudson, LA, 6, 76, 78-79, 81-82, 86, 208

Porter, Rear Adm. David Dixon, 2, 10, 14, 35-40, 42-47, 48-59, *49*, 78-79, 81, 197, 201, 215

Porter, Commodore David, 53

Potomac River, 207

Primedia eLaunch Publishing, 135

prisoners, 6, 93, 99, 130, 135, 197, 208, 220, 240, 257, 271

public history, 200, 202

Rappahannock River, 186-187

Raymond, *xxiv-xxv*, 2-3, *2*, 17, 18, 85, 86, 87, 153, 209

Red River, 79, 132

Reed, John W., 135

Register of the Events from the Foundation of Convent of the Sisters of Mercy, Vicksburg, Miss., 168

Rigby, Capt. William Tutus, 194-198

Riply, W.T., 193

riverine warfare, 200-201

Rhodes, Elisha Hunt, 214

Rosecrans, Maj. Gen. William S., xix, xx, 187, 218, 219, 220, 222-223, 225, 226-234, 236, 238, 239, 240-241, 255, 260-261, 264, 271, 275, 278-282, 284-285

Ross, Brig. Gen. Leonard F., 56

Sanborn, John B., 91

Scotland, Coldstream, 95

Sears, Lt. Col. Cyrus, 197

Secession convention, 157-159, 160, 169

Seddon, James, 177-182, 184-185, 188-189

Selfridge, Capt. Thomas, Jr, 201

Sendai Division, 73-74

Seven Days campaign, 207

Sewanee, 230

Shapland, John, 269

Shelbyville, TN, 219, 220, 264-267

Shenandoah Valley, 77

Sheridan, Brig. Gen. Philip H., 239, 271, 283-284; Sheridan's Division, 270-273

Sherman, Maj. Gen. William T., 1, 5, 10, 13-14, 20, 25, 30, 36, 48-49, 52, 54-59, 64-67, 78, 85, 87, 88, 89, 91-94, 103-104, 108, 112-115, 117, 123, 146, 201, 211, 213; Relationship with McClernand, 64-67, 130-132

Shiloh, Battle of, xviii, xix, 11, 48, 54, 130, 139; as national park, 212

Shipman, A.M., 133-135

Shoup, Brig. Gen. Francis, 196

Sickles, Maj. Gen. Daniel, 174

Sigel, Maj. Gen. Franz, 127

Sisters of Mercy, 168-170

Skull Camp Bridge, 267

Slagle, Oscar, 269

slavery, 138-139, 157-159

Slim, William, 74

Smalley, Rueben, 269

Smith, Andrew Jackson, 151-152

Smith, Lt. Elias, USN, 35, 37-40

Smith, Giles A., 114

Smith, Thomas Kilby, 114

Smith, Timothy B., 21-22, *21*

Smith, Lt. Cmdr. Watson, USN, 56

Smithsonian Institution, 149

South Carolina, Charleston, 95

Southerners, 135

Spencer repeating rifle, 262

Spotsylvania, 204

Springfield Journal, 133-134

Springfield, Illinois, 133

St. Louis (Missouri), 150

Stacey, Charles, 269

Stanley, David, 265-2

Stanley, Steven, 1

Stanton, Edwin M., 132, 218-219

Steahlin, George, 266

Steele, Maj. Gen. Frederick, 89

Steele's Bayou, 56

Stevens, Pvt. Eli, 70

Stevenson, Gen. Carter L., 97

Stewart, Alexander P., 231, 234, 240

Stockade Redan, xx, 5, 31, 105, 110, 112-114, *113*, 115, *116, 117*, 123, 126, 191, 196

Stones River, Battle of, 215, 219, 255, 264, 270-272

Stones River and Tullahoma Campaign, The: This Army Does Note Retreat, 260

Stones River National Battlefield, *216-217*

Strong, George Templeton, 210

Swartz, Brian, 133, 259-262

Swartz, Chris, 259-260

Sumner, Charles, abolitionist, 168

Sumner, Francis Steele, mother, 168

Sumner, Francis S. "Sister Mary Ignatius" 168

Sumner, Henry, 168

Taylor, Lt. Gen. Richard, 79

Tennessee, xix, xx, 260, 262; Middle Tennessee, xviii, 215; Bethpage Bridge, 268; Chattanooga, 215, 220, 259, 261; Columbia, 265, 267; Grand Junction, 200; Lookout Mountain, 261; Manchester, 219, 261; Memphis, 50, 52, 54-55, 65, 80, 135, 200; Wartrace, 219

Tennessee Backroads Heritage, 261

Tennessee Historical Commission, 262

Tennessee River, 11, 261

Texas, 132; Austin, 100

Thatcher, Marshall, 265

Thomas, Maj. Gen. George "The Rock of Chickamauga," 149, 222, 232, 234, 235-236, 238, 261, 278

Tilghman, Brig. Gen. Lloyd, 99

timberclad, 50

tinclad, 50, 56

torpedo, 36, 55

transports, 2, 35-36, 40, 44, 46-47, 55, 56, 58; *Forest Queen*, 40; *Henry Clay*, 40

Trogden, Pvt. Howell G., carrying guidon, 110

Trowbridge, Silas (surgeon), 143, 145

Tullahoma, Tennessee, 218, 219, 220, 271

Tullahoma Campaign, xx, 255-257, 259-260, 262; losses, 220

Tuttle, Brig. Gen. James, 89, 94, 114

U. S. Coast Survey, 53

Underhill, Lt. Stephen E.M., 95-100

Underwood, Pvt. John, 70

United States Regiments
13th Regulars, 5
49th United States Colored Troops, 197
58th United States Colored Troops, 148
United States Colored Troops, 272

University of Mississippi, 171

USS *Baron de Kalb*, 50

USS *Benton,* 37, *39*, 47, 50

USS *Cairo*, *32,* 36, 55, 50, 200-202; preservation of, 202

USS *Carondelet*, 50, 78

USS *Cincinnati*, 50

USS *Conestoga*, 50

USS *General Price*, 37

USS *Lafayette*, 35-40, *37*, *39*

USS *Lexington*, 50

USS *Louisville*, 14, 78

USS *Marmora*, 201

USS *Mound City*, 50, 78

USS *Tuscumbia,* 47, 78

USS *Tyler*, 50

Van Dorn, Earl, xx, 72-74, *73*

Van Meter, Reverend W.C., 133-135

veterans, 194, 261-262

Vicksburg, xviii, xix, 1, 2, 3, 4, 5, 6, 13, 23-28, 60, 61, 62, 64, 66, 67, 75-82, 86, 108, 112, 133-135, 139, 148, 150-153, 154-156, 160, 168-171, 172-173, 176, 177, 179, 198, 210, 219, 260; assaults on 108-110, 121-123, 131; campaign for, 6, *8,* 10, 103-104, 130-131, 182, 186-188, 190; Confederate defenses of, 3, 5, *120*, 123-124; as the "Gettysburg of the West," 205; number of books published about, 213; possibility of sending Confederate reinforcements from the East to defend, 124-125; siege of, 6, 139, 148, 150-153, 194, 210; sources on, 125; terrain surrounding, 122, *126*

Vicksburg National Military Park, 23-34, *24,* 31, 108, 191, 193, 194, 197, 212

Vicksburg National Military Park Association, 194

Vicksburg National Cemetery, 33-34, *34*

Virginia, Fredericksburg, 118; Petersburg, 118, 144; Richmond, 182, 184, 185, 187, 189, 210-211, 212, 226, 255

Walker, Brig. Gen. W.H.T. "Shot Pouch," 86

Wallace, Lew, 129

War of the Rebellion: A Compilation of the Official Records of the Union and Confederate Armies, Series 2, Vol. 26, part 1, p. 37, 134-135

War Department, U.S., xviii, 135

Washburne, Elihu B., 128

Washington, D.C., xviii, 79, 81-82, 135, 211

Washington, Capt. Edward, 5

Watts, Maj. N.G., 135

Welles, Gideon, 51, 54-55

West Point, U. S. Military Academy at, xix, 51-53, 130

West Virginia, xix

West Virginia Troops
4th Infantry, 116

Wheeler, Maj. Gen. Joseph, 222, 230, 231, 238, 264-267, 271, 283

Whitworth artillery, *17*, 18

Wilder, Col. John T., 234-236, 238, 261, 278

Wilder's Brigade, 262

Wilderness, The, 207

Williams, Brig. Gen. Thomas, 30

Willich, Brig. Gen. August, 256

Windsor Ruins, *13*, 14